The 7 Novellas Series

7 Lessons-The Complete 7 Novellas Series

7 Short Stories of Reincarnation and Paranormal Experiences

by

Gare Allen

To Jeff

Enjoy!

7

Sessions

By

Gare Allen

Dedicated to Vicki H. Allen

Session I

"Him? Are you serious?"

Julia chose to ignore Selene's rhetorical disapproval of the man entering through the bar's excessively large pine doors, but Julia's silent disregard did not deter her unsolicited remarks.

"You're staring Jules. What do see in that guy? He has no discernible personality and he's not all that much to look at either."

Jules maintained her quiet avoidance while Selene resumed her attack. "He's in here almost every night wearing the same black leather jacket and smug grin and the only words he manages to utter are 'another beer' and 'time to hit the head'."

Selene's off-the-wall reference to the bathroom broke Julia's gaze that prompted a casual glance upward as she addressed her friend's comments.

"I don't know. There's something about him...almost familiar."

"Well, he should be; he practically lives here."

Jules rolled her eyes at Selene's continued barrage of criticism and continued, half-turned toward the mysterious man but still addressing her life-long friend.

"It's strange. He's not bad looking, not shy but not outgoing either. Nothing stands out but I can't shake the feeling that...oh, what the heck..."

Jules felt compelled to engage her curiosity and acted. She began walking toward the round table in the center of the room where the man had begun drinking his first of many beers with his posse of pals, still cloaked in their leather jackets. They felt the black coats contributed to their rugged exterior but in reality, the cold Chicago air still slightly stung their skin and not coincidentally, the table they chose was closest to the fireplace.

Julia made her approach slowly but never broke eye contact with the man. When she finally reached the table the man stood up, rather sprang from his chair like a jack-in-a-box, managed a wide smile as he pulled off his black cap and over-politely head-nodded, "Ma'am."

Jules stopped dead in her tracks, slightly confused and thought, I'm twenty-five and he's calling me 'Ma'am'?

She decided to move past the man's questionable choice of greeting, chalking it up to nerves and/or a lack of experience meeting women and managed a once-over before she responded.

He stood six foot three inches and boasted broad shoulders with a slender waist. His hair was short, black, thick and strangely in place despite the removed cap. Long sideburns reached toward a larger than average nose but both complimented a strong, square chin. His unusually white teeth beamed from his mouth like a searchlight, yet Jules seemed to find the contrasting attributes working in harmony to create a fairly pleasant, if not unique presentation. Blue jeans, black square-toe boots and a black t-shirt rounded off his ensemble.

Julia introduced herself. The eyes of the man's friends at the table shifted back to their colleague. He was floored. He began to shake in his still cold and wet boots, now somewhat intimidated by the forward engagement of the woman before him. He could not believe the woman he had only seen from afar, indeed, admired from a distance was now introducing herself to him.

For a moment, he lost himself in her radiance.

Julia was exemplary, simple beauty. In heels, she climbed to five foot three inches. Her long blond hair fell down past her tiny shoulders just above her full, C-cup breasts. Tonight, she had on her favorite skirt, bright white, calf length and adorned with light yellow butterflies along the hem. As usual, it was paired with a sky blue short-sleeved blouse that effortlessly complimented her similarly colored eyes. She was often chilly, intentionally leaving her coordinating sweaters at home; proud but not obnoxious about her looks. Her soft blue eyes were her ace in the hole whenever she found the need to convince another to her way of thinking. Like any other night she wore her signature pink scarf, wrapped once around her delicate neck and softly flowing over her left shoulder. She stood a picture, no, a masterpiece of elegance and sweet feminism balancing strength, confidence and beauty.

Somewhere, just in ear's reach, Julia heard Selene clear her throat. The man realized he had been gawking at Jules and had become lost in the excitement and confusion of her approach. Jules smiled, half complimented, half amused.

The man glanced down at the audience around the table, regained his composure and with chest out and shoulders back, he looked Jules in the eyes, flashed that whiter-than-white smile and delivered, "My name is Charles".

Greer's eyes opened to the sight of a ceiling fan directly above him and experienced a fleeting, slight disorientation as he quickly recalled his surroundings and heard the familiar voice of his friend, Sean.

"Dude, you were only out for a couple of minutes. Did you see anything?"

"Yeah Sean, I saw something, alright."

Sean hit the stop button to halt the past life regression disc.

"You were like, out, as soon as the woman on the disc counted from ten to one, man. You were mumbling while you were out but I couldn't understand what you were saying. So, give it up G, what did you see?"

Greer was still reeling from the vivid images, impressions and emotions fresh in his head and heart.

"It was like I was not only viewing the scene, but participating as well." He looked over at his buddy and continued. "I felt like I was the guy, uh, Charles."

Greer described the initial meeting of Charles and Julia and tried to convey the deep emotional connection he felt to them. "It was like I knew them, or was them, or at least him…it's weird, man."

Sean listened intently to his best friend's description of his first metaphysical endeavor into a past life and asked, "So, you saw yourself in a past life? In Chicago? In 1958? How do you know the year?"

Greer got off the couch that he had been lying on since before the regression began and paced the room as he answered. "The clothes, the music, it was late 1950's. Plus, I just get that impression, ya know?"

Sean pulled his neck back and slightly raised his left eyebrow. "So, you got it psychically?"

Greer was getting excited now. "Maybe. I mean, I've had dreams that came true."

Sean was very familiar with his friend's paranormal experiences. Indeed, he had had several of his own. But Sean was only willing to go so far into the experience and began to pull back.

"Dude, she sounds like a hottie. Too bad you can't get that in real life."

Greer was used to Sean putting on the brakes when the circumstances began to breach his non-secular comfort level so he didn't take much from his comment although the look he shot Sean deterred any further jabs.

Greer boasted better than average looks, average height and weight. The frequent visits to the gym provided a good, solid build displayed under his brown hair and green eyes. His "package", as he refers to it, includes a good-paying job, a quick wit and a big screen television even a blind man could appreciate.

For reasons beyond his comprehension, he could not land a relationship with the right girl although it was something he longed for on a daily basis. He often scored dates with little effort and many began well while sometimes even ending the next morning. But Greer was looking for "the one". He wanted that spark, that Lifetime movie, chick-flick relationship that delivered an explosion of realization that you are with the one with whom you will share your golden years; still pining for one another in your quiet suburban home, now empty of the children who grew up to provide grandkids that, upon their visits, provided a sense of satisfaction and closure to your past parenting efforts.

I'm only 31. I have plenty of time to find her.

These thoughts did mollify him, but not for extended periods of time.

"Dude, I know that look. You'd be a ton happier if you were more like me." Sean determined.

Greer quietly responded "More like you?" He respected his friend in many ways but had no desire to mimic his version of courting.

Sean was a player. He was a good-looking, muscular jock right at 6 feet tall, tan and although often not long on words, possessed a quiet sexiness and pair of biceps that served him well. Sean avoided a committed relationship as if it were hunting him for food.

In some ways Greer did envy his pal, but longed for the security and foundation of a relationship. Of course that would include the countless children he would raise. Truth be told, he wanted sons but would love daughters just as much.

He became pensive as he continued to pace his buddy's living room. He lost himself in self-analyzation.

Am I too picky? What if I've already met "the one" and I blew it?

Sean managed to snap him out of his lip-biting, floor pacing, temporary, mental, panic attack by slapping him on the shoulder.

"Buddy, you are way too serious. Relax. Go home, write down what you dreamt." Greer turned and before he could speak Sean corrected himself. "I mean experienced."

Greer's face lightened up as he began to de-stress and put aside his lament on love and asked Sean if he was willing to regress as well.

Sean looked at his Movado watch and upon seeing the time of 10:45pm he obnoxiously announced, "It's a player's ball out there and I'm in the game."

It sounded as silly to him as it did to Greer. Sean's face went back to half-serious. "By the way, you're doing this regression stuff...why?"

Greer really didn't have a good answer but in an effort to provide a response that would end the conversation so he could go home, he tried to recall and recite the sales pitch on the back of the CD cover.

"It's widely believed that past lives give us insight that helps us in our current existence."

Sean looked at Greer and asked both incredulously and rhetorically, "Widely?'

With that, Greer grabbed his keys, left Sean's house, started his white Ford F-150 truck and began his drive home through the streets of north Tampa.

Greer's mind replayed scenes of his regression during the twenty-five minute drive home. He witnessed Julia forwardly introduce herself to Charles.

Very forward, he determined, especially for a girl in the 50's.

His memory displayed favoritism to her image, standing adjacent to the fireplace, smiling. Her striking, blue eyes were kind and confident as the light from the fire illuminated her natural beauty in all its stunning glory.

It was almost midnight by the time Greer arrived home, showered, grabbed a snack and hit the bed sheets. He recorded the events of his experience in a journal and after a few more minutes of Julia's image, tired himself to sleep.

Session II

The next morning Greer awoke to, shall we say, an alert body and although no mirror was in visual range, he most assuredly wore a smile. He proceeded through his morning ritual of a protein shake, walking his black lab, Sobek and doing minor clean-up around his house. The early events took just under two hours. All the while his mind was plagued with fragments of dreams, distorted and incomplete, yet with clear subject matter…Julia.

Thirty minutes later, he met Sean at the gym. Today's workout centered on chest and triceps, with extra focus on triceps.

"It's all about the arms." Sean would say.

After the workout they ended up back at Sean's house. Sean may have been unwilling to delve into the deep recesses of past life memories but he was quite comfortable assisting his friend and, more than he would admit, looked forward to hearing of the experience first-hand.

Sean knew from the morning's conversation, or lack thereof, that Greer's mind was heavy on his experience and without asking, put the disc in the player to continue the regression.

Greer assumed his former position on his friend's living room couch.

The voice on the CD relaxed Greer into a deep trance and implemented a backwards ten to one count. By three, Greer was back in Chicago.

"Would you, um, like to join us?" Charles asked, nervously.

"Well, it wouldn't be appropriate for me to drink on the job." Julia explained, "This is my grandmother's bar. I help out when I can."

Charles' face displayed even more confusion and wonder at this beauty before him. Julia, of course, noticed and inquired as to the nature of his bewilderment.

"Something wrong, Charles?"

"I, um, you're so beautiful, and, uh, you work in this bar? I mean, there's nothing wrong with that. I've seen you here before but didn't realize... I'm just surprised that's all. And, you came up to me!"

Julia looked a bit taken back. "Am I too forward for you?"

Charles struggled to string his words into some sort of meaningful phrasing. "No! No, I mean...no." He sighed and his slumped shoulders told Julia he was feeling defeat in a simple conversation.

She smiled and offered, "I get off at eleven...buy me a drink then?"

Charles picked up his head and with a renewed sense of confidence, replied to the affirmative.

Julia made her way back to the bar as Charles sat down with his entourage and soaked in the admiring glances of his buddies.

Finally, 11pm arrived and Charles and Julia sat at the same round table that witnessed their initial meeting and clumsy communication. For the next four hours they talked about life, love, family, friends, spirituality and any other subject that came to mind. There were no lulls.

The only time silence survived was during trips to "the head". They conversed effortlessly and both enjoyed every moment, but it was Charles who fell silent as Julia began to read his palm.

First, she addressed the nutrient and vitamin information in his fingertips. "A little more vitamin C wouldn't hurt." She informed him.

She flipped his hand over and ran her delicate index finger along the lifeline. "Your life mark is short, too."

Concerned, Charles broke his silence. "How short is short?"

Julia paused before responding and looked him directly in his eyes before saying, "I believe the palm is simply an indication of possibilities. Above everything, we create our reality and nothing is set in stone or unchangeable."

Charles was surprised by the heavy subject matter and Julia's serious take on the lines on his hand. He wanted to ask what she saw for him in his life. Charles put himself to others as strong and independent and indeed he was, but there existed an intimate awareness with very strong emotions just beneath his rugged exterior which no one could perceive. Well, almost no one.

"Charles, what is it? You look uneasy."

Charles smiled and his eyes began to water. Julia connected with the heavy emotion welling up inside of him and perceived the physical changes as well but decided to keep quiet and allow this intriguing man the opportunity to open up to her.

Charles swallowed hard and began. "I've never been able to talk to someone like this." At this admission his wide smile showcased flawless teeth. Julia gasped at their brilliance.

He continued. "I never tell anyone anything that I am feeling and I want to tell you everything! I want to share my dreams with you! I mean, my real dreams; those that I have at night. They mean something. I see things I can't explain but could never tell anyone about them. I feel, so…so…connected to you."

Julia felt a wave of joy rush through her heart. Suddenly this was no longer a first date with a stranger but now a fantastic realization of a deep connection and excitement of anticipation of what would be said next. It felt comfortable and strangely familiar.

"It's really late." Julia found herself saying the words but not wanting to end the night.

Charles then offered, "I feel like, like…"

Julia responded, "Like what?"

Charles continued. "…like I've known you all of my life! I know that sounds like a come-on or even stupid but I do. I feel like I can tell you anything."

At first, Julia didn't respond. She stared into Charles' eyes and allowed herself to listen to her thoughts and embrace her impressions as her grandmother had taught her. She felt a partnership. She felt trust. She felt love.

Charles asked that she share what she was thinking. Part of him couldn't stand not knowing he thoughts but another part of him was relishing her gaze into his eyes so much that he feared her answering his query would end this very intimate, non-verbal moment.

Julia could not reconcile the flood of emotions she felt for this man that she now knew for only five hours. As if on cue, he leaned forward. Julia felt his energy overcome her. Not controlling her, but engulfing her in a comfortable, empowering way. She leaned forward as well. Heads began to slightly tilt opposite of one another; eyes were closing as their lips moved closer and closer…

"Touchdown!"

Greer came out of his trance to the sound of Sean's proclamation of six points. Sean quickly caught Greer's piercing glare as he simultaneously realized that he had interrupted his regression.

"Dude, sorry, watching the game." Sean became a bit less apologetic and remarked, "You've been out for over an hour. Don't you want to catch the game?"

Greer did want to watch the game but he would gladly sacrifice kickoff for a kiss any day; even if the kiss was in a vision.

During commercials, Greer told Sean of the lengthy conversations he or rather, Charles, had with Julia, late at night in her grandmother's bar.

By the fourth quarter the Bucs were typically trailing past the point of interest for both and the big screen went off until the four o'clock game.

Greer continued to refer to Julia in the present tense. "She's so confident and smart. And she is so into me or Charles, I mean. And she's got some kind of sixth sense thing going on."

Sean caught that slip for the fourteenth time during the course of the conversation and stopped him. "Uh, G, you talk about this girl like she is real. You realize that this is just a vision or a dream and basically, not real...right?"

Greer became defensive. "So you don't believe that I've tapped into a past life?"

Trying to keep his friend grounded, Sean responded. "It's possible, yeah. But keep it in perspective. Maybe the trance is more sleep. Maybe the memories are more dreams." Sean paused and looked uncharacteristically serious. "What do you expect to get out of this regression stuff anyway?"

Greer was faced with a very valid question from his best friend to which only the truth would be accepted. His buddy's bullshit detector was finely tuned where Greer was concerned. While he had no intention of lying to Sean, his answer included the fact that he was falling for Julia and was sure to be met with resistance.

In an instant, he would have severed his left big toe to go back in time and refrain from sharing that bit of information with his friend. Sean had several thoughts on the matter and Greer was the recipient of his usual candor.

"Are you kidding me with this?" Sean began. "Dude, she's not real. She's a figment of either your imagination or sexual frustration.

And, knowing your strict adherence to a ten o'clock bed-time, I'm going with lack of sex."

Greer rolled his eyes and said nothing.

Sean took a breath and held up his palm as he continued. "Let's say that she is someone that you knew from your past, a past life even. So what? What is she to you now?"

"I don't know, man." Greer became agitated. "Maybe she is the model for the girl I should be looking for. Maybe I'm seeing this lifetime to understand relationships. I honestly don't know, man. But I gotta tell ya that I'm into her bigtime. And, my friend, this is real. I can't make up this kind of stuff. The way I feel toward her when we're talking…"

"Talking? In the visions?" Sean interrupted, "G, you're crossing a line here between fantasy and reality."

"Sean, you've had experiences too! You know there's other shit out there, crazy shit you said you couldn't explain or..."

Sean interrupted and almost yelled, "Yeah dude, I've seen ghosts but I never fell in love with one!"

Sean's point was made. Greer grabbed his keys and headed toward the door.

"Dude, only looking out for ya."

"I know Sean, I just gotta figure this thing out."

"Later, G."

"Later, Sean."

Greer drove home, gave Sobek his dinner, recorded the day's regression into his journal and watched a quarter of the evening football game until he called it a day.

Sean's right, I do go to bed early.

The next morning was typical. Normal morning cardio, walked Sobek around the neighborhood, shaved and showered and headed to work.

"Good morning, Greer."

"Good morning, Stacy." Stacy was the office kiss-ass. She always found her way to be the first person to greet Greer as he entered the building and often supplied baked goods on ordinary days reaffirming her reputation as suck-up of the year. Greer managed the entire floor and she was bucking for a promotion.

When asked what he did for a living, Greer responded, "I captain a sea of cubicles that perpetuate the lucrative health care system." Whether it was boredom or an attempt at dry, vague humor that fueled his response, he always enjoyed the delivery.

Greer managed to maintain most of the fake smile he had mustered during his greeting with Stacy as he continued his way past his subordinates.

Just outside his office he noticed balloons above Karla's cubicle. Karla is the senior claims adjuster on the floor. She also has, from Greer's perspective, the distinction of having dated him for a lengthy, eight months.

Most only make it three. He once said.

She greeted him with her normal, "Oh, it's you, but I'll force out a smile because you're my boss" expression. "Good morning Greer."

"Mornin' Karla. What are the balloons for?" Greer quickly scanned his memory for her birth date. Surely he wouldn't forget that.

Sure he would.

"I'm moving." Karla explained.

Surprised, Greer asked, "Where?"

"I got a job offer in Daytona."

Greer was shocked. "I don't remember getting your notice or reason that you were leaving."

Karla smiled and said dryly, "I remember being very specific as to why I was leaving."

"Very funny. I meant leaving this job...and Tampa!"

"I know what you meant Mr. Serious. I put my letter of resignation on your desk over the weekend. I'm taking vacation time in lieu of two weeks' notice." She noted the concerned look on Greer's face. "Don't worry; I already set up a temp and Human Resources are already interviewing my replacement."

Greer suddenly felt sad. "Wow, I'm gonna miss you Karla."

Karla looked surprised. "Really?"

She grabbed her box of personal items and walked away with her balloons.

Greer looked around at the nearby cubicles to see a few nosy heads were peering just above the grey walls of their vocational fortresses.

Under his breath as he continued on his way to his office, he muttered, "Yet another woman in my past."

The end of the day came and Monday night football began. Greer met Sean at a new sports bar that opened close to his house and as luck would have it, beers were two-for-one.

About four beers in, Sean brought up Greer's "fantasy girl".

"So…how's your imaginary playmate?"

Greer chose to overlook the sarcasm and cynicism in favor of talking through the situation. For all the confusion and heavy emotion attached to the memories, or events, or fantasies, he needed to sort through it.

Greer had always wondered why Sean became so insightful and well-spoken while drinking. Either the alcohol broke down a barrier to an intuitive, wise man that was normally hidden by the sober antics of a childish jock or, wait, that's it! Greer finally figured it out.

Sean kept his eyes on the game, his hand on his mug and his mouth moving. "Let's play this your way for a minute. I'll buy that in your last "life" you were this Charles dude and you were all about a hottie, Julia, in Chicago, circa 1958. You two have some sort of deep connection and it looks like "love at first sight."" Sean raised two slightly bent fingers up on each hand. "Am I up to speed?"

Greer nodded yes to the server who asked if they wanted another round and duplicated the response to his buddy while adding "They meet in March. And don't air-quote me"

Sean shook his head as he continued. "It seems like you always go after the perfect girl and she never measures up. I've seen you give up on good and go in search of something better. I used to think you just had high standards. But, I gotta tell ya man, given your heavy disposition and deadpan delivery, being picky isn't a luxury you can afford G."

"Heavy? Whaddya mean heavy?"

"Dude, really? You could depress a clown. It's cool though, man. You got that intense brooding thing goin' on and some chicks dig dark dudes, so there's some hope. And, you gained over half an inch in your arms this summer which definitely doesn't hurt your marketability. "

"Sean, can we focus please."

"Oh yeah, your inner-want and all that. G, you have your idea of a perfect woman and she's here. But, in classic Greer style she is totally unobtainable, cause, well, she's not, um…real."

Sean trailed off from his last thought, partly due to the harsh point he drove home but mostly because Greer had a look that could have been captioned, "Wrap it up, Dr. Phil."

Sean treaded lightly but continued. "Let's check the rearview for a minute; there's Amy."

Greer paused and tilted his head as he recalled Amy and only moderately defended the courtship with "She was engaged, not married".

Sean retorted with "But, not available. Then there was Lisa."

Greer smiled at this recollection. "My favorite felony. Stupid fake ID's."

Sean went current for his next example. "Karla?"

19

The smile quickly vanished from Greer's face. "Ouch, bro."

Sean saw the genuine hurt in his buddy's face and switched gears.

"So, what kind of relationship do they have?"

Greer looked puzzled. "What do you mean?"

"Chuckie and Jules. Do they get married? Have kids?"

Greer explained, "I dunno man. I only got to their first kiss, which you ruined, remember?"

"Dude, you can't even get any in your dreams! Regressions! I meant Regressions!"

Greer gave up on the conversation, took another swig of his beer and looked around the bar. He imagined a fireplace across the room next to a round table and visualized Julia standing there glowing, smiling and inviting him over.

After a few minutes Sean snapped him out of his daydream with a familiar slap on the shoulder.

"G, I'll come over tomorrow and we'll put the disc on. Let's see where this is going. Alright?"

Greer nodded in agreement.

Tuesday at work was uneventful for Greer. He was pleasantly surprised to see the temp in Karla's old chair was what Sean would label, "a major hottie", but decided to keep his distance when what appeared to be her boyfriend showed up to take her to lunch.

I don't think it was her husband...no ring. He would later tell Sean.

Greer respected monogamy and the commitment and trust that supported relationships. He considered this perspective to be one of his

20

defining attributes for which he found, the hard way, was not always a great first line.

Five o'clock arrived and Greer met Sean at the gym. After ninety minutes of lifting weights, neither uttered the word "cardio" so they arrived to Greer's house by seven o'clock. Greer relaxed on the couch while Sean powered on the CD player.

"G, before you go back under, what were you saying about this past life stuff again? That the whole idea of reincarnation is experience?"

"Yeah, man. How I see it is we keep being reborn to learn how to live life from different perspectives with varied competencies, beliefs, upbringing and sometimes with physical and psychological limitations or advantages. We get to be a man in one lifetime, then a woman, sometimes we're rich, other times poor, etc. We also come back to work through unresolved issues created through past relationships."

Sean nodded in agreement and added, "So, chances are those closest to you have had lives with you before, right?"

Greer smiled at his buddy's unusual clarity and responded, "It's not a guarantee but I believe it happens a lot, yeah. What are you getting at?"

Sean's cell phone rang. The ringer tone was set at maximum volume. Greer heard "We all wanna be a big rock star..." Sean answered with a quick, "Hey babe, hold on a sec. G, I gotta bolt. Sorry, man."

Greer was disappointed but knew Sean's impromptu date trumped his past life party.

"All good, man. Not really comfortable doing this solo so I'll skip the time warp tonight. Later, Sean."

Greer read for a while and then retired to bed, characteristically early.

Session III

"M-A-G-I-C-K", Charles and Julia spoke these letters in unison.

"Is that how you spell magic?" Charles asked.

Jules explained, "In ancient practices it was. The Egyptians used magic daily like we use the phone."

The planchette slid over to YES. Charles removed his fingertips from the plastic pointer. Julia followed suit and asked if something was wrong.

"It's just strange." Charles began, "I dreamed of getting messages from the Ouija board but I could never see who I was playing with."

"Playing?" Jules asked somewhat surprised. "It's hardly a game, C."

Jules had taken to "C" as a nickname for her now boyfriend of six weeks. Charles initially and clumsily retorted with "J" but quickly decided it was too masculine for such a feminine creature.

"Okay, so the board wants us to do some sort of magic, with a k?" Charles arched one eyebrow and sat back with his right arm stretched out along the back of the couch.

Jules could not resist the comforting seat created by his pose and joined him as she recalled a dream.

"I had a dream last night about some sort of energy booster device. In the dream, I was in a very small room with rock walls and a single torch illuminating the area. A cloaked monk was demonstrating, nonverbally, how to put it all together."

"What did it look like?" Charles asked.

"Well, there was a huge crystal wrapped with copper wiring. The wire was attached to a mirror that had some sort of scroll placed over it. I couldn't make out what it said but I got the impression it was, well, kind of like a wish. Selene seemed to confirm my take on it"

Charles thought for a moment and then deduced, "So, the crystal is supposed to be the battery or power source for the wish? What's with the mirror? And how would Selene know about it?"

Jules responded quickly and in a high tone, getting excited at Charles' early understanding and genuine interest in the dream. "The mirror amplifies the desire, producing creation. At least that is the impression I woke up with. Selene's smart and has an, um, elevated perspective on things."

Greer awoke to a sloppy lick across his cheek from Sobek.

Sometimes this is the most action I get all day. He quipped to himself.

Greer had opted for a personal day off from work. He spent his time pondering his dream of Charles and Julia working the Ouija board. The device that amplifies desire intrigued him so much that he spent over four hours on the internet searching for a reference to such a contraption.

A wish-maker? Next I'll be rubbing lamps. He mused.

Having failed in his research, he opted for an early hit at the gym.

It was just before six o'clock when Greer and Sean finished their workout. After Greer spotted Sean's three hundred and forty-five pound set of five bench presses, Sean hung one arm over the bar, used his towel to wipe his face and instructed Greer to, "Go ahead and drop the bomb".

Greer sheepishly glanced over at him as he removed one forty-five plate from each side and asked, quite unconvincingly, "What do you mean, man?"

Sean narrowed his eyes and launched into a brief personality assessment of his buddy. "G, you're an open book with pop-up pictures."

Greer accepted the remark as another instance of Sean's trademark prelude of humor which would be followed by words that carried certain significance.

Sean continued. "You've been overly nice lately, especially for you. You bought me a protein smoothie before the workout and you're still being super nice…which is becoming weird."

Greer remained silent but his eyes widened as if his plan had been foiled.

Sean resumed. "When you're not being nice you're biting your nails struggling to find the perfect words to say whatever it is you wanna say. So, again, go ahead and drop the bomb".

Greer resumed a focused expression and began. "I had a killer dream about Charles and Julia, man."

Sean looked hopeful. "We're calling them dreams now? Right on, that's progress, G."

Greer shook his head no, corrected himself and explained, "I had a dream, yeah, but it was another session; I was just sleeping. I guess I slipped into it without even trying. It was real, like the other sessions, not dreamlike at all."

Sean silently motioned to the bench. Greer complied and pushed up his set. After ten presses and Sean's direction to "Put some real weight on next time", Greer sprang from the bench and continued while Sean stripped the bar.

"They were discussing this cool way to make wishes manifest. Jules said she got the idea in a dream." Greer paused at the profound circumstance that he was describing. "It's funny, she had a dream that she told Charles, in my dream. Wow, that's like multi-dimensional or some shit, huh?"

Sean tossed Greer his towel, started walking toward the locker room and playfully jabbed, "I'm not entirely sure I wanna hear the rest of your dream but it's gotta beat listening to you compare past lives, dreams and past lives inside dreams so, can ya focus, buddy?"

At Sean's request Greer captured his original train of thought. "Okay, bottom line? I need ya to use a Ouija board with me."

At this Sean stopped, turned and spoke evenly and intensely, "No. Never. Don't ask again."

Greer began to counter his remarks with a somewhat prepared argument beginning with, "Dude, I know how you feel about…"

Sean abruptly interrupted and ended the conversation with "Drop it, G."

Session IV

"You have to work tonight...again? This is four nights in a row, Jules." Charles didn't even try to mask his whining.

Jules continued dressing and chose a response intentionally expressing annoyance. "Like I said last night, and the night before, and the night before that, I promised my grandmother that I would help her out. Besides, the money is good and I don't have a job like you that I can work six months and be free the rest of the year."

Charles pouted as Jules completed her outfit by wrapping her favorite pink scarf around her neck. He then, weakly, defended his profession with, "It's not my fault grass doesn't need cutting all year. A few more weeks and I'll be back at it."

Julia smiled as she simultaneously rolled her eyes, picked up her purse and turned to face Charles. "I'll be home late. I'll miss you, C." She kissed him on the lips and his tension melted away instantly.

Charles closed the door behind her and sat back down on her grey couch. Ruby found his way into his lap confirming Charles' personal perspective that cats often endear themselves to sworn "dog people'. Ruby quickly found his way back to the floor as he rode Charles' hand off the furniture.

Greer woke up on his own couch, fumbled for his phone and noted the time of eight o'clock in the evening.

"I must have dosed off after the gym. I thought Sean wanted to grab a beer at…"

Greer's thought was interrupted by a knock on the door and the subsequent and immediate entry of Sean. This entrance, while abrupt, was quickly overshadowed by his greeting, "What up, G?" Sean flexed an eighteen inch bicep. "This should be illegal!"

Fifteen minutes later the guys were sitting at a high-top table swigging back the first of many cold drafts to come. Eventually someone changed the bar flat screens from ESPN to a syndicated "overweight-comic-with-a-hot-wife" sitcom as Sean made his way back from "breaking the seal". Sensing a disturbance in his all-sports world, Sean rolled his eyes as he found his seat and adjusted his focus to a three-dimensional reality.

"Alright G, get me caught up on the latest with your dream-girl." His face displayed a sudden awareness. "Oh shit, she literally is your dream-girl. Dude, that's funny shit. Kinda sad, but funny."

Greer replied dryly, "Hilarious, muscle-head."

Sean slapped Greer on the back. "Just goofin' on ya, brother. Seriously, you past this shit yet? Get it? Past? Dude, I'm on a roll!"

Greer took swig number one of beer number five while looking nowhere in particular and sounded surprisingly sober as he spoke.

"I had another dream…" He corrected himself, "…or rather, memory of them earlier. It was all mundane stuff; working, money, their cat."

Sean asked, "What is it exactly you wanna see G? I mean, ya wantin' to see them doin' it? You got DVDs for that, brother."

Greer smiled and sat back responding, "And the internet."

Sean retorted somewhat seriously after the clanking of their mugs, "Ya know, porn is supposed to be supplemental. Between your "memories" and "personal online time", I'm scared you're gonna lose touch with reality, brother."

"Is that why you won't work the Ouija board with me? You're afraid of losing touch with reality?" Sean turned his head and glared at his bud as he spoke.

"Dog with a freakin' bone, huh?" At this response Greer backed off. Sean relaxed a little and continued. "Look G, I had a bad experience and it freaked me out, alright?"

"What happened?"

Sean lowered his voice and enunciated every syllable. "Some…thing…bad."

Greer submitted and remained silent.

"Why do you have a Ouija board anyway?" Sean asked.

"It's not mine. That Goth chick left it at my house."

Sean lightened up. "Oh yeah, Dark Dana."

Greer laughed and corrected him. "It was Deanna and we had a few good nights together. Remember, she worked from home and would only come out at night? Everyone wants to be a freakin' vampire."

It was getting late so Sean paid the server and as they got up to leave he quipped, "Classic Greer."

Greer asked what he had said and Sean replied with a slap on the shoulder.

"Later, G."

Session V

Greer wasn't tired when he got home so he took Sobek out for a late walk. Later, after a shower, he sat on the floor with his handsome dog. Sobek nestled his head on Greer's thigh, his brown eyes half closed and looking up only when the belly scratching paused.

Greer's thoughts were audible, if only to Sobek. "Whatcha think, Bek? Am I losing it?" Sobek's lack of response was always a supportive yes or no to Greer, whichever one was more in line with making him feel better.

Finally, he called the night. "C'mon Bekkers, let's go to bed."

Sobek found his corner of the bed as always. As Greer went to switch off the light in the bedroom he noticed the corner of a box under the bed. He knew instantly it was the Ouija board. Bending down, he pulled it out and then sat on the bed with the board in his lap. "Can it work with one person, Bek?"

Sobek was already emitting a low-snore symphony of deep breaths and as always, Greer assumed Sobek would agree with his decision. "Good call, boy, I'll give it a shot."

Greer placed his fingertips on the plastic pointer and paused. "Um, board, speak to me." Greer felt silly after saying this but closed his eyes and began to concentrate on Julia.

He asked another question. "Is there anyone here that wants to speak?" The planchette remained still. "Hello?"

Greer's disbelief was elevated but before he gave up on the exercise he remembered something he was told by Dark Dana or rather, Deanna. "Dammit Sean!" he said out loud.

He recalled that she had them sit and touch knees when working with the board or "witchboard" as she called it. She explained this kept the "energy" flowing and helped with the connection to "spirit".

Greer mused, *"I can't remember birthdays but this I remember? I guess I need Sean after all."*

Suddenly, he had an idea that seemed ridiculous. He reached his feet out and touched his toes to Sobek's legs, hoping to "keep the energy flowing". To his surprise the planchette began to slowly move across the board. Greer remained still as it moved from letter to letter.

S-E-L-E-N-E. Then, it stopped.

"Selene? Who's that?" At this Sobek lifted his head slightly demonstrating a forced if not half-ass acknowledgment of Greer's outburst.

Greer did not immediately recall her name from Charles and Julia's conversations but as he packed up the board and placed it back under the bed, the memory returned.

"Why is she coming through the board? I assume she is passed now but…why?" Greer took this thought to sleep as he finally lied down for the day.

Sobek was way ahead of him.

"I haven't seen you all weekend!" Charles sounded like a frustrated child of nine. Julia however, chose to remain an adult during their exchange.

"I need the money, C. The bar is busier than ever, they need my help and the tips are good."

Charles couldn't argue with income so decided to switch topics in an effort to reconnect emotionally.

"I had another dream last night."

Julia could never resist a dream conversation. She considered them messages from the other side.

She chose to hide her excitement and calmly inquired "Are you wealthy again?"

Charles started pacing the room with demonstrative hand gestures as he launched into his answer.

"Like the other dreams I am filthy rich! I don't know what to do with the all the money!"

"Am I in this dream?"

Charles excitement waned as he responded.

"No." He tried to make light of his answer as Julia's face clearly expressed disappointment.

"I assumed you were out shopping for clothes." Charles smiled and pulled her close for a hug.

"I don't like that I'm not in your dreams, C."

"Shh. I know I get excited about my reoccurring dreams but they are just dreams, Jules. Remember, we create our reality; your words."

Jules smiled and spoke out of the corner of her mouth.

"You do listen…" She pulled back and softly kissed him on the cheek and then made her way out of the front door. "See you later."

"Tomorrow we'll take a bike ride downtown; it's supposed to be warm."

"Sounds great, C. Love you."

The door closed and Charles stood staring for a moment and whispered to himself, *I love you too.*

Charles went to his closet and pulled out the shoebox that contained the items he had been collecting for weeks now.

Ruby immediately stepped on the box. Charles gently lifted her away. He was only slightly annoyed as he had become accustomed to how cats seem to do pretty much what they want.

He pulled out the contents one by one; a mirror, a large white crystal known as selenite and a foot of copper wiring. Charles wrapped the wire around the crystal and then to the mirror. He grabbed a piece of notebook paper and scribbled the words, I wish for money.

Julia was unaware that Charles had his own dreams of the same "wish-making device".

He felt half silly and half exhilarated as he lit a candle and repeated his wish verbally seven times but then reminded himself how much better life would be! No more late nights working in a bar surrounded by guys, guys like Charles, in awe of Julia's beauty. He had caught hell for the times he had "surprised" her at work. Jules called him out on his thinly veiled gesture of protection fueled by jealousy.

Things would be better with money, much better.

Session VI

Greer was walking Sobek in the early morning and pondering, out loud, the night's dream state. "Whaddya think Bek? The dude's crazy right? If he wants more money why doesn't he get a job during the winter months?"

Sobek responded with a hiked leg at the base of a queen palm located at the edge of an unknown neighbor's front yard.

"Yeah, I'd piss on the idea too. And, my pun."

Greer got Bek back to the house, changed and headed to the gym. It was some paid "day of recognition" that allowed for a day off from work, but did not necessitate a family gathering or gift purchase.

Best holiday ever. He would later say to Sean.

Sean sat down with forty pound dumbbells, began his curls and sincerely, asked his buddy, "Remember when we used to talk about girls and football while we worked out?"

Greer understood Sean's less than subtle complaint but was hardly detoured from his train of thought.

"Technically we're still talking about a girl…"

"And weird supernatural past life stuff. You should be a show on The CW, dude."

Greer chose, as he often did, to ignore his buddy's jabs and force the conversation at hand by catching up Sean on the latest events in Chicago.

Sean was starting to find the subject matter mundane and genuinely could not take it seriously.

"Dude, you're kind of a peeper now. You're like, stalking them or something." Sean laughed at his own humor.

Greer assumed the bench and began his curls.

Sean shifted into best-bud mode and got real.

"Look man, I know you think this is some private screening of your past life and you're seeing the dreams or visions or whatever as a personal history but that scares the hell outta me for you. It's fun to have a psychic tell you shit and it's crazy to see a ghost and all that but at the bottom of the day, you are you and you have a reality to focus on, ya know?"

Greer retorted, "I didn't fall down a rabbit hole, man."

Sean accessed his mental files on rabbit holes and his confused expression prompted his buddy to explain.

"It's a fairy tale."

Sean's response was direct. "Give me your man-card. Now."

Greer put the weights down and became even more serious than normal. Sean recognized the look and gave in to the conversation as Greer declared, "He doesn't deserve her, man."

"What, Joanie doesn't love Chachi?"

Greer outwardly appeared annoyed at this comparison but, on the inside he found it hilarious. "*Julia* loves *Charles*, yes, but she deserves someone better."

Sean maintained his sarcastic delivery and asked "Why ya hatin'" on Chuck? Did he hit her or something?"

"No, nothing like that. It's just that his idea of building a life is wishing for money. Julia's so amazing and beautiful. Dude, she's freakin' perfect!"

Sean grew more concerned and his tone indicated as much. He resumed his curls and looked straight ahead into the mirror.

"And here it is, right on schedule."

"What?"

Sean explained as he curled the dumbbells while his gaze remained on his form in the mirror. "Greer finds something wrong with himself or his girl so it has to end. Wait a minute, you do this in fantasies too? Whoa, this is outta my league, you're in shrink territory."

Greer glared. "Really, dude?"

Sean finished his set, put the dumbbells back and leaned on the weights.

"One question, past life boy. Would *you* deserve her? Careful, this might be a trick question."

Greer briefly pondered his friend's query without response. Sean smiled but didn't press for an answer. The guys finished their workout, walked to their respective trucks and then made plans to meet for a beer around eight o'clock.

Sean shook his buddy's hand. "I say you move on from this, bro. Just lookin' out for ya."

Greer got home, made a protein shake, walked Sobek and took a shower. He had the afternoon to himself as usual and found the couch cushion, formatted to his seat, irresistible.

Sobek was at the other end of the couch with similar satisfaction. Greer spun the past life disc on his index finger above his heard.

"Whaddya think Bek, one more spin of the CD?" Sobek didn't hear any trigger words like "treat" or "walk" so he remained motionless and quiet.

"Bek, you're always right, buddy."

Greer got up and placed the disc in the player. He heard the familiar ten-to-one backwards count and quickly drifted off.

Julia's pink scarf would have been blown off had she not tied it twice around her small, soft neck. Her trademark lace accessory was straight out behind her as she enjoyed the cool air on her cheeks. She squeezed Charles' chest partially out of safety, but more for love and comfort.

He continued down Michigan Avenue, beyond thrilled to have the love of his life on the back of his Duo-Glide Harley Davidson bike. The couple enjoyed the clear, high, blue sky above the shimmering lake water on a gorgeous mid-May Chicago day.

For Charles, a ride on a beautiful day is how the world is meant to be seen. Normally he would not have the windshield in use but Jules had insisted.

Too many bugs, C!

In reality, bugs weren't a concern since her right cheek was resting on Charles's back and his wide torso shielded her from any annoying, tiny creatures. Her view was like that of an old movie backdrop rushing by, but she still could make out the art deco sea horses that adorned the bottom of the stunning Buckingham Fountain.

She smiled because inside she was happy and as content as she had ever been.

Charles always felt free and alive on his bike. With his arms extended, his right hand tight on the throttle and his left on the lap, he found a new level of bliss "in the ride" with the fantastic sensation of Jules' embrace.

Time ceased to exist as they continued past Grant Park in awe of the budding trees and fresh life on the ground; "life" that would need cutting from Charles' perspective. The spring air had arrived and with it a feeling of rejuvenation and an exhilaration of love for nature's beauty, that one could barely contain.

Charles' tranquil moment was interrupted by an intrusive group of runners in the near distance who seemingly decided to enjoy the same wonderful weather.

In an effort to avoid the mob he chose to turn right at the next street, just a hundred feet away. As he was turning he saw a small patch of oil or water on the pavement. He managed to avoid the spill only to land the front tire in a deep pothole. The bike bounced out of the hole and the back wheel jumped itself off of the ground which threw Charles off of his cycle. He landed flat on his back and with a hard thud. Remaining conscious and his bike still in view, he saw that the accident before him was far from over. In a nightmare beyond any horror he had ever seen, he witnessed his beautiful Julia being dragged under the motorcycle as it continued down the damaged road.

Her scarf was entwined in the back tire spokes. Her soft face was scraped off by the hot asphalt as she desperately called out for help. Charles could barely hear her pleas, and later would wish he hadn't, beneath the maddening sound of metal clanking and scratching against the hard surface.

The bike finally stopped after another sixty feet and fell silent of the once thriving motor and horrific screams. A resulting display of a motionless, haunting pile of twisted metal and rubber covering a lifeless beauty was the image now engrained in Charles' mind.

Charles could not feel his legs. He screamed for Julia but she did not reply. He cried out one more time, "Julia!"

"Julia!"

Greer woke up on the couch with his hand clutching his chest covering his pounding heart as tears fell from his eyes. Sobek awoke in response.

Greer reached out and scratched Bek's head. "All good things boy, all good things."

He walked Sobek around the block a total of three times hoping the time would help him to reconcile the images in his mind and to accept the horrific sadness of what he was now convinced was a previous incarnation.

Later, he managed to pull himself together and meet his buddy for a few rounds.

It wasn't until after his third beer that Greer trusted himself to tell Sean what he witnessed without losing it.

Sean didn't utter one word as Greer relayed the events he had endured earlier in the day. The continuity of the story of Charles and Julia was undeniable, even for Sean.

Sean waited for Greer to finish and asked him an important question, again.

"Did he deserve her?"

Greer heard the question and managed a tiny smile as he suppressed his overwhelming enlightenment.

"Yeah, it wasn't his fault. He loved her so much and his intentions were good, man. No one is freakin' perfect and we set the bar way too high for ourselves and others. Doing that dooms any relationship to failure."

Session VII

Ruby leapt into Charles' lap. The familiar sound of the lid being removed from the tuna can ignited a conditioned response to be present at once for a cat's feast.

Charles spooned the fish into the small yellow, plastic bowl like he had done a hundred times before.

Like Jules had done a thousand times before.

As Ruby ate, Charles began his usual mental dialogue. He reminded himself that he never did like cats. Indeed, he was a dog person, although he had never adopted one into his life.

A supportive friend that doesn't judge and is always happy to see you. He would muse of the dynamic between a man and his loyal canine.

Mostly, a loving dog companion would have erased some of the loneliness that he had endured; at least until Julia had taken stage in his life.

Painstaking feelings of guilt and a distorted sense of duty forced him to create a hospice for his love's pet.

"What torture", he brooded. "To care for a living reminder of the love of my existence, now missing from my life, imprisoned in this wheelchair…alone, again."

His dramatic mental lament waged on for hours, as it had so many yesterdays and would for so many tomorrows.

The open construction area that claimed his love's life was void of the signage and barricades that could have prevented the accident and the loss of his Julia.

The police report helped win a lawsuit settlement that allowed Charles the cruel repetition of a mournful day and funded a continuous, intense experience of the repeated sorrow.

A loud knock on the front door broke his pensive retreat into desolation. In his haste to reach the door his chair rolled over the yellow food dish that had been licked clean and abandoned by a now satiated feline. Pushing himself up with his left arm he was able to turn the doorknob and swing his front door inward, affording him the ability to claim his weekly arrival.

The delivery boy had taken to wrapping rope around the boxes to enable Charles easy retrieval from the immediate hallway.

He managed, as always, to pull the boxes to the kitchen. Their contents played a vital role in his daily ritual as the cigarettes supplied a steady distraction between swigs of whisky.

At day's end, every day's end, Charles fell asleep in his chair. Ruby nestled in his lap and often purred in unison with his deep snore. It seemed he had obtained his animal companion after all and unfortunately, he was sadistically aware of the cruel irony.

Ruby lifted her head, peered through her sleepy eyes and sang a low meow while looking nowhere in particular.

Selene and Julia were two faint light images not five feet from Charles. For several moments they watched him sleep with Ruby curled in his lap. Time sadistically stood still as Jules took in the scene until she was finally moved to speak.

"I want to be reborn with him, Selene."

Selene remained uncharacteristically silent as Jules continued. "In the next life…we need to do this again. Do it differently…do it right." Her voice became hauntingly desperate. "Our time was so short. We weren't able to…"

She began to plead. "Tell me we can come back! Oh, my Charles."

"Greer, wake up."

As the fog from his eyes quickly cleared, he scanned his surroundings and accepted the memories of the previous night which had begun to flood into his mind. "Club. Sean bolted. Way drunk. Hottie! Name? Oh Hell…"

"Uh, good morning." Greer began.

"Good morning. How are you feeling? You kept talking in your sleep."

"Yeah, all good."

Suddenly an overweight tabby leapt onto the bed and landed in Greer's lap.

"Whoa, big fella, eh?"

"Her name is Jewel. Doesn't the pink bandana give it away?" responded the quite attractive, young woman with whom Greer was recalling as his "score".

Sean's words, not mine! He would later say while throwing his pal under the bus.

Greer stretched one arm above his head and continued to pet Jewel as the beautiful woman climbed back into the bed.

He struggled to reclaim her name as it danced on the edge of his mind.

Greer embraced a profound sense of understanding as the name, Jewel and the pink bandana transcended coincidence. He mentally thanked whoever or whatever was allowing this fantastic, spiritual experience to unfold.

The attractive woman placed her hand on Greer's pec and admitted, "I never thought I would end up like this with you, I mean, after working for you and all."

Greer almost shouted as his memory was fully restored and sprang upright on the bed, knocking his bedmate to the side, "Now I know! You replaced Karla! You're Ashley!"

"You just now remembered who I am?"

"No, no, I mean…no. I just can't believe it's you. I didn't think you were…available. I thought I remember your boyfriend taking you to lunch?"

"That was my brother visiting from Chicago. Since I moved down here he visits me a couple of times a year".

Greer smiled ear to ear. "You're from Chicago."

Continued in 7 Regressions-Book 2 in The 7 Novellas Series

7

Regressions

By

Gare Allen

The 7 Novellas Series by Gare Allen

Book One-7 Sessions

Book Two-7 Regressions

Book Three-7 Apparitions

Book Four-7 Abductions

Book Five-7 Projections

Book Six-7 Predictions

Book Seven-7 Reflections

Also available on amazon.com

The Dead: A True Paranormal Story

Dedicated to the Fourth Norris of the Garrisons

Regression I

"Tell me your ghost story." Greer took another swig of his beer and then leaned forward while awaiting Sean's response.

"Really? I've been outta town, haven't seen ya in weeks and that's what you wanna talk about?" Sean was slightly annoyed and more interested in hearing about his buddy's relationship status so he quickly changed the subject with a sharp query referencing Greer's historic destructive pattern.

"Did you find something wrong with the new Jules, yet?"

Greer initially chose to address the remark maturely but in the same instant changed his mind. "Her name is Ashley and you know that. Dick."

"Guessing that's a no. Right on, G. Is it three months now?" Sean was really happy for his bud as the guys clanked mugs to Greer's reply.

"Yup, it'll be three months next week. It's going well. Taking it slow…ya know."

Sean remained silent and widened his eyes expectantly while his friend searched for his next words.

Greer could not deny the incredible connections between what he now calls "that Chicago life" and today. As a result, he was determined to do things right. It was truly a gift to see the decisions of the past unfold as an opportunity for learning and, of course, heed the warnings of failed actions.

Greer remained vague. "It's all good man."

Before Sean could call foul, the server brought another unordered pitcher to the table. Just after pulling up the already too tight, short sleeves on his grey t-shirt to ensure a good view of the recently worked biceps, Sean delivered a trademark line to which the attractive server had become accustomed. "It's like you know me."

The server turned to leave while replying, "That's why I'm walking away."

Greer laughed. "Smooth, muscle-head."

"She'll be back."

"Uh, yeah, to bring the check."

Sean shook off the rejection; in truth it was quite easy. He turned his ball cap backwards and quickly resumed the subject of Ashley. "So, what are the cliff notes on Greer hearts Ashley?" At this Sean formed a heart with his hands and held it over his chest.

After a short look around the bar Greer straightened his back, raised his left eyebrow and brought his friend up to speed.

"My Facebook status would be 'In a relationship with Ashley, taking it slow while I try to not repeat the mistakes of the past.' Honestly man, just trying to be cautious and see how it plays out. She's awesome, digs me and all that. So far, so good. Now, Chicago won the cup, you lost the bet so, again, tell me your ghost story."

Greer had never been able to get his buddy to explain his aversion to Ouija boards but now, he had to fess up.

Sean filled the guys' mugs with more draft beer and downed his full mug. A second refill later he looked across the high-top table and began. "When I was fifteen, we found out our house was built on an old Indian burial ground. Strange things happened in the middle of the night-"

Greer interrupted, "That's the storyline in Poltergeist."

Sean began again. "There was this neighbor kid, Damien, and he was super evil and -"

"That's the character in The Omen."

Sean paused, turned his head slightly to the right while keeping his left eye on Greer and offered, "Burnt guy with a dirty sweater attacked me in my dreams?"

"Dude, what the hell?" Greer gave up on the conversation in favor of another citing more recent events. He was prepared for his buddy's reaction to his news and launched into his announcement without letting him off the hook completely. "I'll allow the side-stepping for now but you promised, man."

Sean rolled his eyes but said nothing. He was accepting the avoidance as a big win since his friend was uncharacteristically letting it go without much of a fight.

"He'll back off if he has something about himself to talk about, temporarily, anyway." Sean would inform Ashley during dinner several weeks later.

Greer continued. "I did more regressions."

Sean froze with his mug halfway to his mouth and glared directly at his friend. Sean saw Greer was about to continue and delivered the first of several, abrupt interruptions. "No."

Their subsequent exchange went like this:

"I know what you think about-"

"No."

"Sean, it's all good I just got this-"

"Nope. Stop talking."

"Dude, I bought a certificate to get regressed and over the last few weeks I've had-"

"Un-freakin-believable. Is the new Jules in on this, too?"

Greer responded with clenched teeth. "Again, her name is Ashley. And, again, dick."

Sean used one hand to down the remaining beer in his mug while the other hand simultaneously reached for the pitcher. After downing half of his refill he moved the pitcher to his immediate right and, intentionally sounding like a young child stated, "Mine".

Greer waited patiently until Sean gave the green light to continue. After a short pause Sean sighed, checked the time on his Movado watch and spoke calmly and plainly to his best bud. "It's still early, I don't have to work in the morning so I claim this high-top as ours until you explain this whole regression insanity."

Greer was ready to respond; excited, in fact, to finally fill his buddy in on his latest past-life experiences.

Sean halted Greer's motion to speak by holding up two fingers. "Before you start, I have a two-part question. First, I thought you were done with the whole Chicago/motorcycle/pink scarf/wheelchair drama."

"That's not a question."

Sean's neck straightened and his eyes narrowed as he asked, "Really?"

Greer quickly chose to behave and asked, "What's your other question, brother?"

"Does the new, pardon me, does Ashley know about the…um…experience you had?"

Greer paused to ensure his boy was done speaking. After a few seconds when it appeared safe to take the floor, he did just that. "I am done, I mean I have moved past, pun intended, the whole Chicago deal. I learned a lot from that experience so figured I'd see what else I could uncover. I tried the same regression disc but nothing happened. So, I went to a metaphysical bookstore and paid for seven previous incarnation viewings. "

"Viewings?" Sean was now slightly intrigued but kept his tone even, detached and monotone. He carefully navigated the conversation with short responses and just enough ridicule to appear skeptical but not deter his buddy from continuing.

"Yeah, they call them viewings because you see them during a light hypnosis."

Sean remained in character. "Light?"

Greer explained. "This lady, Beverly, is a regression expert. She works with people suffering from trauma occurring early in life or in some cases previous lives." Greer began to sell the idea as if he would collect a commission. "Man, she has a degree in psychotherapy and she's been doing past life recall for over twenty years so I gave her a chance and bought seven regressions."

Sean motioned to the server for another pitcher. "Hang on G, we'll need another before you stroll down past life memory lane."

Round three of freshly poured draft beer was underway a few moments later and Greer prefaced the specifics of his first regression with a quick how-to. "So, I am pretty much conscious but she does this guided meditation which puts me, like I said, into a light hypnosis. It's similar to the guided meditation on the disc I used but this is more controlled. I can hear her as she directs me to go back to previous incarnations. She explained that you have to train the subconscious to travel there; meaning move the focus out of this current lifetime."

Sean remained quiet and kept his thirst quenched. Greer interpreted Sean's silence as comprehension and continued. "In order to do that, you use visualization to take the subconscious backward. I chose to see myself on a boat in open waters. As the boat moved off and began to disappear into the horizon, I would see images form.

Beverly then asked me questions and took notes on what I was seeing. My subconscious would offer different scenes from that lifetime. I understood that they were snapshots of pivotal moments which gave me a general feel for the circumstances of that particular life. Since my goal was to understand relationships, the hope was I would see the events of those incarnations with regard to my family, friends, etc. Make sense?"

Sean burped. "Longest…intro…ever."

He counted off the following points finishing with an index pointed at Greer. "You're awake, snapshot memories, ya wanna be a better boyfriend. Got it."

Greer had become accustomed to Sean's trademark summation and was pleased that Sean was listening even though he often had one eye on the flat screen tuned to an ESPN channel.

"And no, I haven't told Ashley about the regressions."

Sean arched an eyebrow at his admittance.

Greer remained focused. "Do you want to hear about the first viewing?"

"Sure, man."

Sean filled his glass and retained both eyes on his buddy as Greer described the scenes in his mind during his first viewing.

Sorcha crouched amongst the unfamiliar children, their legs and arms intertwined with one another. There were hundreds she supposed. She had lost count but it was day number nineteen with four more to go in the bottom of a dilapidated boat she could not even remember boarding. All she could recall in her dehydrated, food-deprived state was waking up to men in her bedroom, yelling, smelling of the sea and claiming her as their property. One of them began to stroke her soft, blond hair. Feeling violated she screamed out for her parents only to feel a sharp pain across the back of her head. That was her last memory until this boat.

She still wore her nightgown but it was now tattered and stained with blood and soiled with dirt. A girl of twelve, having grown up with some means in Ireland, now found herself literally piled upon sickly children that were her own age and younger. The smell of urine, feces and decaying bodies burned her nose while the motion of the boat sickened her with every movement. She would vomit if she had any food in her stomach.

"You were a chick?" Sean laughed, not being able to resist an obvious poke.

"That's your big takeaway so far? Really?" Greer ignored his juvenile humor and jumped to the next scene.

Sorcha had been working twenty-hour days in a sugar colony. She came to understand that she was now a slave, having been sold and transported in that horrible boat to the West Indies, specifically the island of Saint Kitts. How long had she been there now? A month, maybe, she guessed to herself.

If she slowed they whipped her. She ate once a day, at the end of the day and was given very little. Often she would fight off the other children as they tried to steal her food. She would sometimes taste the sugar embedded under her fingernails; a sweet treat in contrast to the tasteless mush provided as their singular daily meal.

She continued to lose weight pushing those endless, heavy carts of sugar from morning until night and though her once shiny blond hair was dirty and tangled, she retained her posture and never spoke back, even when they hurt her. Her pristine upbringing was evident even in slavery. So clear was her station that she was abducted once again from her bed, a slab of concrete flooring that often failed to foster sleep.

"Whoa bro, what the hell?" Sean was clearly not enjoying the telling of this particular viewing. Greer moved the story along to the next scene promising it would get better, but not by much.

It had been three weeks since her abrupt removal from the sugar colony. She was treated much better in her owner's home but she knew her place. She had overheard them talking that first night when the man who had brought her to his home told his wife that she would be compliant or replaced. The man had her bathed, groomed and dressed in a clean, pretty pale blue dress that was similar to the ones she used to wear and missed so much. Sorcha understood from their conversation that she was a gift for the man's wife; a slave-girl to tend the house.

The man was especially proud of his "find" as she didn't appear to be a commoner and, once clean, was visibly presentable to guests.

They referred to her as "girl", never caring to ask her given name. For the next seven months she worked hard to please her owners. Meals increased to twice a day affording her more energy to clean the floors and walls, tend to the dishes after their hearty meals and, of course, the daily laundering.

It wasn't clear until Sorcha began to vomit and bleed from her nose and eyes that she had contracted Yellow Fever. Her owners kept her isolated in her room. Days passed as she lied on her bed, much more comfortable than the concrete slab she had endured, not that she found any kind of comfort in her current state. She suffered from nausea and drifted in and out of consciousness until her heart finally gave. Sorcha passed early one morning, less than three years after her arrival to the home. Her owners found her shortly afterward and had her removed to be tossed into a nameless grave.

Sean was truly moved and saddened by the story partially by his own brotherly, protective instincts which he possessed for his younger sister and certainly by the descriptive account of Sorcha's miserable servitude. In his best effort to hide his true feelings he simply uttered, "I gotta pee." He left the table.

Regression II

Sean returned from "breaking the seal" and before he was back in his seat, he heard, "Tit for tat brother."

Sean played dumb looking toward their server and asked, "She's got tats?"

Greer was not deterred by his lame joke and sat back with folded arms and expectant eyes beneath raised eyebrows.

Sean finally gave in. He filled his friend's mug, topped off his own and then began telling a terrifying story from his childhood.

"I was thirteen I think. I had a neighbor buddy who lived next door that I hung out with all the time. He was cool, called him Dewey 'cause he always had a Mickey Mouse t-shirt on. Anyway, it was summer and a new kid moved in across the street. Everyone kept sayin' that he was weird."

Greer lifted his mug but before taking a drink asked, "Weird, how?"

Taking an opportunity to both own the stage and keep his focus despite the increasing pitcher count Sean curtly responded, "You'll find out if you let me tell the story G." Greer smiled out of the corner of his mouth and remained quiet.

Thirteen year old Sean was basically a younger, smaller version of the adult model. His factory settings included an affinity for sports and teasing girls which would remain active throughout early adulthood. His blond hair was short, not than anyone ever saw it beneath the ever present Philadelphia Philly's baseball cap.

His childhood buddy, Dewey, had dark brown hair and was drawn to music. High school would provide him the chance to play the snare drum in the band that would perform on the same field into which his buddy, Sean, would later sink his cleats.

On one warm July day, boredom, Sean's go-to instigator of trouble, fueled an interest in the new kid across the street. The knock on Dewey's door yielded a cold soda and, after a very brief explanation of his mission, "Let's go meet the new kid", the boys made their way across the street.

As was the case with most kids during the summer, their parents were at work, having left their children with older brothers and sisters who allowed a very, very long leash and reacted only to specific alarms of crying and bleeding.

"Solid parenting" Greer said under his breath.

Children often bypass any preliminary screening of new friends so a few minutes after they'd knocked on the door, the boys were inside playing video games in the bedroom of the new kid, who going forward would be known as Mark.

Mark was tall for his age of fourteen reaching five feet and six inches. His hair was dark black with thick, bushy eyebrows and pale skin.

"Need some color." Sean would often suggest as if it were not obvious.

"You guys wanna see somethin' cool?" Mark asked, as if any red-blooded child could ever resist the calling of 'somethin' cool'. There was no verbal response but the joysticks froze and both boys waited, wide-eyed and now somewhat fidgety from the caffeine in their sodas. Mark swung the end of his single bed out of place until a painted symbol was in view.

Dewey and Sean gasped in surprise but Sean quickly needed more, "What is it?"

Dewey tugged on Sean's arm and said "Man, we should go."

Mark asked Dewey if he knew what it was. Dewey was growing more uneasy staring at the symbol painted in red, blood red from a child's frightened, imaginative perspective and clearly permanent on the originally light-tan carpeting.

"We gotta go." Dewey grabbed his almost empty soda and made his way to the front door.

Sean was more confused than scared but quickly followed Dewey after a quick "See you later, Mark."

Sean caught up with Dewey halfway across the street. "Dew, what was that?" Sean grabbed Dewey's grey, Mickey Mouse shirt sleeve to stop his momentum, seeing clearly that his buddy was upset.

Sean thought for a second then offered, "I think it's some kind of star."

Dewey stopped panting, leaned toward Sean and informed him, "It's a pentagram."

Greer sat staring at the "grown-up" Sean. He had stopped telling the story and it was clear that he was taking in the scene.

Taking in the scene meant he was checking out any new arrivals, female that is, in the bar as Greer's mental Sean-to-English dictionary explained. After a few more silent moments Greer finally spoke up. "Do I gotta put disc two in or something?"

Sean laughed and motioned for another pitcher, number four if anyone was counting.

"Can I have some of this one?" Greer jested while subtly suggesting that his boy slow it down, but Sean was alert and only slightly sloppy. Unbeknownst to Sean, out of care and concern for his boy, Greer had taken his keys during his assessment of the building crowd.

"Great, now I gotta pee." Sean hardly acknowledged Greer's announcement and he was back quickly, very eager to hear more.

"Wouldn't you rather tell me about the next regression?" Sean felt he was being clever playing to Greer's inability to pass up a chance to share a story and while it may have been obvious intelligence, he definitely got wood on the ball.

"Ok, big man, last pitcher and last story." Greer pointed at his buddy and added, "Until tomorrow."

Sean remembered it was Friday night and Saturday was wide open after the morning gym hit so a power nap was mentally scheduled. He had missed his buddy over the last few weeks and even though the guy had a one track mind lately with crazy past life stuff, he was fun and they always had a great time together.

"Plus, I need someone strong enough to spot me." Yeah, it was pure brag.

Greer filled the guys' mugs and just before he spoke, Sean asked, "What year was that?"

"What year was what, Drunky-McDrunk?"

"Not drunk G, just in a good mood. And I missed my boy. It's good to be back in Tampa."

Greer smiled at the alcohol fueled yet sincere sentiment. "Missed you too, brother." Greer realized what Sean was asking.

"Oh, you mean the first life? Man, that was like late17th century stuff. I don't have an exact date or anything."

Greer moved the pitcher closer to himself while mocking Sean with, "Mine". After a sharp laugh Greer launched into the viewing of the next incarnation in his series of regressions.

Pascal was sweating profusely. He continually wiped the water from his face but his whole body was drenched with moisture.

Few wore beards in the legion but his pioneer unit was given special treatment for the extreme risk associated with their role. It was they who provided the entrenchments for battle. It was they who cleared obstacles under enemy fire to make way for the infantry.

Pascal was fast with an axe and shovel. He was a large, strong man, twenty-three years of age standing six feet and four inches and weighing two-hundred and fifty-five pounds.

"What are we talking here G, French Army?" Sean asked jumping ahead of the story.

Greer replied, "Yeah, but more of a combat engineer than a soldier." Sean's face reflected understanding and respect which prompted Greer to continue describing the scene.

In 1859 during the Battle of Magenta, he fought against Austria under the command of Napoleon III.

"I didn't know there was more than one." Greer would later confess.

Pascal was digging a trench with four other pioneers when suddenly they heard shouting and had sand kicked in their faces, effectively blinding them to the enemy who now stood with clear advantage above them. Ordered to drop their tools and climb out, their guns were confiscated as they were arrested and taken prisoner.

"Alright, my buzz is officially gone now. Do any of these 'viewings' have happy endings?" Sean paused and a silly smile emerged on his face. "Hehe, I said happy endings."

Seeing that Sean was lost in self-appreciation of his humor and the night was quickly coming to an end, Greer described the final scene.

He'd been in an underground jail with fifteen other Frenchmen for over two weeks now. The days had passed slowly as Pascal fell victim to fatigue and sickness. One by one the men had curled up in corners to die. In another four days, only Pascal and one other would still be living, if you could call it that. His lungs were filled with dirt and his wounds from the abusive guards now festered with infection. Light-headed and longing for a release from the torture, he recalled the endless nights spent drunk in the local tavern, wasting away his time and money. He needed to do something with his life and make it mean something.

In his last moment of clarity he pondered his choice to join the army, to do his duty to his country and more, what he had forsaken…a family of his own.

Sean waited a moment before speaking. "G, these are sad lives."

Greer paused as well, barely masking his own realization of the same conclusion before responding, in his characteristically serious tone, "I know. C'mon, I'll drive you home."

Regression III

Eight o'clock in the morning came early for the guys but they claimed a bench at one minute past the hour even despite swinging by the bar to get Sean's truck.

"It's all about dedication, G." Sean would say.

Greer intentionally spoke loudly and delivered an overly enthusiastic, "Let's get at it, Sean!"

Sean's somewhat squinted eyes and unusually slow reps of chest presses helped Greer gauge the level of hangover.

About a seven on a scale of one to ten. He would later tell Ashley.

"Spot me." At Sean's request, rather a barked command, his workout partner complied.

The guys managed a "solid hit" which in Sean-speak meant the pecs were ready to be poolside. Per their Saturday ritual they grabbed a protein shake at the juice counter in the back of the gym and sat down to chat.

"Whaddya got goin' on today, G?"

"Gonna see Ashley today, hang out, watch a flick, I don't know. Date stuff, I guess. You?"

"Not sure yet. I know what I'm not doing…drinking draft beer."

Greer laughed and reminded his friend that "One day your metabolism isn't gonna let you do that nonsense without cardio."

Sean frowned at the truth in his statement. "Cardio…the other "C" word."

Just then several small children ran past them on their way to the play area where their parents could leave them and get an uninterrupted workout.

"Funny, the next lifetime I saw had a lot of kids."

Sean arched one eyebrow. "Kind of a weak segue, G but go ahead and lay it on me."

"Man, this one was really short snapshots." Greer displayed a proud face and looked nowhere in particular before saying "And, it appears I am quite...active in this particular life, if you know what I mean."

"Buddy, I always know what you mean...unfortunately."

"You're home! Look what I made you!"

Richard had just walked into the house. He had not even set his briefcase down when the youngest of his children came running, rather sprinting toward him, with a varied mess of colorful crayon lines and circles on a small white sheet of paper.

"It's a picture of all of us and our house. See, there's the door and windows and..."

Richard wasn't even looking at the picture as she continued to point out the chimney for their house with no fireplace but was already leaning down to kiss little Sarah on the head.

"Thank you, pumpkin, I love it. I'm going to put it on the fridge with the others." At this little Sarah beamed with delight and her six-year old face wore a sweet smile of happiness.

Sean finished his protein shake while creating a loud, obnoxious sound of air being pulled up through the straw. "You're a Richard."

"Dude, are you ten years old?" Greer resumed his story of snapshot scenes and once again put the latest childish remarks of his buddy out of his mind.

"Hold the ball like this, with your fingers on top."

Richard held the football up until Eddie moved his small fingers along the laces as instructed.

"Okay, pull it back past your ear and throw it forward."

The ball wobbled out of Eddie's nine-year old hand but he obtained forward momentum and the celebration ensued.

"Great job, Eddie!"

Eddie was laughing in celebration of his accomplishment. Richard hugged him and told him that practice will make him even better. Eddie ran to pick up the football. They would spend another hour and a half in the backyard throwing the pigskin and celebrating every near spiral.

"Look, Perfect Dad, I do appreciate the cheerier story-telling compared to yesterday's gloom-fest but how many more kids are you gonna tell they can be president one day?"

Sean's genuine interest in the more promising lifetime was characteristically masked by his smartass remarks.

Greer decided to not tell his bud about the teenage girl, Emily, who had blossomed into a beautiful young woman and was just discovering boys. Emily would embrace life as an adult armed with spiritual love and compassion and the conviction of her father.

He also passed on recanting the viewing of the oldest, William, who had just begun college and was hopelessly in love with his high school sweetheart.

Classic jock gets the smart, pretty girl. Greer thought to himself. *It's a beautiful love story that would continue for the remainder of their lives.*

"You're off the hook, brother. Come by tomorrow and we'll hang out." answered Greer.

Sean gave Greer a familiar slap on the shoulder and responded, "Will do, G-man." The guys made their way to their respective trucks and drove off.

Once home, Greer was greeted by his ever-happy black Lab, Sobek who licked his face and then motioned his body toward the front door. He mused that Sobek wanted to say, "Real happy to see ya but just downed the water bowl so leash and collar, now!"

Greer took his big boy around the block a few times and lost himself in his thoughts. Reviewing all of his previous incarnations he noted the wildly different personalities of each.

I guess that makes me more well-rounded? He hoped, anyway.

When they got back to the house he retrieved a new toy from the cabinet. It would take Sobek less than four minutes to not-so-surgically remove the plastic treasure within, the grand prize that delivered a high-pitched tone which was music to Sobek's ears...the squeaker.

Greer had read that toys helped relieve tension, stress and aggression but he mused that Sobek mostly enjoyed the process of leaving white cotton-like carnage all over the living room floor for Greer to clean.

Sobek sank his teeth into his new, soon-to-be shredded, stuffed toy. This time it was a mallard duck. The wings were the first to go...in a record eleven seconds.

Greer left a much focused Lab to his task and took a needed, post-gym shower.

Thirty minutes later he was clean, dressed and walking through a carpet of white stuffing snow. Greer easily spotted a proud black Retriever lying in the middle of the soft sea of filler, falling fast to sleep.

Greer smiled at his content canine and headed out to meet Ashley for lunch.

I am so coming back as a Lab next life.

The two met at a small, Spanish café.

"Love me some deviled crab!" Greer would announce as if anyone who had ever eaten with him didn't know that he would order it.

Ashley just smiled, genuinely amused at his infrequent and welcomed excitement at food. She was finding Greer to be sweet and affectionate, if not often distracted by his pensive nature. She knew him well enough to know he was a good guy; a little unsure of himself, but his intentions were good.

"So, he's a little broody; look at him, he's hot." Ashley's best friend had once said to her.

The pulled pork and rice arrived along with the center of the meal, the deviled crab. Ashley moved the bottle of hot sauce to Greer's side of the table without being asked. Greer smiled as if to say, "It's like you know me."

Ashley verbally spoke, "I know you well enough now, Greer."

Greer must have had an unsettled look on his face as Ashley continued. "Relax. I didn't go through your garbage or anything."

Greer laughed as he often did at her amazing sense of humor. He sat back chewing his first mouthful and looked across the table. Ashley was beautiful in an understated way.

I had to elaborate quickly on that remark but I skated through. He would later tell Sean.

Ashley had soft, light brown hair atop deep, blue eyes. She was slender and fit standing just at five feet tall. Her silky hair reached past her shoulders and today was pulled back to accentuate her delicate cheeks and permeating smile. Not too much jewelry, not too much make-up…yeah, understated. Today she wore a white spaghetti-strap top and blue Capri pants. Greer scanned the restaurant mentally and confirmed that she was the hottest girl there.

Man, that's so Sean.

"I missed you last week; I didn't get to see you at all. Was work keeping you late?"

"No." Greer answered, without thinking.

His quick reply now warranted a subsequent reason and he wasn't entirely sure he was ready to tell her about the regressions.

"I mean, yeah. Work was…busy."

Smooth, G.

Ashley didn't buy his vague response and playfully dug. "Big project at work?"

"Um, just a lot of stuff that took time, ya know?"

"Like what?" Ashley could see the serious look on his face as his mind began to work hard for a reply and was having fun reeling in her fish.

Greer did not want to lie. But a lie of omission is still a lie.

"Not if you say nothing because then you're omitting everything so it's all good." Sean would later rationalize.

The guy makes some crazy sense sometimes.

"Greer?"

Greer mentally came back to the conversation and offered as little specifics as possible. "I was doing a personal project after work. It's crazy stuff, kinda embarrassing so…ya know."

Ashley nodded and smiled. "Vague, but honest. I'll take it."

Greer found her confidence and respect of privacy insanely attractive. He would show her just how much later that night and never get to watch a movie.

Regression IV

Sunday morning arrived and after spending the night together, Ashley found herself playing with Sobek on the living room floor. She had cleaned up all of the toy's stuffing left on the floor by the time Greer made it out of bed.

Shirtless, wearing blue boxer briefs, he stretched his arms high above his head. His tattoos accentuating his bicep muscles, he stood almost posing and remarked, "You cleaned up? That's not gonna hurt your approval rating."

Ashley was accustomed to Greer's detaching humor after intimacy so accepted the borderline rude crack at face value and played along. "It's cute that you think you'd be asked." She shifted her attention back to Sobek. "I'm taking this incredible dog home with me, by the way." Ashley scratched Sobek's chest and he lifted his head as if to say "That's the spot."

Greer smiled as Sobek's tail began to move.

Ever the happy lab.

At the sound of the doorbell Sobek sprang up off of the floor as a startled Ashley came to her feet. As usual, his deep base bark alerted Greer, and most likely several neighbors, that someone was at the door.

Greer opened the door to see his buddy, Sean in white cargo shorts and a brown, just-barely-fits-but-can't-take-another-wash, t-shirt.

Sean came in and saw Ashley gathering her belongings. Greer introduced Ashley to his best friend. Having heard way too much about

Sean she pretty much had his number. Sean decided to behave for which his buddy would later thank him.

"It's very nice to meet you, Ashley."

"You too, Sean." Ashley found his overly nice tone tailored for her comical and called to Greer while still smiling at Sean.

"Greer, gonna go now. You guys have fun."

Greer retrieved a pair of gym shorts then walked Ashley to her car. When he returned back into the house he found that Sean had assumed Ashley's former spot on the floor and was giving Sobek, what Greer called, if only to his dog, lovin's and scratchin's.

He dared anyone to say something about it.

Greer closed the door and mentally counted seconds. One one-thousand, two one-thousand, three-

"Dude, she is freakin hot! Right on, G!"

And there it was. Greer wore an annoyed expression. "Man, you saw her when she temped at the office."

"Yeah, but from a distance. And she stayed the night? Sweet!"

His tone was playfully condescending. "Yes, Sean, adults do that sometimes. And afterward, they continue to act like adults."

Sean put his nose to Sobek's snout and managed to baby talk between lab licks, "Mr. Maturity. Yes, he is."

Greer filled Sobek's food dish and instructed, "Sobek, go eat. Sean, ass on the couch."

"Uh-oh, I think I'm in trouble 'Bek."

"Whaddya wanna do today?"

Sean thought for a second. "Hang at the pool?"

"Right on. Let's do some breakfast first." Greer returned with two bottles of water, two protein bars and an agenda.

"Hey, what happened after you guys saw that symbol and left the neighbor kid's house?"

Sean dropped his head. "Man, can I just email it to you?"

Greer wasn't gonna let up and Sean already knew it. He pointed at Sean as he commanded, "Pentagram on the carpet, back at Dewey's house...go."

Dewey immediately went to his room and sat on his bed while Sean stood directly in front of him. A beautiful white Angora cat found his way into Dew's lap as if he knew he needed comforting. Dew began to stroke the soft, white coat of his feline companion.

"Hey, Amadeus." At the mention of his name the cat relaxed his body and began to purr.

"Dew, what's that symbol mean; that pentagram?"

"I saw something on T.V. about it. It's a five-pointed star." Sean flashed a proud smile as if to say, "See, I said it was a star." Dew continued. "They said it could be good or bad depending on how it was drawn."

Sean was not surprised at his friend's understanding as Dewey had always been a straight-A student and had often helped Sean with his homework after school.

Dewey struggled to recall the exact specifics of the star. "I think he said if the top of the star was facing up, it was good. If it was down, it was bad." Dew paused and Amadeus playfully swiped a snow-white paw at his Mickey shirt which prompted Dew to resume the petting.

Sean was pondering the star. "So, what does it do?"

Dewey clearly remembered this answer from the television show and was a little over excited in his response. "It's a doorway!"

Sean wrinkled his forehead. "A doorway to where?"

Dewey didn't know the answer but he did remember one related point, "Dunno, but it lets stuff in too. They talked about evil spirits and stuff."

Suddenly the conversation went from intriguing to silly for Sean. "Man, that only happens in the movies."

The boys were hungry so they went to raid the kitchen and just like that, the conversation was over as they moved on to Dorito's and more soda.

"Wow, did the neighbor kid, Mark, know what the symbol was?" asked Greer.

Sean took the last bite of his protein bar and responded with his mouth full, "He would in a few days." Sean took the opportunity to appear annoyed at Greer's interruption. "Can I continue? Thank you. Alright, flash forward a few days."

Sean and Dewey were playing Atari's then impressive, Asteroid game at Sean's house when they heard loud banging on the front door. It was Mark.

"Guys, you gotta help me. Come see!"

Their interest in the video game waned instantly and the three boys made their way across the street. Inside they followed Mark up the carpeted staircase to his bedroom to find that the door was closed.

Sean wiped the sweat from his forehead. The short run coupled with the summer heat and their heightened anticipation had everyone's heart racing.

Just outside his bedroom door, Mark turned to Dew and Sean and warned them, "You can't tell anyone. You gotta swear!"

The guys made cross signs with their fingers across their chest and nodded in compliance.

Mark opened the bedroom door slowly. Sean was almost on top of him, anxious to get inside the room and immediately felt a chill. He soon realized the room was cold, a good fifteen degrees colder than the hallway. Dewey entered slowly behind Sean and once through the door his eyes were focused squarely upon the bed that had been moved back into place. Although the star was not visible he somehow knew it was still there and it made him even more uneasy.

Mark stood staring at the bed. While it was only a minute, it seemed like much more before Mark spoke.

"Wait a second, it'll happen again."

The three boys stood in silence with their eyes transfixed on the bed. A few seconds later they saw movement from under Mark's bed. The room dropped another ten degrees. The hairs on the back of the boys' necks stiffened as they tried to discern what was emerging from beneath the mattress and box spring.

At first, it looked like a worm. Then, it appeared to be several worms. A moment later and after another ten degrees drop in the room's temperature, the boys could make out the image of disfigured fingers on a hand crawling outward, as if walking itself toward them. Sean could now see his breath due to the cold freeze in the air.

Mark broke the silence. "I think it's after me!"

All at once, they turned and ran from the room, out the front door and back to Sean's house. They locked the front door and sat knees to chest with arms wrapped around their legs on Sean's living room couch.

Dewey was the only one who spoke. "I guess this star is…bad."

"Holy crap, man. Did that really happen?"

Sean finished his water, "Yup. Crazy, huh?"

"I get the fear factor seeing that as a kid, hell, as an adult! But, how does the Ouija fit in?"

Sean was done storytelling for the day. "To be continued…"

Greer wasn't going to press him and let it be, for now.

I've gotten much better at backing off. He proudly determined.

The guys drove to Sean's condo and after filling the cooler with "provisions", they found two empty chairs at the property's pool. Sean quickly removed his shirt and stood, some would say posed, for a moment as he took in the scene.

"Decent view."

Greer knew that to be Sean-speak which meant there were several "eight's and above in viewing distance." Ashley would later roll her eyes at hearing the translation.

Greer removed his shirt and confessed, "Having a chick moment, don't judge."

Sean glanced over, "What's your issue, Sally?"

Greer put his hand on his stomach, "I'm one slice of pizza away from a second airline ticket."

Sean grimaced and warned, "It's all the Starbucks macchiatos, man. Switch to black coffee or find another crutch."

Greer always admired Sean's ability to provide solid advice inside a slam.

The guys took a quick dip and then made their way back to their chairs.

"Let's get your daily dose of crazy out of the way. What happened in the next life? SuperDad again? SuperMom?" Sean laughed at his own humor.

Greer, as a matter of course, ignored the jab, recalled the fourth viewing and relayed it to his bud.

"Go to your room and play while the adults visit, honey."

"But, Mom!"

"I'll be right back." Joey's mom promised her male "guest" as she escorted her ten-year old son upstairs to his room. Once there, she sat next to him on the bed.

"I need you to be good for me, honey. I have a friend over and we need some adult time."

"I don't have anyone to play with, Mom."

"You'll make some new friends soon, Joey. We just moved here so give it some time, Sweetie. Play with your toys and use your imagination. Remember, we can go anywhere and do anything in our minds."

They had moved in and out of small apartments ever since Joey could remember. His mom would work six days a week and on the seventh she would have "adult time." Joey would shut himself in his bedroom at her request. She was always working to provide for her son. Joey's mother possessed few skills having left school early due to a pregnancy at sixteen years of age. Committed to caring for her son, she took any kind of odd job and, although Joey didn't know it, would beg for food or money, if necessary.

Joey's father was long gone from the picture, also having been just sixteen years old and too scared to deal with what life presented to him.

Joey spent the majority of every day in his bedroom, reading and playing with toys but mostly got lost in his imagination as his mom had encouraged.

Lost in his imagination, he would see himself as part of a Calvary fighting off Injuns! He wore a blue uniform with a yellow neck wrap and rode a dark brown horse named, Rescue.

Other times he would imagine that he was a pirate sailing to remote islands with a treasure map. He would follow simple directions like twenty steps away from the water and seven steps north of the tallest palm tree until he saw the opening of a small cave. Darkness engulfed the first thirty feet of the cave until small holes in the cave walls illuminated chests of gold and silver that were all his!

In the mornings he would walk to school and at his mom's direction, return home, lock the door, eat, do homework and play until bedtime. His mom would work late for any extra money and sometimes he would go days without seeing her.

Greer stopped talking.

"That's it? Sad, lonely child. Nothing else?" Sean asked.

Greer smiled, "You almost seem interested, Sean."

"Not really. I was just wondering if the kid remained this side of Norman Bates."

"I don't know, man. That's all I saw."

"I thought you said you got a few snapshots of each lifetime?"

"I did, mostly, but for Joey's life this was all there was. Guessing that was the significant part?"

For the next hour or so the subject matter changed to football, their unimpressive golf game and The Walking Dead. The guys enjoyed their time by the pool, relaxed and bull-shitting with one another.

Regression V

A little later, it was Sean who circled back on the past life revival. "Was the next life any better?"

Greer grinned while realizing his buddy was not aware that he was outwardly showing interest.

"Yeah, wanna hear about the next one?"

"Is it sad and depressing like the last one?"

"Worse." Before Sean could object, Greer began.

Little Cindy combed her long, red hair frantically as she rushed to the hallway. Prospective parents had arrived looking for a daughter. Cindy knew the drill all too well, having been in the children's home for over five years now.

She was told that she was four when she arrived but cannot recall much before that, even her mother for that matter. Indeed, most of her life had been at this home.

Cindy lined up with seven other girls and recalled the rules clearly: stand up straight, smile, do not make eye contact and never speak unless spoken to.

She knew the older she was, the less likely she would be picked to go to a family. She overheard one of the home's workers say that, "Once they're over ten, they may as well settle in."

Cindy was still nine years old and very hopeful. However, the competition was getting tough. Four of the other girls were very young, between four and six years of age.

A well-dressed man and a beautiful yet sour faced woman in their early thirties walked the line of young girls as if window shopping for clothes. They conversed with each other, seemingly void of concern that the young girls could hear every comment and consideration.

"The younger, the better." The woman stated to her husband without even trying to whisper.

Cindy could feel the tears well up inside of her but she kept her composure and beautiful smile. The girls were finally excused to their rooms while one of the four year old girls was introduced to her new parents. Cindy fell onto her bed and cried into her pillow until she fell asleep.

Several months passed and Christmas time arrived. During that period, Cindy had turned ten. She had abandoned all hope of having a family and turned to food for comfort. Easily twenty pounds overweight and gaining, she would take anyone's leftovers and even stole food from the staff's eating area.

The home's workers were often mean to her or simply ignored her in favor of the younger children. The holidays saw many treats fill the worker's breakroom area so she had a bounty to pick from during her raids.

There was one bright moment on the horizon, however, as charities would bring donated gifts on Christmas Eve to the less fortunate children, like Cindy.

Finally, the big day arrived and strangers brought presents for each and every one of the parentless boys and girls.

Cindy opened her gift to find a generic doll with curly, red hair. She loved it. Not many other girls had red hair and she'd always felt different. She loved her new doll and took it straight to her room.

But her happiness would be short lived. After the charitable patrons left, the staff went room to room and collected the donated toys for their own children, which left the devastated orphans sad and crying on Christmas Eve.

"Dude, what the hell? Cindy the fat, red-headed orphan? Are you kidding me with this?"

Greer couldn't argue the sadness of the tale but assured Sean that she finally found happiness in a loving home, just one year later.

All four of the adopted children ranging from ages eleven to seventeen gathered in the living room to meet their new sister. Their foster mom introduced Cindy as she hugged her with one arm while everyone in unison welcomed her.

"Hi, Cindy!"

Their greeting made her beam ear to ear. Never had she felt like she belonged.

All of the children had their share of chores and their foster mom, being in her late fifties, had some physical limitations requiring help from time to time. Her goal was to provide a loving, supportive environment and parent the children with education while setting clear rules and guidelines.

Cindy's intelligence blossomed and she graduated in white, in the top of her class. She had long since lost the extra weight being quite loved while growing up with her brothers and sisters in Rhode Island, no longer in need of the false comfort of food.

Sean cracked open a cold beer and handed it to Greer. "Here, I can't imagine living in that head of yours but this might help."

Greer laughed and put his head back, soaking in the Florida sun.

Several hours later the guys had emptied the cooler and were faced with the choice to get more or call the day. Since Ashley had recently texted and Sean failed to claim the interest of any of the "eights," it was an easy choice.

Greer left the pool to the sound of Sean's best impression of a whip and the direction to let him know "when his mom would let him come out to play next."

A few hours later Ashley was eating dinner with Greer at his house.

Sobek patiently waited for something, anything to fall from the table to the floor. He had been conditioned that Greer would always ensure that some form of red meat or fowl would make its way to the ground level. Until then, he would drool quietly with ears forward, awaiting his treat.

"No, you don't spoil him at all." Ashley clearly read the scene.

"He's my boy! Plus have ya seen him light up when there's red meat on the menu? Definitely, a Labradorus Rex."

Greer hand delivered a piece of steak. Sobek gently took the meat while his tail wagged behind his ninety pound body.

Ashley enjoyed the interaction and the sincerity of her boyfriend's love for his dog.

"You guys have quite the bachelor pad here. Have you always lived alone?"

"Yeah, I got this place right out of school. I was gonna room with Sean but then I thought about what it would be like to room with Sean...so I didn't."

Ashley laughed, well aware that it was a friendly jab at his buddy's lifestyle. For all of Sean's nonsense he was good counsel for Greer. He kept him grounded, indeed more secular and hopefully realistic in his perspective, "recent" past lives, notwithstanding.

I can't watch him twenty-four-seven. He would later explain to Ashley.

The couple finished their meal and after a quick clean up found their way to the couch. Greer sat in one corner while Ashley snuggled up next to him with her head on his shoulder, feeling quite content and secure inside his outstretched arm.

She ran her finger along his bicep which she, without asking, had been repeatedly told measured seventeen inches. Ash was impressed with the artwork of his arm tattoo but admittedly a little scared of the Egyptian crocodile-headed portrait of Sobek.

A large crocodile with sharp, white teeth and cold, reptilian eyes seemed to stare into her soul. Complete with royal head dress and claws, he held a staff that stretched down just past the band that spelled out his name and was connected by small ankhs on the underside of the arm.

Sobek, the dog, found the opposite corner of the couch and took complete ownership of the cushion. He glanced at the couple with his brown, droopy Lab eyes before resting his head on the armrest. It would be only seconds before he was asleep.

Ashley shifted her gaze to Greer who was smiling at Sobek's retirement to slumber only to find that Greer was also showings signs of fatigue, having half-closed his eyes.

"You guys call it quits early around here."

Greer came back to life. "Naw, I was just resting."

Ashley looked back at his tattoo. "So, what's the fascination with Egypt?"

Greer paused because he had never been asked that question. Even Sean had only remarked, "Sweet tat. Egyptian, yeah? Nice." For Sean, that was practically an interrogation.

Greer suddenly made a connection. "Now that lifetime makes more sense."

Ashley heard the words but had no idea what he meant. "What, Sweetie?"

Greer decided to open up and get Ashley up to speed on "Past Life Project 2013."

Sean is still proud of that designation.

First, he clued her in on the Chicago lifetime with Jules and Charles. He described their deep love for one another during a short three months together and the terrible loss of Jules' life after the motorcycle accident.

"How long did Charles live in that wheelchair?"

"Eleven years."

"All alone?"

Greer nodded to the affirmative as Ashley felt a strange sadness for him or them if she accepted the premise. Her sadness turned to annoyance as she recalled the then confusing reference Sean made one day while on speaker with Greer.

"New Jules, I get it now." Her annoyance remained as she glared at Greer.

Not knowing, and honestly accepting that he never will fully understand how to handle an upset girlfriend, Greer charged forward with a description of each lifetime as he recalled them during his viewings with Beverly.

He told her of Sorcha, the young girl enslaved in a sugar mill that was removed from one life of enslavement and delivered to another.

Then, he relayed the military misfortune of Pascal in the French Army who joined to add meaning to his life and was eventually captured and left to die.

Seeing Ashley's arms had uncrossed, he continued confident that Sean's comment was no longer an issue.

Next was Richard or SuperDad as his buddy had termed him. He spoke in reverence of his loving parenting and dedication to his children's development.

Fondly, he described little imaginative Joey, or at least the little he was able to recall and the lonely hours spent inside his head in his bedroom.

Ashley was sitting back on the couch, wide eyed and while intrigued, quite surprised at Greer's endeavor.

Finally, he told her of Cindy in the children's home and the loving foster mother she found at the age of ten that afforded her the courage and education to grow into a bright, confident, young woman.

Ashley was moved by all of the personalities and their stories. Admittedly, she struggled with the surprise that this otherwise average football loving, gym going, beer drinking guy had such a strong interest in something so metaphysical and chose to left-brain her perspective.

"So, if I'm following this right you have an Egyptian life coming up?"

Greer straightened his back and pointed affirmatively at his beautiful Ashley. Overwhelmed with happiness that she not only held an interest, but was asking for more, he took the stage to tell her of the next recalled lifetime.

Regression VI

Ashley sat back and stretched her arm over the top of Sobek, stroking his thick black coat. Sobek barely noticed and continued to emit a low snore.

Greer absorbed the imagery before him of his loving and supportive girlfriend sitting next to his loyal, amazing dog.

A cold pitcher and the Bucs in the playoffs and I'm in the best beer commercial ever. He mused to himself.

Once again lost in his thoughts, he was able to regain his focus after reading Ashley's expectant and slightly impatient expression. Wasting no more time, he told her of his time in ancient Egypt.

Merkharu sat motionless, one hand resting on the arm of his golden throne and the other holding a staff topped with an ankh, the Egyptian symbol of enduring life. Adorned with a royal beard fashioned of gold and attached to his royal mask, he appeared stoic and menacing. He was shirtless, wearing a white skirt and two tight arm bands that dug into his muscular biceps.

In truth, he weighed only one hundred and seventy five pounds and stood five feet nine inches, yet not short for very ancient Egypt. Protective, masked guards stood erect and silent on either side of him.

"So, you're a Pharaoh? No offense but isn't everyone a king or someone famous when they talk about past lives?" Ashley was now showing her skepticism but still intrigued. "I was probably Cleopatra."

"Was a Pharaoh." Greer corrected. "But, not just any Pharaoh. It's going to get a little 'out there' so stay with me."

It was a little "out there" a while ago, Sweetie...

Merkharu was outwardly detached while in a deep pensive state and recalling his ancestry. The people were frightened as bright, shiny objects descended from the sky. Their landing, while eerily quiet, was overshadowed by the emergence of tall, humanoid creatures. Physically, the differences were minor and the awe at the sight of their flying crafts soon waned as they struggled to comprehend their ability to communicate with their minds rather than their mouths.

The visitors allowed the indigenous crowd to find the courage to approach them. After some time they embraced the strangers from the sky and their fear began to subside. Soon, their presence became commonplace.

Gradually, the aliens offered insight to the use of gems and crystals and eventually pyramid power. They used the power of their minds to move massive rocks into place, thus creating immense structures that were astrologically aligned. The impressive power producing pyramids tapped into a cosmic magic that is now lost to the changed constellations in the sky.

Their mission seemed to be one of universal philanthropy. Having won the people's trust, they began to copulate with the Egyptian woman.

Merkharu was the first of eight of his kind. A half-breed, revered as a miracle to the Egyptian people and a success to the aliens despite his loss of height due to the union of physiology.

Twenty-four years after his birth he ruled the people of ancient Egypt. True, indigenous Egyptians worked as slaves while the other seven half-breeds practiced magic as priests.

The aliens left Earth only after leaving clear instruction for Merkharu to procreate with indigenous females and continue the new line of the more intelligent, capable human. His offspring were only one quarter alien but the abilities were in the DNA; the very goal of the now departed visitors.

His specific agenda dictated Merkharu's actions for another fifteen years until his human frailty allowed a dental infection which traveled to his heart and eventually took his life. He left behind countless children that he never knew, having lived life on Earth void of the human experience of a family unit.

Ashley's incredulous expression said it all. Greer felt compelled to explain himself.

"I'm not saying I believe all this, Ash. I'm just sharing what I have experienced." He added, very unapologetically, "At your request."

Ashley ignored the last remark and was pleased that Greer was sharing a part of himself so openly. She stood up, moved toward her boyfriend and kissed him lovingly before leading him to the bedroom.

The couple made love and fell asleep in each other's embrace.

The next morning they left for their respective jobs with a promise to see each other Tuesday since Greer informed her that he was busy on Monday.

"We're doing bi's and tri's today; can't miss that!" Greer declared.

Ashley mentally questioned his choice of priority while Sean found it commendable.

After their Monday workday ended and their arms were sufficiently exercised, the guys found themselves, post workout, back at Greer's house mixing creatine, protein and several other powders that advertised the promise of muscle mass. It was a cool evening so they found their way to the outside deck with Sobek in tow.

Greer recapped the Egyptian lifetime for Sean, talking quickly to deter any lulls that would most certainly be met with unflattering comments about aliens and white skirts. When he was done telling the story, he received the following:

"Did you nail Cleopatra?"

Greer shook his head. "What's wrong with you?"

Sean laughed and reached for his shaker. He air toasted his buddy and declared "Good hit today, bro."

Greer returned the gesture. "So, finish your scary story."

Sean rolled his eyes and then decided to get it over with. He swung his patio high chair around so that he was facing his best friend and commanded Greer to "raise your right hand and repeat after me."

Greer complied, half-smiling and awaiting the fresh nonsense about to be delivered.

"I, broody Greer, swear that, after today, I will never ask Sean about his ghost story, ever again. If I do, I will be subject to a beat down...MMA style."

Greer laughed and repeated his words, mostly verbatim.

Sean took another drink of his muscle building chemical concoction and then relived the scariest night of his life…thus far.

Dewey and Sean sat on an old green sofa that clearly needed to meet the edge of the driveway but was deemed "basement worthy" by Mark's dad. The sunken room was ten by ten feet with a small window behind the boys' heads.

Mark retrieved a folded chair from the corner and positioned it facing the couch. He then placed a board, a Ouija Board, on the small glass top, coffee table between them.

Dewey displayed a similar look of concern for the board as he had when he saw the pentagram under Mark's bed. Sean took note of Dew's discomfort and watched as Mark lit two candles before turning off the single lamp in the room.

Just then, the basement door swung open.

"You're supposed to be watching me! I'm telling!"

Mark's younger sister, Becky, had become bored with the replacement sitter, the television. But, Mark knew the drill. "If you're quiet, I'll let you stay."

And, just like that, Becky was silent and standing against the wall, quite content feeling like a big kid and learning early how to get her way.

Feeling uneasy in the dark room, Sean rubbed his thighs nervously and asked, "So, Mark, what kind of game is this?"

Before Mark could reply, Dew answered. "It's a Ouija Board; you talk to ghosts with it."

Mark then demonstrated. "We all place our fingers on the pointer and ask questions, like this." Mark placed his fingertips on the plastic planchette and waited for the other boys to do the same.

Sean was first to reach his hands out and managed to get all of them on except his pinky fingers. "Do they all gotta be on?"

Mark just shrugged and mumbled, "Should be OK."

Dew joined his buddies and almost every edge of the pointer was covered with a finger. Immediately the plastic piece moved to the center top of the board. The swift movement caught the boys off guard and they all removed their fingers.

"Who did that?" Sean assumed it was Mark.

"I didn't move it! I swear!" Mark looked at Dewey.

"Don't look at me!"

The boys spent another few moments trading accusations until their excitement and anticipation overruled their initial fears. Placing their fingers back on the pointer, they resumed their connection as Dewey made note of something.

"Look, it moved to the picture of the pentagram on the board." Not seeing any significance in the remark they resumed their "game."

The planchette moved swiftly in a figure eight motion. Or, it resembled the symbol for infinity; contingent on your perspective.

The boys watched, wide-eyed as it effortlessly glided across the slick board. Anticipating the continuous movement with no thought to its meaning, they found it easy to keep their fingers on the pointer. A sense of calm was instilled as the sensation continued for another minute without incident.

Then, Mark asked a question. "Is anyone here?"

The pointer moved to "YES" and then resumed the figure eight movement. Sean and Dewey looked to Mark for this next question.

"Are you a ghost?"

Again, the board answered "YES."

Mark found the building conversation promising and decided to quiz the ghost.

"What's my name?"

The pointer moved from letter to letter.

M-A-R-K

"What's my birthday?"

J-U-L-Y-7

Mark looked up at and excitedly stated, "That's my birthday!" He looked down at the board and continued his queries.

"What is the star under my bed?"

D-O-O-R

"A door to where?"

H-E-L-L

At this, the boys all removed their fingers and sat back, wide eyed and with growing trepidation.

The room dropped a good ten degrees in temperature. Dewey took instant notice. "Uh-oh."

Sean, ever one for the obvious, declared, "This can't be a good idea, guys."

Unaware of what was being spelled out, Becky stood silently against the wall trying to understand the "game" the boys were playing.

Mark's fear was turning to anger. He was tired of being scared in his own bedroom. He begged the guys to ask one more question. They reluctantly put their fingers back on the pointer. Wanting to confront this ghost Mark asked, "What is your name?"

L-U-C-I-F-E-R

Suddenly the board jumped six inches off the table. The guys quickly pulled their hands back as if escaping a tripped mouse trap. Becky's long blond hair stood up straight above her head. She screamed, frozen in terror. A whirlwind of freezing air rushed through the basement extinguishing the candles which left the children in total darkness. Becky continued to scream; her voice became hoarse but still deafening.

Mark stumbled in the dark to find his way to the lamp in the corner. He felt someone grab his hand and pull him the opposite direction.

"Let go so I can get to the light!" he pleaded. He pulled and pulled but could not break free. The hand holding him was cold and strong.

Suddenly, the room was illuminated to show Sean was half on and half off the couch, pale faced and motionless. Becky was still against the wall while her hair slowly fell down back into place. Dewey was standing next to the lamp that he had just turned on.

Confused, Mark looked at each of the other children one by one. "Who was grabbing me?"

No one responded.

"Which one of you grabbed me?" he practically yelled.

In almost perfect unison they responded, "Wasn't me."

"That's the story, my man." Sean got up to head home.

Greer stood up, at a loss for words.

First time ever. Sean would later say.

He could see that telling the story had brought back some uncomfortable memories.

"See ya, Sean."

"Later, G.

Regression VII

Greer texted both Ashley and Sean that he had taken a half day off of work to see Beverly for his seventh regression. Their replies were easily recognizable.

"See you tonight, Sweetie."

"Is she hot?"

"Are you ready, Greer?" He assumed his place on the black, leather, inclined chair with his feet on the rest and nodded to Beverly.

She was an attractive woman with soft brown, straight hair and smart, square glasses. Definitely in her forties, Beverly emitted a soft smile and soothing tone. Her low cut blouse, under her dark blue pant suit, still rocked out the hourglass, but this side of cougar. Greer realized he was sizing her up.

Dammit Sean!

Beverly's familiar, calming voice allowed Greer to quickly relax and, without direction, he envisioned the boat on the open waters. He was, sadly, reminded of Sorcha during her depressing voyage to slavery.

"Allow any intrusive thoughts to leave your mind." Beverly offered as if aware of his current mental state.

Images began to form on the horizon as his mind's eye displayed a vision.

Charles swallowed hard and began. "I've never been able to talk to someone like this." At this admission his wide smile showcased flawless teeth. Julia gasped at their brilliance.

Greer opened his eyes. "Uh, yeah, I've seen this one."

Beverly looked up from her notepad and asked, "Are you sure?"

Greer grinned and held back a chuckle as he replied, "Very sure."

Beverly simply suggested, "OK, let's try again."

She talked him through the same visualization steps until Greer spoke.

"I see Joey, again."

Beverly was confused. "Are you sure?"

"Yes, but it's different this time; he's a grown man, but I know it's him."

Beverly jumped on board. "What else is different?"

Greer smiled ear to ear. "He became a writer!"

Joey, now Joseph, was submitting his latest article to the New York Times Editor. Greer could see that he was well dressed as he made his way out of the Times' office and rejoined what appeared to be his wife. Strangers to him, but not his brilliance, paused to tip their hat and offer their praise for his work. The scene ended.

Greer was pleased as he had felt that the original viewing of this particular lifetime was limited.

Beverly felt that a revisit to a previous session wasn't a full viewing and offered to take him back one more time. Once again, he saw a familiar face.

Richard looked around his hospital bed at the faces of his fully grown loving children, Sarah, Eddie, Emily and William. They were leaning over their father while holding his hands and crying.

Richard recalled the day he had adopted each one of them and how he fought the system each time while assuring them that a single father could raise them in a loving and supportive home. He made it his life's mission every day to give those innocent children a foundation of support, the education needed to succeed, and a fighting chance out in the world that they could not have received all alone.

Greer sat up reflecting with bittersweet understanding.

Beverly shifted into therapy mode. "Greer, are you up to discussing the viewings?"

His eyes glanced up and displayed what Beverly noted in her file as a "cautionary but curious response to the affirmative."

He remained quiet, now feeling somewhat overwhelmed by the sad continuity of his lifetimes.

Sensing his emotional response, she chose to be simplistic and do what she does best which was allow Greer to answer his own questions. Beverly suggested, as if knowing his thoughts, "Let's look at them one at a time."

Instantly loving her structured approach, Greer's shoulders raised and he looked up and to the left and then began.

"Well, first there was Sorcha. Honestly, I didn't really relate to her."

"How did that lifetime, rather how did she make you feel?"

Greer thought for a moment. "Sad. Like a lot of the incarnations."

"Good, let's focus on this one for now."

Greer really had nothing else to offer so he spoke out of expectation. "She had a good attitude."

Beverly just looked at him.

He added, "Guessing I'm missing something, huh?"

Beverly smiled and switched gears. "What were the pros and cons of her lifetime?"

Greer was surprised at her process but was not going to question her. No, he would leave the inevitable ridicule to Sean.

"Well, the cons are easy. She was enslaved, treated poorly and alone. She even died alone."

Beverly made notes and maintained her patient and encouraging smile. "And, the pros?"

"Not many of those."

"Try to be objective, Greer."

He considered her slightly improved circumstances. "She was removed and placed in a home; still a slave but not subject to beatings and hard labor."

Beverly sensed a potentially important aspect of the lifetime. "What caused those circumstances to improve, Greer?"

"A worker. He took her home to his wife." Greer's face expressed an obvious struggle to see the importance of the man so Beverly asked about the second lifetime.

Greer recalled the incarnation. "Pascal? Another life alone, dying alone. That's a theme! A very sad one, but a theme, nonetheless."

Beverly flipped a page and continued writing. "What else?"

Greer was adopting an intellectual perspective of his regressions and was seeing them through an objective viewpoint while growing excited at the apparent common threads.

"His dying thoughts were of regret that he didn't have a family."

Beverly made more notes.

"You're gonna have a book when we're done." Greer quipped.

She continued writing. "Uh-huh. What about the next lifetime stands out to you?"

"The next life was Richard. Initially I saw that he had four kids but I now know that they were adopted. And, they loved him, until the end." Greer smiled and then resumed his trademark serious look. "He wasn't ever married, was he?"

Beverly remained silent allowing Greer to continue.

He spoke more to himself than her. "He was single but not lonely. I mean, he died surrounded by his family." Greer made a connection and blurted out, "Cindy!"

Beverly's hand was cramping but she kept writing. Greer continued to audibly work through his thoughts.

"Cindy was alone but then found a family thanks to her adoptive mother. Before that Richard adopted four children. It's almost like I lived both perspectives, ya know?"

Beverly smiled. "To me, it is like you lived both perspectives."

Greer continued without addressing her remark. "They longed for a family. So did Pascal, but he didn't get the chance to make one." Greer paused, remembering his life in Egypt. "Merkharu didn't have a family although he had many children and he was alone most of the time."

He became focused on the specific recurrence of being alone. How many times had he worried about never finding "the one"? He was often detached and kept Ashley at arm's length, choosing to see her only two to three times a week, just to ensure he could keep a temperature check on their relationship. He was picky or particular depending on how he wanted to rationalize his defenses. It was no longer fun dissecting the lifetimes to the same sad realizations. He was choosing the pessimistic perspective and becoming lost in a classic Greer, pensive moment and Beverly reacted.

She put down her pad and leaned forward, very motherly, and asked Greer to listen to her.

"The fear of being alone is often fueled by abandonment. I believe it doesn't matter if something happened in your past or past life, it stays with you."

Greer responded slightly despondent. "Set up for failure?"

"Absolutely, not. We make choices and set priorities in our lives. Pascal decided his life and death would mean something, and it did despite his regret of never having a family. Had he made it out of the war he may very well have found a wife and had children. But he set the priority of making a contribution to the world in a very important war."

She continued. "Richard gave all of his love and attention to those children in need. And, they gave it back, as you saw. Being loved and not being alone isn't only accomplished in a romantic partnership, Greer.

There are benefits to being alone. Look at Joey, who became Joseph, an accomplished writer as a result of his time spent in his own imagination. What you viewed as a sad childhood was a breeding ground for creative and adventurous thought.

Even Cindy finally found her loving family unit with people who were strangers the day they met. She learned that family is not defined by blood but by support, encouragement, acceptance and unconditional love. Understanding that ensures you are never truly alone."

Greer's perspective had been widened and he allowed his comprehension to settle a moment before he spoke. "Merkharu was alone but leaders often are. His priority was his agenda and from that angle, he had a successful lifetime."

Beverly swayed her body slightly from left to right, half agreeing with Greer. "He did choose a priority and that did not change. I don't like to measure viewings as successful or unsuccessful. I prefer to focus on what we can learn from our past to help our future."

Greer thanked Beverly as she walked him out of her office.

He paused at the door with one last thought. "I recognize the people in some of those lives that helped as best they could. Joey's mom encouraged his imagination. Cindy's foster mom was every bit a real mother to her. Richard's kids were at his bedside at the end and even the man that took Sorcha home removed her from a worse situation."

Beverly made a mental note to add this to Greer's file before responding, "Are you aware of those helpful people in this lifetime?"

Instantly seeing a vision of Ashley and his best buddy, Sean, in his mind's eye, Greer beamed a wide smile.

"Yeah."

The story continues in 7 Apparitions-Book 3 in The 7 Novellas Series by Gare Allen.

7

Apparitions

by

Gare Allen

The 7 Novellas Series by Gare Allen

Book One - 7 Sessions

Book Two - 7 Regressions

Book Three - 7 Apparitions

Book Four - 7 Abductions

Book Five- 7 Projections

Book Six- 7 Predictions

Book Seven- 7 Reflections

Apparition I

Slowly, Greer managed to successfully pull his numb arm out from beneath Ashley's resting body without waking her. For the next few minutes he stared at the ceiling fan, flat on his back, as he welcomed the blood rushing back into his left arm, tingling as it regained feeling. He pondered the increased frequency of this event, as Ashley had been staying over two to three times a week as of late.

He glanced at the alarm clock, which sat immediately to his right on the night stand, and noted the time of three forty-five a.m. Welcoming back possessed mobility of all his fingers, he turned to check on his sleeping beauty.

The light from the street lamp beamed in through his bedroom window and allowed Greer a familiar point-of-view; its soft glow illuminated Ashley's glistening light brown hair, from an angle that just missed her eyes, enabling her to maintain a peaceful slumber.

She sleeps like the dead. Greer had recently told his best friend, Sean. *The running of the bulls wouldn't wake her.*

Greer stared a moment longer at his beautiful girlfriend and ran the back of his feeling-restored hand along her soft cheek. Though she remained sound asleep, the sensation of his touch stimulated a head turn away from him, with her body following, thieving what little comforter Greer had been using.

I'll try not to take that personally.

Still lying on his back, he closed his eyes and began to drift into a light sleep. He was beginning to feel chilly, another familiar occurrence as his partner was, as usual, wrapped in a cocoon of all his warm bedding. A moment later, having just about drifted out, he felt a severe drop in temperature in the room. He opened his eyes, surprised to see a building fog. Despite blinking and rubbing his eyelids several times to clear the haze from his vision, the same fuzzy perspective remained. A continued decline in the air's temperature was followed by the realization that he had lost complete control of his body. He struggled to move his arms and legs only to lose the battle to a frightening realization of complete paralysis.

Am I dreaming?

Thinking, rather hoping with all his might that he was having a nightmare, he told himself to wake up. No longer could he swallow, blink or even breathe. The fog now completely surrounded him, blocking any view of his bedroom, including Ashley, not that he could turn to look.

Was she aware of what was happening? Was she paralyzed too?

Unable to turn his head or call out, he felt a full-on panic attack. His heart pounded hard within his chest while terrifying fear engulfed his sense of being. Feeling trapped inside his own body and unable to move, created a smothering wave of claustrophobia that prompted an even more rapid heartbeat. The room, now permeated with a blinding white haze, fell hauntingly silent as he experienced a loss of hearing to accompany his horror. Greer yelled inside his mind for help, for Ashley, for the ability to move!

A few more seconds, which felt like minutes, passed as the horrific torture endured. Staring at the white blanket of smoke, he became light-headed and was convinced he was going to pass out, or worse.

Just when he thought he would surely lose consciousness, assuming he was truly awake, an image began to form directly above his frozen face. An outline of a large head pushed its way past the white barrier and materialized before Greer's wide, dry unblinking eyes. Retreating mist revealed a terrifying sight to which Greer, immobilized and helpless, was forced to witness.

A demonic visage now stared down, barely an inch above him. Its leathery skin was folded over, both burned and scarred. Giant, blood red eyes directed a primal, piercing glare into Greer's soul. Pointed teeth, brown and crooked, jutted from its mouth. Inside his head, Greer screamed in terror at the monster before him. The devilish apparition seemed to be studying Greer's motionless form as he floated up and down, moving ever closer to Greer's terror-stricken face. Coarse, wire-like hair on the chin of the evil being brushed against Greer's cheek and, with their mutual contact, his physical senses returned. Greer inhaled a welcomed breath of air, but was overcome by a foul stench he would later describe as a mixture of death and decay. Audible, low growls emanated from the creature as Greer finally blinked his aching eyes. Despite numerous attempts to blink the image away, the demon remained. Panic and fear instantly transformed into anger.

Feeling his mobility restored, he jumped up with outstretched arms, and lunged for the demonic intruder before him. The demon growled loudly as it was pushed upward and away from the bed by a set of forceful hands. A sensation of extreme heat emanated from the creature's soft, mushy skin. The monster hissed as it turned, revealing a long black tail with small red spikes which whipped around and knocked the alarm clock from the night stand. In a flash, the demon disappeared beneath the bed; the fog pulled along with it, and leaving no trace of its presence.

Greer ran to the wall and quickly flipped the light switch to the on position.

Ashley, awakened by the light, rolled her body back toward Greer's side of the bed. Pulling her soft hair away from her deep, blue eyes, she witnessed her boyfriend, who wore only a pair of boxer briefs, gasping for air. Wide-eyed, he stared at the bottom of the bed, trying to make sense of his terrifying experience.

The lamp's illumination demanded Sobek's attention as well. He waddled, sleepily, into the bedroom doorway and glanced upward at Greer. He tilted his head slightly, bearing the typical inquisitive Labrador expression; this demeanor was duplicated by Ashley, who had sat up in the bed, oblivious to what Greer had just endured.

"Bad dream, Sweetie?"

Greer collapsed himself downward onto the edge of the bed. As his breathing returned to a normal cadence, he glanced to the floor and saw the alarm clock, on its side, displaying a time of three forty-seven a.m. In disbelief, he exclaimed, "Two minutes?"

Sobek responded by taking several steps forward and sloppily licking Greer's left cheek which, despite what had just occurred, managed to bring half a smile to his face.

"Wanna talk about it, Greer?" asked a very sleepy, unaware Ashley.

Greer scratched Sobek's neck and then got up, turned off the light, crawled back into bed, and kissed his girlfriend on the forehead.

"Go back to sleep, Ash, we'll talk in the morning."

Sobek reluctantly found his way back out to his bed which had been moved to the living room to accommodate Ashley's presence overnight.

He actually tried to fit all three of us in the bed. She later told one of her friends.

There's plenty of room for all of us. He had told Sean.

Greer stared at the ceiling, reliving the traumatic experience repeatedly in his mind's eye. He argued with himself that it had to have been a nightmare.

But it was so real! And the clock was knocked to the floor! It seemed like it was surprised to see me or was curious about me...the way those piercing red eyes looked at me!

After another hour of confused inner dialogue he fell asleep from mental exhaustion.

The alarm clock, still on the floor, sounded precisely at seven a.m.

Ashley moaned. "It's Saturday Greer, why did you set the alarm?"

To which he simply replied, "Gym."

Greer took a quick shower then mixed a concoction of fruit, protein powder and several muscle building products together in a blender. He drank this as he walked Sobek around the block, his mind heavy on the nightmare, or nightmare-ish experience.

By eight o'clock he'd come back home to find Ashley getting dressed and gathering her belongings.

"Are you heading out, Ash?"

Ashley stopped, sat on the edge of the bed, placed her hand to her right and motioned for Greer to join her.

"I am, but not before you tell me about last night."

Just then, Sobek made his way onto the bed and from behind, lathered Ashley with a lick along her right cheek. At this she laughed and turned enough to reach Sobek's soft, black coat; making use of her nails to lightly scratch him as he had become accustomed to enjoying during her visits.

Greer smiled at the familiar scene of Sobek and Ashley's loving interaction, but was quickly distracted as he noticed the alarm clock, once more.

Ashley looked at him expectantly. "Well?"

Greer paused, still staring at the clock, and withdrew into his mind.

Was it just a nightmare? Did I knock the clock to the floor by accident?

He turned to see Ashley's raised eyebrows, which he had learned, the hard way, were a signal of waning patience.

I don't want to scare her and she already thinks I'm half nuts with all the past-life regression stuff. She didn't see or experience anything so how could it have been real?

Greer finally chose a response. "It was just a bad dream and I don't remember much about it. I must have hit the clock without realizing it."

Ashley managed a half-smile while observing her boyfriend, who had once again, held back in a conversation. She continued scratching the neck of Sobek, who had sprawled across the bed on his side, eyes half-closed and quite content. While she didn't necessarily believe Greer was lying, she was sure he was not telling her the whole truth.

It'll take a few conversations, but I'll get the story eventually. She would tell her friend later that day.

Ashley maintained her patient demeanor and allowed the short conversation to end...for now.

"I'm gonna get going. I'm meeting some friends later. See you tonight?"

Greer, relieved and foolishly confident that he would never need to share his experience, grabbed her overnight bag and walked his girlfriend to her car, with his faithful dog in tow.

Ashley bent down to address her favorite canine much like she would an infant, "I'll see you later Sobeky, yes I will!" Sobek wagged his tail and lowered his head to receive one more head scratch.

Greer waited as Ashley finished her doggie goodbye. She stood up and leaned in to kiss him.

"Have a good workout. Tell Sean I said hello."

They kissed and set a time of seven o'clock to meet for dinner.

Thirty minutes later Greer was at the gym, beginning his first set of back pull-downs, having just finished telling Sean his tale of the demonic visitor.

Sean immediately declared the event a bad dream and then delivered a jab as a matter of course. "Was it the Ghost of Christmas Past? If so, present and future are next and 'Future Greer' will be the real nightmare."

Greer finished his set and switched places with his workout partner. Sean turned his hat backwards and began his pulls while Greer responded, a bit impressed.

"First of all, points for the literary reference. Second, it wasn't a ghost; it was a demon or something evil…definitely not human."

Sean, having finished his set, customarily swapped places with Greer after taking the liberty to increase the weight. Sean removed his cap and ran his hand through his short blond hair while checking out the "scenery" and offered some Sean-sight to his buddy.

Sean-sight is like insight except it comes from Sean so ya gotta speak his language. He explained to Ashley later at dinner.

"Man, it's just leftover past-life, dream symbol, astral, alien, science fiction, horror movie sweat."

Greer breathed out between reps, "Ya know, just because ya string a bunch of words together, it isn't necessarily a sentence."

"You get my point."

And Greer did. Sean was suggesting that his buddy was purging the recent months' experiences of past life regressions along with consistent exposure to metaphysical readings, programs and books.

"Focus on real life for a while, ya know, like Ashley?"

Greer was surprised. "Since when are you on Team Ashley?"

Sean was ready for his set and motioned for Greer to move. "Since the whining about not having a girlfriend stopped."

Greer pondered Sean's assessment and landed on the same airstrip. "A release dream, eh? That makes sense." Greer applied the theory to another dream. "I guess the recurring dream could be something that needs to be released too. But, what?"

Sean was slightly interested but more focused on the workout. "You have the same dream over and over?"

Greer took a swig of water. "Yeah, for years now. It must mean something."

"Of course it does. Can we focus now?"

"You've never had a recurring dream?"

"Yeah, G, I dream that we focus on our workout."

Sean then noticed a bruise on his friend's neck. "How'd that happen, man?"

Greer turned his head sideways to see it in the adjacent mirror. "Not sure, must have bumped into something, or, I dunno. Been there over a week now, thought it would be gone by now."

With that, they moved on to another subject and the next exercise.

Apparition II

Thirty minutes later, the guys finished their workout, bought a couple of protein shakes and chatted on their way out to the parking lot. Back muscles sufficiently worked, they made plans to meet poolside on Sunday, and then departed for their respective homes.

Greer arrived to his house after a stop at the grocery store to buy food and wine for the evening meal. Having put away the groceries, he decided to take a much needed nap. Calculating he'd managed a mere four hours of sleep due to, what he now deemed, a nightmare of epic proportions, he was hoping for another two.

After a hot shower he retired to bed and set the alarm for five o'clock to allow sufficient time to prepare a dinner for Ashley. Once in bed he immediately felt the heavy leg of his dog in his gut as Sobek made his way, literally, across Greer to his, or, some might argue, Ashley's, adjacent spot.

Feeling just a little irked he uttered, "Thanks, buddy."

Plenty of room and the unusual access to the comforter fostered an initially perfect slumber and within minutes they were both sound asleep.

They enjoyed a solid hour and a half of undisturbed rest until Greer felt a chill on his left cheek. Lying on his right side, he opened his eyes to see the alarm clock on his dresser, instantly reminding him of the hideous creature's tail, whose image was ingrained in his mind. He pulled the comforter up to his neck and tried to clear his mind for a few more minutes of rest.

Just as he closed his eyes, Sobek emitted a low growl. Greer reached back to pet his pup, without turning his body, to comfort and quiet his canine companion, but the snarling increased in volume until it became a bark. Greer turned around to see his now fully awakened Retriever quite alert and staring at the ceiling.

"What is it, boy?"

He scratched the greying muzzle of Bek's square Lab face in an attempt to relax his agitated dog as the room grew colder. With no effect, he then observed his dog's eyes dart from the ceiling, to the end of the bed, and back to the ceiling again; despite the intermittent barking, his expression appeared more inquisitive in nature.

Greer resumed his scratching while looking at the ceiling and back down to the bed, but saw nothing. He glanced back at Sobek to find his ears folded back, his hind end raised and his impressive canine teeth on display. While simultaneously growling a full-on warning tone, Sobek stared straight past Greer toward the end of the bed.

Feeling another decline in temperature, Greer began to panic as he experienced a full emotional recall of last night's evil intruder. Slowly, he managed to turn himself in time to witness a full apparition appear, hovering just above the edge of his bed.

Sobek's growl became a fitful whine as if he also feared the vision before them. Greer gaped at the unbelievable sight; breathless and in shock, his frozen stare registered every detail of the ghostly appearance of a...woman.

Greer locked eyes with the lady suspended just above his bed and only a terrifying arm's reach away from him. Oddly, his fear slightly subsided as he observed her bloody face, to his surprise, displaying fear and confusion.

Sobek sounded an uncomfortable bark despite the continued comforting petting, all eyes transfixed on the floating female. Inhaling a needed breath, Greer continued to study her.

He beheld a fairly attractive woman in her early fifties, despite the blood running down her face. Her brown hair lay flat; one side coated with bodily fluid and an obvious gash. Scrubs…he noted that she wore blue scrubs.

Shocking himself, he held control of his senses long enough to blurt out, "Are you a doctor?"

He studied her face as she appeared to not only comprehend his question but attempt a response. Her mouth moved but he heard nothing.

"What did you say?"

She moved her lips again, this time with outstretched arms, as if making a plea. Fear gave way to hopeful interaction with this human entity, as Greer tried to communicate with the apparition. Even Sobek fell quiet, but continued to maintain a visual lock on their late afternoon visitor.

"Are you hurt?" Greer initially felt stupid for asking, but she was responsive, if not audibly.

Later he would defend his query as reasonable due to the deep bloody wound in her upper forehead.

Again, the suspended lady moved her lips but released no sound.

"I'm sorry, I can't hear-", Greer stopped mid-sentence as the room suddenly filled with a white, almost blinding light. Within a few seconds the brightness forced his eyes shut.

Not again.

Sobek broke his silence releasing several alerting barks and then abruptly stopped.

Greer opened his eyes, scanning the room. The woman was gone with no indication of her ever having been there, along with the overwhelming white light. His once concerned dog was now wagging its thick, black tail, looking up, with no trace of fear or aggression to be found.

The alarm clock sounded.

Yeah, I'm up.

Greer made his way, in a bit of a daze, to the kitchen where he satiated Sobek's appetite. He chilled a bottle of Riesling, and then prepared a meal consisting of baked chicken, asparagus and brown rice, his mind reflecting heavily on the ghostly experience.

It had to be real. This is the second time something like this has happened and I was awake this time, I know it! He continued to mentally review the scene. *She seemed confused as to where she was. She was injured, her head was bleeding... Who was she?*

He was just about to break out the wine for an early start when the doorbell triggered a series of deep base barks from you-know-who.

Greer took a breath and told himself to forget about the ghosts. He then opened the door and allowed a canine love attack to ensue on Ashley.

"Hey Sobeky, how's my big boy?"

"Ok Bek, don't eat my girlfriend. Down, boy." Greer instructed in a tone that was hardly serious.

Sobek retreated as directed which gave Ashley the ability to enter, where upon she immediately landed a kiss on her boyfriend's cheek.

"Hope I'm not late. There was a bad accident on the way here that had traffic backed up for at least a mile."

"Nope, you're good. Hungry?"

A few moments later the couple sat enjoying each other's company at the dinner table, with Sobek present in his usual spot at Greer's feet, patient and quiet…for now.

Greer paused with fork in hand to take in the beauty across from him. Ashley had her soft, brown hair pulled to one side, hanging just above the narrow slope of her shoulders. Her blue, short-sleeve top accentuated her delicate frame. She was more than pleasing to view and certainly enough to remove the memory of the day's events, including the apparitions…mostly.

"You look nice tonight."

Ashley smiled. "Thank you, Greer." Noting that Greer wore his signature black V-neck shirt and blue, straight-cut jeans, she delivered playfully, "So do you. I see you went with black tonight."

Greer grinned, fully aware of his need for an expansion of color in his wardrobe.

"You're lucky I even have a shirt on."

To this, she could not argue.

He has something against clothes; his idea of modesty is boxer shorts. She had told some of her close friends.

"How's the chicken, Ash?"

Ashley choked back a laugh. Greer served baked chicken almost daily with rice and asparagus. She had endured this meal more than half a dozen times. While homemade and very tasty, it was redundant. Eager to avoid his protein-carb-ratio, muscle building lecture again, she simply replied, "Delicious."

Ashley leaned back, having finished her meal, took another sip of her sweet white wine and asked, "So, what was the nightmare you had last night?"

Greer was caught off guard and looked away before responding. "It was nothing." He focused on the dog under the table. "Here ya go Bek, the last piece of chicken for ya buddy."

Not distracted by his tactic, Ashley pressed him. "Sweetie, you were out of bed and out of breath with the alarm clock knocked to the floor. What happened?"

"I had a bad dream and I must have knocked the clock off the dresser...I guess."

"What was the dream about?"

Greer looked away and shrugged his shoulders, "Not sure, I really don't remember." Sensing she was not buying his story, he switched tactics. "So, what did you do today?"

Ashley took another sip of wine and looked nowhere in particular before responding, as intentionally casual as possible, "I had lunch with a friend."

Greer took the bait. "Nice. Where did you go?"

Ashley swirled the remaining wine in her glass and chose an innocent expression, then delivered, "Richard took me to a great Italian place. The pasta was made fresh and the service was excellent."

Greer froze. He glared at Ashley with narrow eyes, allowing a pause for his mental huddle.

What the hell? Relax, don't seem jealous. Just ask questions.

Suppressing a reality-TV level emotional outburst, he softly asked, "Um, who's Richard?"

Enjoying her character's continued, and mostly innocent, deference, she took her phone out of her pocket, scrolled through her read texts and replied, "Oh, just a friend." She glanced up to see that the blood had rushed to her boyfriend's face. "Red on the outside, green on the inside?"

Greer managed a level of restraint that surprised even him. "Uh, how do you know him?"

As if sensing an impending explosion, Sobek got up and found his bed in the living room.

Ashley decided to not implode the evening but instead land the plane and make her point. "He's a friend visiting from Chicago. I'm close to him and his partner, Mike."

Greer visibly relaxed at the realization that there was no threat in that scenario. While the tension left his fists, and his fingers once again were relaxed and accepting the flow of blood, he nodded while boasting a relieved grin.

"I'm sorry G, I should have told you." Ashley called him "G" when she needed him to feel at ease. He initially retorted with "A" but decided it was too masculine for such a feminine creature and settled on Ash. "It's important to communicate in a relationship, don't you think?" She tilted her head slightly while leaning back in her chair, enjoying a final sip of her wine.

Well played, Ash…well played.

Greer accepted defeat, got up, grabbed the half empty bottle of wine and both their glasses. He leaned over the top of his beauty and kissed her on the forehead.

"Yes. And I'm sorry. Going forward I will be very forthcoming." He promised. "Let's go relax in the living room."

Their exchange over, Ashley snuggled next to Greer on his brown, oversized couch. Sobek raised a tired head briefly, and then drifted off beside them, on his personalized bed.

Ashley was feeling the effects of the alcohol and closed her eyes. *TV it is then.*

Greer retrieved the remote and flipped on the flat screen displaying a local news station.

"A fatal accident resulted in the death of one driver on North Dale Mabry Highway earlier this afternoon..."

Ashley opened her eyes at hearing the news report. "That must be the accident that caused the traffic back-up." She closed her eyes again and thought no more of it.

The reporter continued. "The investigation into the accident is not complete but we are able to tell you that the deceased driver was a local nurse. Police are not releasing her name until the family has been notified."

Greer felt a chill run down his spine. He turned to Ashley, only to find that she had fallen asleep, curled up against his side.

Apparition III

As Ashley slept, Greer pondered the possibility and disturbing likelihood that the ghost he saw just hours ago could be the very woman the news had been discussing.

I guessed that she was a doctor but the scrubs could mean a nurse also. Ok, let's say that it is the same person. Why the hell was she in my bedroom?

He debated another hour before waking her up. "Wanna watch a movie?"

Slowly she came to life while holding her hand to her head. "Sure. But, no more wine."

She didn't need to worry as Greer had finished off the bottle while she peacefully rested.

They watched "The Lake House" and enjoyed each other's embrace until they retired to bed.

I don't know man, something about a magic mailbox. He would later describe the flick, in very little detail, to Sean.

Greer climbed into bed but discovered his girlfriend had quickly fallen asleep, mere seconds after her head had hit the pillow.

"Uh, good night, Ash." He spoke in his normal tone, knowing full well that it would not disturb her. Rolling over on his left side, to face Ashley, the relaxing effect of the wine won over his conscious state.

After a few hours Greer felt a familiar chill on his right cheek. He reached down for the comforter to find that his girlfriend had once again thieved the covers. He'd just closed his eyes and had begun to fade out when he felt a second, colder chill.

Here we go.

He allowed his right eye to survey the room and then the second eye followed in turn. He sprang upright when he caught the sight of an elderly man standing at the foot of his bed.

Greer's first thought was to wake up Ashley, but then reconsidered. He stared at the apparition for a moment and noted the details. Before him appeared a man, easily in his eighties, maybe even nineties, with thin, white, slicked back hair, and dressed in a three piece suit and matching black tie. His skin was pale, almost translucent.

He's just standing there, like he's waiting for something. He seems...peaceful. Greer thought to himself.

Greer had been startled but, surprisingly, was not fearful. There was a sense of calm about the bedroom which only intensified once the blinding, white light returned. Its brilliance engulfed every square inch of the room, just as it had when the nurse was present. Just before the image of the man was bathed in light, Greer observed his parting expression; a smile.

In a flash, everything was baseline again. The temperature in the room returned to normal, no white light, no man, woman or devil for that matter. Ashley continued to sleep soundly, oblivious to what had just transpired.

These aren't dreams. I don't know what they are, but they are not dreams.

Pondering the latest apparition, he sat in the dark as Sobek wandered into the bedroom.

"You're a little late, buddy."

Bek wagged his tail a few times at the sound of Greer's voice. Sniffing nothing of interest in the air, he retreated back to his bed in the living room.

His mind weary, Greer lay back down on the bed. It would be over an hour before he fell back to sleep. He laid there, cold and shivering from a lack of covers, failing to make a connection between the three apparitions, until mental exhaustion shut down his mind, and his body, finally, followed suit.

Eight o'clock arrived and Greer was greeted with a morning kiss upon wakening and then, much more. Afterward, the couple enjoyed breakfast together, or at least Greer's concept of a morning meal.

I get yogurt, a banana and bottled water. If I complain, I gotta hear that 'abs don't get made in the gym, they're made in the kitchen'. So are grumpy bagel-loving girlfriends. She would text her best friend later that day.

Ashley and Greer said goodbye around noon. His afternoon free, Greer sent a text to Sean that he was on his way over. Thirty minutes later the guys were poolside, shirtless wearing sunglasses, soaking in the sun.

Greer described the visitations of the injured and presumed dead woman as well as the well-dressed elderly man.

"So, you're dreaming of ghosts now? Is this more past life stuff?"

Greer corrected his buddy. "No, they're not dreams. I thought they were, but now...they're just so real, man. And no, they have nothing to do with past life regressions. At least, I don't think they do." Greer paused. "To be accurate, I saw two ghosts and one demon and it seems to only happen when I'm sleeping."

"Which...makes them dreams." Sean retorted trying, as always, to keep his friend grounded. But, knowing that Greer would only move past the issue by talking it through, Sean kept the topic alive. "Has Ashley seen anything?"

"No, she slept through them. Sobek sensed the woman though, so I know that one was real."

"A white horse with an erection isn't a unicorn man. There may be another explanation."

Greer laughed at the classic Sean-sight moment. "You said you saw a ghost once didn't you?"

Sean grimaced. "You remember that? We've had to take bolt cutters to your gym lock twice because you forgot the combination, but that you remember?"

Greer ignored the jab. "When did you see the ghost?"

Sean reluctantly recalled the event. "It happened after that night we'd all played with the Ouija Board. I went back to Mark's house and he was down in the basement. We started talking about what had happened when we felt the cold blast of wind, the candles all blew out and his sister's hair had stood on end. The board was still on the coffee table. Mark couldn't sleep because he saw something under his bed and his room was always freezing. He asked me to work the board with him again, but I refused. I was still freaked out over what had happened and wanted nothing to do with that thing. Mark kept begging me, man, but I wouldn't give in. He lit the candles, turned out the lights and tried to work it by himself. As he was trying, I looked in the opposite corner of the room and saw something."

"What did you see?"

Sean expressed his annoyance at the interruption, just to be a dick. "Can I continue so you can find out?"

Greer rolled his eyes, took a swig of his bottled water and leaned back in his chair, but said nothing. Mentally, he spoke a few choice words.

"Thank you." Sean resumed his story. "So, I'm seeing this movement in the corner and it starts to take shape. Mark is still screwing around with the board and doesn't notice it. I just stared at the figure until it finally stepped out of the dark and into the candlelight. I looked over at Mark, but he still hadn't seen it."

Greer waited as Sean drank some water and intentionally delayed the story.

"Oh, come on man!"

Sean continued, now genuinely creeped out over recalling his childhood experience. "G, I swear to you that standing in front of me was a Native American Indian with a full head dress, feathers and war paint…the whole deal man."

Greer sat up. "An Indian?"

"Yeah man, an old mean-looking Native American Indian. He looked like a chief or something. He just eyed me for a minute or so then looked to his left at Mark and then back at me. Then, he did it again. Mark was still messing with the board and didn't seem to notice the Indian at all. After like the third time the Indian held up his hand, palm facing outward, and said, 'Stop.' Mark looked up, put the board down and responded, 'Yeah, I guess it's not gonna work.' He thought that I had said to stop! Back on the other side of the room, the Indian was gone! He had just...vanished!"

Greer was about to ask another question when his phone alerted him to a text. He punched in his access code to view a message from Ashley.

"Is that Mrs. Greer checking in with ya?"

Greer raised an eyebrow and barely smiled. "*So* not there yet. She's just saying hi and telling me to have a good day at work tomorrow."

Sean went deadpan. "That's sweet. Ready for some lunch?"

By lunch he meant beer.

"Yeah, sure man." They both began to gather their belongings.

Ashley's text had distracted him from Sean's story. While he brushed off the "Mrs." remark, he couldn't deny the warm feeling that overcame him as he'd read her text. The sentiment was kind enough, but he was remembering last night; that one glass of wine and how she'd fallen asleep on his shoulder with her soft hair brushing against his neck. Her scent, her humor and her no-nonsense delivery, he admitted, were all very alluring and attractive to him. He looked up to see Sean staring at him.

"Whoa, you're falling for her, aren't ya?"

Greer realized he had lost himself in fond reflection and his face surely wore the emotion so he chose to remain silent, unlike his buddy.

"My boy's all grown up and he's chosen a mate."

"A mate? Really, dude? Yeah, next week we're gonna shop for caves."

Sean laughed and slapped his buddy on the back as they walked to their trucks. Fifteen minutes later they were seated at a high-top in a Sports Bar where they'd spend the next two hours watching ESPN on the flat screens, swearing each consecutive beer would be their last.

Apparition IV

By four o'clock the guys had switched to water and by six both had safely returned to their respective homes.

Greer took his big dog around the neighborhood for an evening walk, allowing him the opportunity to hike his leg on pretty much anything standing still and everything previously marked. Once back home, he took a shower and found the oversized couch cushions too inviting to pass up. Sobek jumped up beside him, in lieu of his own bed, as if he knew the rules were different when it was just the boys at home.

Greer scratched his canine's thick black neck. "Let's unwind for a few, then we'll get dinner buddy."

Within minutes they were both napping.

Roughly an hour later, Greer woke up to a chill. Without any covers on the couch he crossed his arms in an attempt to get warm, and then remembered what generally followed a drop in temperature lately. He jumped up, anticipating the worst. Fortunately, it was just the air conditioner kicking on. His movement prompted Bek to awaken as well.

Greer joked, "See any ghosts, Bek?" Sobek stretched his big paws out in front of him with no regard to the question. "Me neither, boy. Let's eat."

He filled his dog's bowl with a single serving of a grain-free, no by-product, and breed-specific food before heating up a leftover chicken breast with a side of veggies for himself.

After a quick kitchen clean-up, the guys found their way back to the couch where Greer felt compelled to check in with Ashley over the

135

phone. His hope was that she would enjoy the sweet gesture; the muted television commanding only a small portion of his attention, notwithstanding.

"Hey, Sweetie."

"Hey Ash, just thought I would check in and see how your Sunday was."

"Aw, that's sweet. It was nice. I drove over to Clearwater to visit with friends, had an early dinner, and got back a little while ago. How was your day?"

"All good, hung out with Sean some, now back home. Bek says hi."

In truth, Sobek was enjoying a mini post-meal snooze on his bed.

"Aw, tell my Sobeky I love him."

"He says he wants to meet Jewel." Greer joked.

"Yeah, I'm pretty sure he doesn't see a difference between cats and chew toys."

"Good point. On second thought, let's not find out."

"Oh, I meant to tell you about a dream I had last night."

Greer was intrigued. "Dream or nightmare?"

"Dream, why do you ask that?"

"No reason. What was it about, Ash?"

"I dreamt that I was in a white room with nothing but a bed in the center. The walls and floor were pure white but the bed sheets were a deep red. I kept hearing voices and they sounded like they were coming from the bed. I stepped closer to the bed and the voices became louder. I got closer and again, the volume of the voices increased. I was just about to the bed when I felt someone touch my shoulder. I turned around to see an old man smiling at me. Then, I woke up."

Greer said nothing but his mind was racing.

Surely this can't be the same old man I saw? Is the white room the white light I saw? Why is the bed red?

"Greer, are you there?"

"Yeah, sorry, I was just thinking about your dream. What do you think it meant? Do you know who the old man was?"

"I'm not sure. I didn't know the old man, but I wasn't scared of him. Maybe a little surprised to see him. The voices were a little creepy, but I couldn't make out what they were saying."

"How was the old man dressed?"

"He had on a suit. Why do you ask?"

Greer's jaw dropped. He regained his focus. "I've read that the symbolism of dreams is often in the details."

Ashley decided to poke fun. "Really, Mr. Dream Interpreter? So, what do the details in my dream mean?"

He recalled the specifics of the one book he read on the subject while sucking down a Starbucks Macchiato a few weeks ago. "Well, a suit is a uniform, symbolically speaking anyway. So, the man was dressed for something, an event of some kind, or attending something important. The white room is a positive symbol. White is purity, cleansing, and so forth. The red bed, I dunno. A bed is usually security; ya know, the sanctuary of your bedroom, and all that. A red bed suggests something is wrong with it or, I dunno…" He trailed off from this last thought genuinely confused at the mixed symbolism.

Ashley thought for a second before responding. "Ok, but I'm still not sure what the dream meant."

"Yeah, me neither." While, in truth, he had some idea why she had the dream, he dared not share this for fear of scaring her, at least not yet.

"So what does it mean when you have the same dream over and over?"

Greer knew this answer as he specifically researched the reasoning for his own recurring dream. "It's a message, an important one, or a memory."

"A memory?"

Greer treaded lightly. "Yeah, maybe one from early childhood that was suppressed or even further back."

"You mean a past life?"

"Uh, yeah."

Ashley took a playful jab at him. "It always goes back to a past life with you, doesn't it?" Before he could respond Ashley got another call. "Sweetie, my Mom is on the other line. Can I call you back?"

"Sure, Ash."

"OK, bye Sweetie."

"Bye."

Greer unmuted the television and channel surfed for another hour or so before calling it a day; but not before sending Ash a text that he would talk to her tomorrow. Her response included an apology, for not calling him back, as her call with her parent went long.

His final reply of the exchange was, "No worries and good night."

Greer downed another twelve ounces of water, brushed his teeth and made his way to the bedroom. He set the alarm clock, turned off the light and climbed into his bed, resting flat on his back as usual. Sobek walked in a few seconds later and leapt up on the mattress, surprisingly agile for a dog his size, and laid at the foot of the bed. He looked back at Greer with droopy eyes, before resting his square head between his front paws.

Smiling, Greer told his boy, "G'nite buddy."

His mind raced with the notion that Ashley had dreamt of the same old man that he had encountered as a ghostly apparition.

He endured broken sleep for the next four hours. Each time he tossed and turned he would scan the room for anything strange and, well, anyone.

His kidneys doing their job, he had to use the bathroom. In the dark he stumbled to the toilet and relieved himself. Walking back into his bedroom Greer noticed Sobek's tail wagging while he stared into a corner opposite the doorway. Greer followed Sobek's line of sight to see a feminine figure emerge from the darkness, her image self-illuminating and quite lucent.

Sobek released a happy, excited bark. His tail was whipping back and forth, while Greer lost himself in the stunning sight before his eyes.

She was beyond beautiful. He told Sean the next day.

Indeed she was. Before him stood a radiant woman with straight, jet black, waist-length hair, that shimmered like diamonds. Her dark, inviting eyes displayed a mixture of affection and familiarity. She wore just a hint of a smile, which further elevated her already impossibly high cheek bones. Around her neck dangled a shiny gem, a garnet, from a thin silver chain. Greer would discover later that garnet was his birthstone, having been born in the month of January.

The woman's motionless, lithe body was adorned in an ivory white gown; form fitting, it was attractive, but not seductive and its length just touching the floor. Hands held loosely together at her waist, she waited patiently while Greer finished his observation. When he'd managed to sustain an ocular connection at last, he absorbed from her such a loving, knowing expression that he desired nothing more than to reach out and embrace this angelic creature. He took one step forward, and then she spoke.

"Seal the door."

Greer took the step back, his face awash in confusion.

She repeated, "Seal the door."

He somehow found the courage to speak. "Um, what door?"

The exquisite woman glanced down, and then vanished. Sobek yelped as if disappointed.

"I know what ya mean, boy."

Greer sat down on the edge of his bed and stared at nothing in the dark.

I'm losing it.

Finally, he shook his head and lay back down. He replayed this recent, and by far, most pleasant apparition repeatedly in his mind. He eluded sleep, involuntarily, and groaned when the alarm clock sounded.

Apparition V

An early morning coffee hit and an energy drink after lunch enabled him to make it through most of the work day.

Exercising the "Boss's Prerogative", he left early to swing by the house, let Bek outside for a bio-break and feed him an early dinner. By five forty-five he was mustering all his energy to spot Sean's chest presses while filling him in on the latest ghostly appearance.

Greer spoke of the visit and cryptic message that he'd received from the beautiful woman. His face was drawn and tired from a lack of sleep.

Sean realized the experiences were now beyond coincidence and something, whether good or bad, was affecting his buddy.

"Man, are you positive these aren't just nightmares?"

Greer's tone was tense. "Positive."

The guys switched places. As Sean spotted his workout partner, he ran through his current, and much summarized, understanding of events.

"So, you've seen four ghosts in your bedroom. The room gets cold when they appear and one wants you to close a door?"

Greer pressed his final rep of the set, then racked the bar and corrected his friend. "Three ghosts, one demon and the room didn't get cold this last time." Greer found this last point interesting as he spoke. Regaining his focus, he continued. "And she said to seal the door, not close."

Sean raised an eyebrow. "Is there a difference? What kind of door?"

Greer was annoyed and spoke directly. "I dunno man, but not gonna argue over a synonym. That's what she said."

Sean recognized the increased stress level so temporarily abandoned the subject and focused on a strong workout, pushing his partner with heavier weight, to help relieve his tension. After the last set of decline presses he tossed Greer his water bottle and towel and asked, "Feel better?"

Greer, catching his breath, replied to the affirmative. And, he did feel better. They grabbed their workout bags and headed out to the parking lot.

Sean stopped at Greer's truck and resumed the conversation.

"I believe you when you say they aren't dreams, alright? But can you tell me how you know the difference?"

A fair question.

"I've had this recurring dream for years now. I see what's happening from the point of view of the "me" in my dream, but it's more like a movie, instead of reality." Greer paused, recalling the definition he'd shared with Ashley. "Or, a memory." He asked of Sean, "Recall a memory of something that happened and see it in your mind. It's like a silent movie, right? Those people, or things, or ghosts, or whatever they are that I have been seeing are real. Other senses are activated, meaning I feel my bed underneath me and I hear Sobek growl and...it's just different man."

Greer trailed off from mental and physical exhaustion, as well as frustration.

Sean pretty much understood his explanation but had nothing to offer, except his curiosity. "What is the recurring dream you have, G?"

Having had the dream multiple times over the years it was easy to recall. "I'm a young, Native American Indian on a horse, and my tribe and I are attacking a wagon train. The men and women are mostly unarmed so we slaughter them easily and quickly. One by one, they fall to their deaths from our arrows, and when they are all dead, we begin to retreat. I look back and see movement in one of the wagons. A young girl removes a blanket that she had been hiding under and looks at the mass murder of her family and friends. With tears and a devastated expression, she looks right at me. I pull out an arrow, place it in the bow and raise my weapon. We maintain our mutual stare as I pull the arrow back, aim…then I wake up."

"Whoa. How many times have you had this dream?'

"I had it a dozen or so times growing up but over the last year I've had it at least once a week." He paused and appeared even more serious than usual. "I always wake up seeing that little girl's scared expression in my mind."

Sean's heart went out to him. He squeezed his buddy's shoulder and told him to go home and get some rest. They then left the parking lot in their respective trucks.

Living closer to the gym, Sean was home in about ten minutes but sat in his truck for a moment pondering Greer's experiences.

Seal the door. Where have I heard that before?

It was close to eight o'clock when Greer pulled into his driveway and was surprised to see Ashley waiting for him in her car. She got out of her white Honda Accord holding what appeared to be take-out.

"Hey Sweetie, I brought you dinner." She held up a white bag of food, smiling ear to ear as she approached Greer. He melted at her sight.

I was out of chicken breasts so it was perfect timing. He told Sean the next day, downplaying how much he had reveled in her sweet gesture.

"If there's a deviled crab in that bag I'll marry you."

"Sorry, Italian night."

Greer gave her a kiss as he opened the front door, "Well, let's get our pasta on!"

Once inside he grabbed the bag from Ash so she could greet the black canine beast who had already knocked her halfway down to the floor. Her delightful laughter made him smile as Sobek playfully bounced around her, landing wet licks on her cheeks.

Greer, feeling ignored, took in the scene. "I'm home too, Bek."

Ashley gently held each side of Sobek's grey mug and baby-talked, "The Big Man is feeling neglected, yes he is."

Greer laughed as he placed the food on the table and retrieved plates and silverware. "Give him one of the toys in the cupboard, would ya, Ash? That'll keep him busy while we eat."

Ashley provided the pooch with a multi-squeaker, plush squirrel that promised "hours of enjoyment."

"More like ten minutes." Greer quipped.

The couple ate and thoroughly enjoyed their dinner together. Greer wanted to show appreciation for her gesture so intentionally restricted from his vocabulary the use of words such as heavy, carbs or fat with relation to the pasta-heavy dinner.

She can eat anything and not gain weight. It kind of pisses me off. He thought to himself.

"Can you stay over?"

Ashley frowned, "No, I have to get up super early for work tomorrow."

Greer was visibly disappointed. "Alright."

She leaned forward on the dining table, clearly seeing the fatigue in his eyes, and asked, "So, you still having nightmares?"

Greer thought for a second. Last night's encounter was hardly a nightmare, real or otherwise. Staying true to his gender's default setting, he accepted a technicality as truth. "No."

"Uh-huh. So, you've been sleeping well, then?"

"More or less."

"OK Sweetie, if you're not going to talk to me, then I'll go."

Greer was very tired after the heavy food and while he did not want to fight, he wasn't sure he wanted to share his experiences with her until he had some answers. "It's all good, Ash."

"Actually, it isn't. I'll talk to you later, Greer." She got up from the table, grabbed her purse, said goodbye to Sobek, and left.

Greer sat at the table stunned.

Our first fight. Was I wrong? I'll ask Sean tomorrow. WOW, did I just say that? Now I know I'm tired...

He took Bek out for one last walk while pondering Ashley's strong reaction.

What am I supposed to tell her? I see dead people?

He returned home, showered, set his alarm and went to bed early in hopes of catching some shut-eye.

Extreme fatigue allowed him to quickly attain a deep level of sleep, that is, until awoken at three-thirty in the early morning to an icy cold sensation upon his face. Still lying on his back, he opened his eyes in time to see his breath fog in the freezing air.

Abruptly, he heard a low menacing growl. Reaching down and petting Sobek's thick black coat he said, "Easy boy." The growl continued. He looked around the room but saw nothing. He began to shiver from the frosty air permeating the room. Suddenly, from beneath the bed a winged creature flew up and hovered in the air.

"What the hell?" Greer yelled.

Though he would only see it for a few seconds, he could make out four wings on its back and a wasp-like stinger hanging low behind it. Its face resembled that of a bird with small, yellow eyes and a sharp, narrow beak. A low buzz emanated from the clear wings.

Sobek lunged from the bed with his jaws open and attacked the monster. The insect-like creature coiled in fear, let out a high pitched whine, and disappeared beneath the bed leaving its attacker to land on the floor.

It took only seconds for the air in the room to return to a comfortable temperature, but a little longer for Greer's heart to resume a normal beat.

Sobek climbed back into the bed, and while still on alert, he no longer growled.

Greer sat in bed for some time before he finally grabbed his phone, determined to focus on the real world. He noticed an unread text that had arrived the previous night from Sean.

Hey G, I remembered something about sealing a door, call me tomorrow.

He put the phone down, made a mental note to call his buddy on the way in to work and laid back down, more angry than frightened at this point.

He was pissed that apparitions were haunting him, he was angry that Ashley was upset with him and he was furious that he couldn't get a good night's sleep.

After a few more hours of staring at the ceiling, he got up and took Sobek out for an early walk. The next hour was spent searching the internet for stories and postings from people with experiences similar to his own. Reading countless tales of ghostly encounters shed no light on what he had been experiencing or why.

After a shower and a quick breakfast, he left for work, and called Sean on the way.

Apparition VI

"What's up, G?"

"Mornin' Sean. What's goin' on?"

"Man, I thought of something that I had forgotten about closing, I mean, sealing a door. Remember I told you about that guy Mark who lived across the street from Dewey and me when we were kids?"

Calling to mind his buddy's childhood experience, Greer didn't like where this was going. "Yeah…"

"Ok, so Mark had that giant star painted under his bed, right?"

"A pentagram, yeah…what about it?" Greer grimaced as the unsettling details of Sean's story flooded back to him.

The giant, red pentagram painted on the carpet beneath Mark's bed, the disembodied hand which crawled out from there too, the freezing temperatures in the bedroom and how terrified Mark was to sleep in his room. Yeah, it was difficult to forget at story like that.

Sean continued. "Pentagram, star, whatever. Anyway, Dewey told me it was a doorway and that it needed to be sealed; that was the reason Mark's house was haunted."

Greer was silent.

"You there, man?"

"Yeah, Sean. I'm just not sure where you're going with this."

Sean was confused that his friend was not following him. "G, if ya got a star, I mean, pentagram, in your house, then that could be why you're seeing all those ghosts."

"That makes sense buddy, but pretty sure I don't have any pentagrams anywhere."

Sean was certain he had solved the mystery and pressed a little. "Do me a favor G, just check all around your bedroom. That's where the ghosts have been, right?"

Greer apathetically replied. "Yeah, that's where they've been."

Sean detected the disinterest in his buddy's voice so he wrapped up the chat. "Just tryin' to help ya, man. That's all I could come up with unless you've been doing rituals or playing with a Ouija Board or something. Catch ya later, Big Man."

Sean hung up before Greer could reply.

Ouija Board? Holy crap, I completely forgot!

He turned the truck around to head back home, and then made a call to the office letting the staff know that he would be working from the house instead.

It was the second execution of "Boss's Prerogative" this week, if anyone was counting.

Arriving home, he practically ran into the house. Sobek looked up, sleepily, and wagged his tail as he watched Greer make a beeline for his bedroom.

He rushed into his room, knowing exactly where the Ouija Board would be. Dropping to his knees, he reached under the bed and pulled out the "game" box. He placed it on the mattress and removed its cover; the board revealed, it confirmed what he had suspected the entire drive home. Staring back at him, centered on the top of the board, was a pentagram.

He dropped the board to the floor and sat on the edge of the bed, wallowing in what he later described as "believed disbelief".

Later, when Ashley asked why he even had the board to begin with, he explained that it had been left behind by a gothic ex-girlfriend. Sean often, or rather, always referred to her as Dark Dana.

She wasn't sure which part of that explanation she liked the least so chose a polite smile in lieu of a response.

His pragmatism returning, Greer took a deep breath and, said, aloud, "Ok, so I have to seal the door." He paused. "How do I do that?" Then it hit him. "Beverly!"

He pulled his wallet from his back pocket and searched feverishly through an array of various cards.

Sobek wandered in wearily, his internal clock favoring sleep, and stretched out on the floor. Greer glanced over at him.

"Rough day, buddy?"

Finally, he'd found the business card he had been looking for. He read the first couple lines of print: Beverly Lee: Past Life Regression Therapist and Spiritual Healer. Locating the phone number in the bottom right corner, his call to her office was answered by a polite, female receptionist.

"Hello, Beverly Lee's office, how may I help you?"

"Hi, can I talk to Beverly?"

"She's currently in a session, can I take a message?"

Greer left his name, phone number and relayed his sense of urgency without going into, well, any detail.

"Are you a current client?"

Greer paused before responding. "Yeah, I've been there seven times."

"I'll give her the message."

He paced the room with phone in hand, talking to himself, more specifically, trying to talk himself down from "Worry Mountain".

She'll know what to do, it's gonna be fine.

He stepped over his slumbering canine and proceeded to the kitchen where he swigged a full glass of water. His thirst quenched, he made his way to the living room to relax on the couch. The ever-comfortable plush cushions immediately helped him, as always, to unwind. Waiting on a return call from Beverly, he'd eventually sunk into repose.

His impromptu nap was short-lived, however, thanks to an abrupt intrusion of Sobek's loud, alerting barks. Following the racket of his bellowing guard dog, he got up, grabbed his phone and made his way back to the bedroom. Bek remained on the floor but was now staring intently across the room. Greer followed his gaze, until his own line of sight fell upon the subject of Sobek's discomfort. To his utter disbelief, he saw a small, grey creature with an enormous head. It had big, black eyes and only a slit for a mouth as it stood by the opposite wall. The alien entity, who measured less than four feet tall, remained motionless and silent. Greer noticed an aroma of formaldehyde in the air.

Disturbed, Sobek rose and barked again, posturing but not attacking. The short being tilted its gigantic head slightly in response and disappeared through the wall. Stunned, with his jaw hanging open, Greer gawked at the wall in a familiar state of incredulity.

Breaking the silence, which more than startled him, Greer's phone rang. Unable to still the shaking of his hands, he awkwardly moved the phone to his ear without taking his eyes off the wall.

"Hello?"

"Hi, is this Greer? It's Beverly Lee."

He took control of his focus, relieved to hear from her. "Hi, Beverly. Thank you for calling me back."

"My pleasure, how can I help you?"

Greer explained that he believed he needed to seal a doorway, opened by a Ouija Board and asked if she could assist.

"Let's talk about this, Greer. I have a one o'clock open, can you make that?"

"Absolutely."

"Great, see you then."

"Thank you, Beverly."

He arrived at her office early, in frantic anticipation of help.

Beverly wore a tailored pant suit with her recently colored, and now grey-free, dark hair pulled into a tight bun. She remained silent while taking notes as he shared with her his ghostly experiences, including today's encounter. Once Greer was finished, Beverly looked directly at him and warned him in a borderline condescending tone that,

"Ouija Boards are not toys. They are literally portals and can be very dangerous. Entities on the other side see them as an opportunity to visit our world."

Greer was visibly taken aback. "Ok, uh, sorry. I don't want to use it; I want to get rid of it. That's why I'm here, Bev."

"It's Beverly." She exhaled, relaxing just a little while taking off her reading glasses and pointing them at Greer. "I'm sorry to be so blunt but I've seen many cases where people get hurt using those boards."

Greer was growing impatient. "I understand. Do you think all the apparitions I saw came through the board?"

She put her glasses back on, crossed her legs and looked down at her note pad.

"No, but some were probably drawn to it."

Greer remained expectant and wide eyed but said nothing in the hopes she would elaborate.

"Let's review them one at a time."

These therapists love their structure. Greer smiled at his own thought.

Unbeknownst to him, she had her own inner impression. *I'll try to keep it simple for him.*

"Your first encounter was with a demonic entity, yes?"

"Yeah, I couldn't move. The room was freezing, it filled with a white fog and the thing looked like it was studying me or something. Then it disappeared beneath my bed."

"Good, it sounds like he went back through the doorway."

"Why was it so cold?"

"It takes an incredible amount of energy for them to manifest physically on our plane so they absorb much of the energy out of the air which drops the temperature. Sometimes, and apparently in your case, they extract energy from people, leaving them temporarily paralyzed."

Greer accepted her explanation and endeavored to remain calm. "That makes sense. It's unsettling, but it makes sense."

Beverly continued. "The next encounter was with a woman whom you believe had been in a recent car accident, a nurse?"

"Right, we saw the news report and, well, obviously I can't be sure, but it's a helluva coincidence if it wasn't her. But why would she be in my bedroom?"

Beverly's face softened. "It's believed that when we pass over we see a white light, essentially a doorway. The board is just that and they are drawn to it, like a beacon."

"She didn't disappear under the bed like the demon did. The room filled with white light and she vanished." Greer clarified.

Beverly smiled. "It sounds like her white light appeared and she moved on."

Greer considered the old man. "Guessing the same thing happened with the well-dressed elderly gentleman then?"

Beverly thought for a second. "He would most likely wear a suit at his funeral."

Greer again accepted the logic, although hardly comfortable with the circumstances, he moved on. "What are your thoughts on the beautiful woman that warned me to seal the door?"

"I'd rather hear your thoughts." She replied, shifting full gear into therapist mode.

"She wasn't scary at all. And she warned me so she appears to be looking out for me."

Beverly waited a few seconds while displaying an expectant stare. "Like a...?"

Greer felt a little silly but replied, "Guardian Angel?"

"Or a Spirit Guide." She explained the roles guides play in our lives and how they often look over entire families, not just single people.

"Have you not considered that someone is over there, looking out for you, Greer?"

He looked up then quipped, "That can't be a fun job."

Beverly looked back down at her notes, "No." She smiled to let him know she was joking. "Did you happen to ask her name?"

"No." His mind moved on to the next apparition. "So, the next thing I saw was that bug-like creature."

Beverly curled her lips. "It sounds...unpleasant."

"It was just hovering when Sobek went after it, then it flew back under the bed."

Beverly looked concerned now. "The frequency of the apparitions is alarming. With so many encounters, the doorway must be very wide and very bright." She lightened up a bit. "At least you saw that they went back under the bed and presumably back through the portal to their own plane."

Greer was growing concerned. "How many do you think had come through when I wasn't there?"

Beverly ignored the question. "Now, are there any other details from the most recent encounter with the alien?"

Greer tried to remain grounded. "Aside from it looking like the classic TV grey alien that people in rural areas have claimed to eat dinner with? No."

She ignored his comment. "Did it communicate at all?"

"No." Greer did note something that he felt he should share, however. "There was a strong smell of formaldehyde in the air and it sent a chill down my spine. It was like it reminded me of something scary."

Beverly responded, very curious. "Of the five senses, smell has the strongest recall. Did you have an unpleasant experience when you were young; maybe in school, using formaldehyde?"

Drawing a blank he replied, "No, nothing. I dissected a frog once but I didn't lose any sleep over it."

Beverly made one last notation with an underline, then flipped her notepad and continued writing. Several minutes later after sitting in complete silence, Greer spoke. "Uh, Beverly, are you going to help me seal the door?"

As if on cue she ripped the page from her notebook and handed it to her client. "You need to burn the board. Here are the instructions."

Greer reached out to take the sheet of paper. She pulled it back slightly. "Follow these directions to…the…letter."

He nodded in compliance prompting her to release the paper from her hand.

Apparition VII

After thanking Beverly, he drove straight home to dispose of the board. Having read the steps she outlined, he gathered the tools needed to achieve his goal which included: a box cutter, a metal bucket, a lighter, sea salt and a shovel.

First, he cut the board into seven pieces.

The number seven has biblical significance. The seven days of creation, seven deadly sins, and so on. He later explained to Sean.

Then, after placing them in the metal bucket in the backyard, he lit them on fire. The blaze burned black for a second, at least he thought it did, and then common reddish-orange flames danced in the pail until they burned themselves out, leaving nothing but blackened soot behind. Greer poured the salt in the bucket and said a prayer for protection.

First time…ever.

He then buried the canister and its contents deep in the ground.

The deed done, he returned inside to find his canine buddy waiting at the door.

Strangest thing on a daily to-do list for two-hundred dollars, Alex. He quipped.

Greer washed his hands and then went into the living room, with a Lab just two dog-steps behind him. They occupied their favorite cushions on the sofa; Sobek was able to relax almost instantly, thanks to some enjoyable neck scratches.

Greer hoped that his efforts would now rid him of the ghostly apparitions and subsequent lack of sleep. But even more pressing on his mind, and conscience, was Ashley. After considering her perspective, he understood that she felt left out. She was extremely fond of Greer and wanted to know him more. He didn't intentionally keep her at a distance, but by not sharing his life, he was not allowing their relationship to grow. He'd kept the recent encounters from her, but now, he was ready to share them.

You said you wanted to know…

He'd prepared this retort in advance to her inevitable discomfort regarding the demonic visitors.

The text he'd sent to her read like this: "Hey Ash, I'm sorry for keeping things from you. Hoping we can talk, got lots to tell you. Can you come over?"

She was impressed with the direct apology but kept her response simple:

"See you soon, Sweetie."

Greer felt confident that he had fixed his ghost problem and would, no doubt, clear things up with Ashley, later.

So, with all good at the homestead, he shot Sean a text thanking him for the advice with the pentagram.

"See, I know stuff, G." Greer knew this to be Sean-Speak for "You are very welcome".

On his wat to the kitchen to grab a protein drink he noticed a light coming through his bedroom door at the end of the hallway. Thinking it must have been on all day he grimaced and headed there instead.

As he entered he was floored to, once again, see the beautiful woman, who had instructed him to seal the door. The brilliance that had caught his attention was the pure white glow which surrounded the angelic creature. In her ebony waist-length hair and ivory gown, she stood, smiling at him. Unlike the intrusion of the demonic entities, his bedroom was temperate and aglow with a purity of loving essence that bathed him in warmth. Fear, anger and worry vanished from his heart and mind. He basked in the brilliance of oneness within her loving light.

Eventually his senses were focused back to reality, when she'd broken the silence.

"The door is sealed." She smiled, proudly, the garnet around her neck gleaming as if alive.

Greer's mind raced to make sense of her existence despite the fact that the doorway was now closed. As if she'd planted it in his mind, he instantly understood that her heavenly presence needed no door.

"You really are a Spirit Guide, a Protector, aren't you?"

As if confirmation of his understanding were her exit cue, the glowing woman began to fade.

Greer suddenly remembered Beverly asking if he had learned her name. He blurted out, "Wait, what's your name?"

She continued to vanish but just before her visual presence was erased from his sight, she softly answered, "Selene."

Greer, again, sat on the edge of his bed, shocked by her response. Her image completely gone, the room returned to a normal illumination.

He pondered Selene's presence, both now and in Chicago, in a past life. His pensive retreat would last only a moment, as the doorbell triggered Sobek's howling announcement that someone requested entry into the kingdom.

Opening the door he found Ashley's kind, smiling face. He quickly stepped outside to give her a long kiss, pulling back only to offer another apology for his behavior. She was pleasantly surprised by his choice of greeting, both physically and verbally. He took her hand and led her inside where she could endure the over-the-top, but much anticipated, doggie-welcome.

Greer retrieved two bottles of water from the kitchen and then returned to the living room to find both Ash and his dog on the floor.

Sobek's face displayed half-closed eyes and a pink, wet tongue hanging out of the left side of his snout, quite blissful as the recipient of a belly rub.

"Are you hungry, Ash? I could make us some chicken."

In her mind she said, *God no!* She chose to audibly reply, "No, thank you, Sweetie."

She got up and joined Greer on the sofa, while Sobek found his bed to continue his very relaxed state.

Ashley rested her hands in her lap after turning herself to face Greer. "So, what's been going on?"

"Brace yourself, Ash." At hearing this, her neck stiffened.

Greer chose full disclosure. He told her of the ghosts, the demons, the alien, Selene, the Ouija Board and his belief in dream messages.

Relaying every tiny detail of his encounters and all but arguing his determinations and explanations of the events, or rather he and Beverly's conclusions, he spoke without pauses. When finished, he waited patiently as a silent Ashley wore a blank look, still absorbing the download.

I thought for sure I was gonna be her "worst ex story"…but she stayed. He later told Sean.

To which he replied, slapping his buddy on the shoulder, "My brother, you're definitely somebody's 'worst ex story'".

She was finally able to organize her thoughts. "Ok, um, just a few questions."

Greer remained cautiously quiet.

"So, while I was sleeping, there were ghosts and demons in the room?"

"That's why I didn't want to tell you, Ash. It freaked me out too."

Ashley made a connection. "The dream I had about the white room and the old man…was that the ghost's doing?"

"I think so, yeah."

"So it wasn't a dream?"

"I asked Beverly about it and her thought process was that you were sleeping during the encounter but still aware subconsciously, which produced the dream." Greer remembered another point. "Also, she said the symbolism of the bed being red was a warning. I didn't know what she meant, but now it makes sense since the board was under the bed."

Ashley was trying to integrate the metaphysical reasoning. "I can't believe I didn't wake up, though."

Greer once observed her sleep through her alarm for twenty straight minutes, but chose to respond with another factor. "You had some wine that night, remember?"

She nodded, remembering, and then switched gears. "What's with the little green man?"

Greer corrected her, "Little grey man, actually."

Ashley glared at him.

"According to Beverly they use the same types of portals to travel in and out of our plane."

Ashley was becoming overwhelmed trying to accept what Greer was telling her. She had always considered ghosts and alien encounters science fiction or fantasy.

"Sweetie, this is a lot. Are you sure you weren't just dreaming, at least, some of this?"

Greer chose to let Ashley dictate her level of acceptance and not push the issue. "I am not one hundred percent positive about anything, Ash. All I know is what I experienced and I'm trying to make sense of it the best I can." He couldn't resist one last remark. "And suppose I was dreaming it all. Dreams mean something. You even said that you had a recurring dream, didn't you? Doesn't that tug at you, just a little, that it has some kind of importance?"

She couldn't deny that she had often wondered about the recurring dream.

"Yeah, I do wonder why I have it so frequently."

Greer asked softly, "Will you tell me about it?"

164

"Well, in the dream I'm a little girl. It must be in the Old West because I'm in a wagon with my parents and we're traveling with many other people to a new town. Suddenly, we're attacked by Native American Indians. I hide underneath a blanket and when I look out, everyone is dead. The last thing I remember is looking to my left, I see a young Indian on a horse with his bow pulled back and an arrow aimed right at me. Then, I wake up."

Greer was speechless.

Ashley got up from the couch. "Excuse me, Sweetie; I have to go to the little's girl's room."

He sat back, blown away by the synchronicity of their recurring dreams. He thought to himself. *How is it possible for two people to have the same dream but from their own personal perspective, unless it truly is a memory...a shared memory? Another shared lifetime?*

Ashley returned holding her phone. "I have to go, Greer. Can we pick this up tomorrow?"

Perfect.

Greer walked her to her car with his four-legged buddy.

Ashley kissed Greer on the lips. "Thank you for being honest." She tilted her head slightly. "Might be a little heavy on the weird and creepy...but honest." She then noticed the marks and discoloring on his neck. Softly tracing them, she asked, "How did you bruise your neck?"

"Not sure, Sean asked me about it too. It just sort of appeared."

She brushed off her concern. "You probably did it at the gym. Tell Sean to learn how to spot you correctly."

They both chuckled and said goodbye. Ashley reached down and allowed Bek to lather her cheek while she scratched his scruff. "Bye Sobeky!"

Greer raised an eyebrow. "I hope you carry wipes with you."

"Dinner tomorrow?"

"See you tomorrow, Ash."

Greer went back inside for a fairly usual evening. He mixed some tuna and rice, with a dash of parmesan cheese, in a bowl for dinner.

See, I don't always have chicken. He would later tell Ashley.

After supper, Sobek took the day's final tour of the neighborhood's palm trees. Then, Greer took a shower and watched syndicated television until he was ready for bed.

Lying in bed and thinking about the strange encounters over the past week, he felt relieved that the door was now sealed. He would no longer be visited…at least he hoped not.

Sobek jumped up and, as a matter of course, nailed him in the belly with his massive paw. Greer winced in brief pain.

"Thanks as usual, Big Boy."

Finally, able to clear his mind of concern, Greer fell into a peaceful sleep.

It would not be long before he was disturbed from his much needed slumber by a sharp pinch above his shoulders. Startled, he opened his eyes, but realized he was restricted from movement. He felt cold, metal bars around his neck and forehead. Steel straps bound his chest and legs while he lay tilted at a forty-five degree angle, on a hard metallic bed.

Where am I?

While his body was illuminated, complete darkness engulfed the area around him. He could hear the scraping of metal and low whispers but could see no one. Instant panic prevailed as he tried to move his head, only to once again feel a sharp pain in his neck. He yelled but no sound came from his mouth, all the while inhaling the intense aroma of formaldehyde.

Suddenly, out of the darkness, emerged a figure. Its motion seemingly triggering illumination from above, he could now see a small, grey alien being. Its huge head tilted, looking up at him like an inquisitive dog. Greer's heart felt like it would pound out of his chest.

Out of the corner of his eye, he could just make out the small being climbing up toward him. It held a small metal tool similar to a fork, only shorter and sharper. It leaned closer to Greer until he felt the sensation of cold metal, then excruciating pain shooting down from the back of his head to his toes, causing him to silently wail in agony. Greer caught one more glimpse of the alien as it moved back into his line of sight allowing him to observe a short, hairless, grey creature with large, round eyes and a slit for a mouth.

Greer woke up screaming in his bed. Sobek jumped up, startled from his slumber.

Terrified and struggling to catch his breath with a pounding heart, Greer sat up. He was soaked in sweat and desperate to discern reality from nightmare as he sniffed the aroma of formaldehyde in the air.

The story continues in 7 Abductions-Book 4 in The 7 Novellas Series.

7
Abductions

by

Gare Allen

The 7 Novellas Series by Gare Allen

Book One- 7 Sessions

Book Two- 7 Regressions

Book Three- 7 Apparitions

Book Four- 7 Abductions

Book Five- 7 Projections

Book Six- 7 Predictions

Book Seven- 7 Reflections

Abduction I

"Are you ready to begin, Greer?" Beverly intentionally spoke in a soft, soothing tone.

The only honest response to her question was an emphatic "No!" But, since he was desperate for answers, he reluctantly replied, "Ready."

She sensed the trepidation in his voice. After unbuttoning the tailored jacket of her navy blue pant suit, she leaned forward in her chair which sat perpendicular to the sofa that he'd tensely positioned himself flat upon, and prepared to start the session. She removed her reading glasses while careful not to mess her dark hair that she'd smoothed seamlessly into a tight bun, and offered a reassuring smile before she spoke.

"Remember, Greer, you are completely safe here. I will be with you every step of the way. Now, breathe in through your nose to the count of six and then out through your mouth for the same duration."

Greer complied and executed the familiar relaxation technique he had used during his past life regressions.

Beverly continued, "Feel the tension exit your body through your fingertips and toes. Your mind will now disregard any intrusive thoughts or concerns. Relax and focus on the sound of my voice."

Several minutes of quiet, controlled breathing eventually led to the desired state of calm tranquility. The released stress was apparent in her client's relaxed mouth and unclenched jaw, as well as the departure of those worry inspired wrinkles which lined his forehead. Satisfied with his state of relaxation, she had a green light to move forward.

"Greer, I am going to count backwards from five to one. When I reach one, you will be able to recall any memory that you wish. You will have complete control of your recollection and will be only an observer, not a participant, and therefore safe from any harm. Do you understand this, Greer?"

"Yes."

"Five...four...three...two...one. How do you feel, Greer?"

"Good."

Beverly was accustomed to the often limited description of his feelings and continued. "Recall the small alien creature you saw in your bedroom and hold that image in your mind." She paused for a few seconds and scrutinized his face and body for signs of discomfort. Seeing none, she continued. "Now, ask your subconscious to take you back to your very first encounter with this being."

Immediately his head jerked to the right while his fingers dug themselves into her brown sofa.

Beverly reacted quickly. "You are safe, Greer. Memories cannot harm you. You will see them as if you are watching a movie or television program. Do you understand?"

Accepting the premise of safety, he released the cushions from his grip and his muscled body once again appeared peaceful.

"Describe for me Greer, in as much detail as possible, what you see."

"I'm in a metallic chair. It's cold and uncomfortable. I'm reclined and, I don't see any restraints, but I'm paralyzed. I can't move at all!"

Beverly's tone was confident and consoling as she replied, "You are safe, Greer. You are only watching, do you understand?"

No longer fearful, he replied, "Yes."

"What else do you see, Greer?"

"The room is dark, except for a light above me. I can hear movement but I can't turn my head. I feel like I'm moving, like I'm on a plane or ship. Wait...out of the left corner of my eye I can see some movement!"

Greer paused as he recalled a short, grey being appear at his side. "I can see the alien!"

"Please describe the being, Greer." Her glasses back on her face, Beverly was simultaneously taking notes as she spoke.

His lips curled as he relayed the unsightly description. "It's short, maybe four feet, with grey shiny skin and big dark eyes. It doesn't have a nose or ears and there's a slit where a mouth should be."

"Good, Greer, you are doing great. Now, what is it doing?"

"It tilted its head down at me, like it was nodding or bowing at me. That's weird..."

"Greer, is it speaking to-"

"NO!" Greer screamed, interrupting Beverly's question.

She responded quickly and effectively. "Greer, listen to me, you are safe. Nothing is happening to you. You are only observing a memory. Do you understand?"

"Yes."

She waited a moment, allowing him to catch his breath and resume his relaxed state before he explained his outburst.

"The alien put a sharp needle in my neck. It hurt like hell!"

Beverly observed and noted a healing bruise on Greer's neck that, unbeknownst to her, Sean and Ashley had inquired about over a week ago.

"Are you able to continue, Greer?"

"Yeah, I'm good."

"What do you see now?"

Though his eyes remained closed, Greer's face expressed confusion. "It stepped back, I can't see it anymore. What does it want?"

Greer raised his hands for his face, and rubbed his eyes just before opening them.

"Perhaps we should end this session as you seem fatigued. You did great, Greer." Beverly smiled and exhibited, what Greer chose to believe, a proud expression. "I do have just a few follow up questions while the images are fresh in your mind. Are you up for that?"

Greer got up and paced the room. The folding of his hands behind his neck prompted his tattoo to peek out from beneath the short sleeve of his signature black, V-neck t-shirt. He looked at Beverly and responded, "Sure, but I got one for you first. These are just dream memories, right?"

Warmly, she replied, "That's what we are trying to figure out, Greer. Are there are any other details about the alien that you can recall?"

Greer thought for a moment as he ran his hand through his short, dark hair. "It didn't seem to have any clothes or covering and I didn't see any, uh, genitals. Other than that…nothing more than what I already mentioned. I only saw it for a minute; before it stuck me with that needle!"

At that statement, Greer raised his hand to rub the left side of his neck as if he had just received the puncture.

Beverly continued to take notes while asking her next question. "How would you describe your feelings while disabled in the chair?"

Greer walked back over to the sofa. "Disoriented, for sure. I felt like I had just woken up and found myself completely helpless. So, at first, I felt more confused than anything. Then, I was scared."

Greer sat down as Beverly asked for specifics, "Did you feel like you had been in that chair before?"

"No, it was definitely a new experience. And, alarming. Don't forget alarming."

Beverly smiled out of the corner of her mouth. "What emotion did you experience when you first saw the alien being?"

Without hesitation he responded, "It freaked me out!"

Beverly raised her eyebrows as she made more notes. "So, fear. What else, Greer?"

Moving past his initial emotion, he was able to ponder the short interaction with the small, grey extraterrestrial. "It seemed, I don't know, curious…like it was studying me or something."

"Are there any other details that you can recall, Greer?"

"No, nothing." He surrendered to his mental fatigue and got up to thank Beverly. "I appreciate your help with this stuff; I just wish I remembered more."

She smiled while choosing more appropriate words over the ones she truly wished to express. "Well, this 'stuff' is what I do, Greer, so it's my pleasure. The process will become easier for you and you'll recall more details with each session."

Oblivious to her facetious remark, he left her office while promising to return the next day at the same time.

It'll take a week's worth of sessions but we'll get to the bottom of this. She had promised him during their initial consultation.

Moments later he was driving his white Ford F-150 truck north toward the gym, consuming a protein bar and bottled water along the way. The ride lasted only twenty minutes, which gave him time to reflect on the day's events.

Greer emerged from the locker room, and was met with the usual pre-workout beverage fueled enthusiasm he had come to expect from his buddy, Sean.

"Monday is International Chest Day. Happy Holiday G-Man!"

Greer laughed while thinking to himself, *And we're off...*

Sean did a warm-up set while Greer put on his gloves. "I called your office this afternoon, G, and they said you had left early today and I couldn't get you on your phone. Everything good, man?"

Greer hadn't mentally prepared himself for Sean's reaction to what he would later refer to as his "total recall" of alien abduction, so he switched topics, fast.

"Yeah, all good man. How was your weekend?"

Sean relinquished the bench to his workout partner while replying, "Good. Went fishing, caught some trout and snapper." He paused. "Hey, are you still seeing ghosts?"

Greer held back his initial response once he observed a serious expression on Sean's face had replaced the typical smirk of a smartass that he had come to endure in favor of the friendship. In truth, he found the guy hilarious and their "bro-rule of mockery" states that if it was funny, the court would allow it. Sean has yet to lose a case.

"Nope, thanks to you, man. Looks like getting rid of the Ouija Board did the trick."

He asked about ghosts, not aliens. Greer thought to himself, very much splitting the hair.

Sean nodded and added another plate to each side of the bar. "Got me?"

Greer positioned himself behind the bench to spot him. "Got ya."

Three hundred and fifteen pounds went up and down ten times.

"Good set, brother."

Sean nodded a "thanks" while regaining his breath.

Again, without words, they removed one forty-five plate from each end of the bar and replaced them with twenty-five pound plates. No judgment.

Greer delivered a strong set of ten reps prompting Sean to deliver, "If you can do ten slow, you have to add weight to grow." Greer suspected he was more proud of the rhyme than the sound concept of muscle growth but couldn't argue his assertion.

Sean circled back on the subject. "So, you don't think you'll see any more ghosts?"

Greer had struggled to gain Sean's audience when his experience with the apparitions occurred so the two follow up questions easily raised suspicion. "I don't expect to. Why are you asking?"

Sean stood facing his friend and looked left to right as his mind worked very hard to search for the words of admittance that he would never have the chance to utter.

"Holy shit! You've seen a ghost!" Greer said, just a little too loudly.

With a deadpan expression, Sean responded, "It's kind of sad how much that excites you. And I've seen a ghost before, remember?"

"Yeah, I know but you were just a kid. I didn't know that you were still able to see them."

Sean elevated the weight on the bar and, just before beginning his next set, promised, "I'll fill you in after the hit, bro."

The guys worked through another twelve sets which consisted of incline presses, decline presses and flies until they both succumbed to muscle failure. After mixing post-workout powder and bottled water on the tailgate of Sean's truck, he, without being prompted, told his buddy about his recent experience.

"I was on my way to work, sitting at a red light at an intersection. I looked in the rearview mirror, and, no lie, man, there's a freakin' Indian sitting in my backseat. I was like, what the hell?"

Greer took another swig of his protein drink before asking, "Was it the same Indian ghost you saw as a kid?"

Sean sat on his tailgate. "Might be man, looked like him. By the time I turned around he was gone so I only saw him for a few seconds."

Greer drank the remainder of his liquid supplement. "Have you seen him since then?"

Sean shook his head. "Nope." He paused before continuing. "What's crazy is I turned back around and the car behind me was honking because the light had turned green but then a car flew through the intersection from the other direction and ran the red light. Had I gone through at the light change, I would've been t-boned." Sean looked at his watch. "Man, I gotta run. Thanks for the hit, G."

Greer shook his buddy's hand goodbye. "Glad you're safe, my man."

"Me too, G, me too."

Abduction II

Greer arrived home to find his faithful black Lab, Sobek, more than ready for a walk around the neighborhood. They took the usual route which measured just under half a mile. This was ample time to enable the territorial Retriever to mark, rather, re-mark his originally marked, landmarks.

Thirty minutes later the surrounding area was sufficiently scented with Sobek's presence, so they returned home.

Greer took a quick shower and then heated up some chicken and broccoli for himself and filled Bek's bowl with his grain-free, salmon-based dog food. Both ate quickly for no particular reason and with their appetites quelled, they made their way to the living room and relaxed on the most comfortable, brown sofa that Greer's ass had ever met.

The day's events over, his thoughts returned to Ashley. He hadn't spoken with her all day and missed his gorgeous girlfriend.

After dialing her number, a smile spread itself across his face, compliments of her affectionate greeting. "Hi, Sweetie!"

"Hey Ash, how was your day?"

"Good, how was yours?"

"All good...I just got home a little while ago."

"Oh yes, Mondays are a long day due to the holiday." Ashley joked while, unbeknownst to Greer, rolling her eyes.

"So, is anything new with you?"

Greer paused. "Got some stuff to tell ya".

Understatement.

He asked, "How about I fill you in tomorrow? Dinner?"

"That sounds great. I hate to cut this short, but I have another early day so gonna get ready for bed. But, I'm looking forward to seeing you."

"Me too. G'nite Ash."

"Good night, Sweetie."

Greer decided to call it a night as well. "C'mon Bek, let's go to bed."

He managed a few hours of slumber in between snapshot dreams of being restrained by bizarre alien creatures.

The alarm sounded early. Very early.

Sobek was agreeable to a morning walk at dawn, finding that it didn't interfere with his daily agenda of naps and toy homicide.

To compensate for his plans to leave early to make his appointment with Beverly, Greer arrived to work at six-thirty a.m. With the assistance of morning coffee, he'd completed all of his daily tasks and made significant progress on his current projects.

He continued to manage his time effectively so that by five after the hour of three o'clock, with Beverly at his side, he was breathing in and out to the count of six and enabling himself to recall that, which he had forgotten.

"What do you see, Greer?"

"I'm immersed in some type of thick liquid. But I'm not choking; somehow I can still breathe."

"You're doing good Greer, what else can you see around you?" Beverly was logging every word in a recently purchased iPad, having abandoned her usual pen and paper method.

Greer continued. "The gel-like substance is clear so I can see that I am in some kind of shallow pool. There are other people with me, six or seven of them. We're all naked. Everyone appears confused and one of the women looks terrified."

Beverly attempted to stimulate his other senses. "Greer, can you hear anything?"

"I can hear a lot of different voices, but I can't quite make out...sorry, it's all white noise."

Beverly tried again. "You're doing great, Greer. Do you smell anything?"

Greer grimaced, though his eyes remained closed. "There's a strong odor of...formaldehyde. Why would...?" He paused.

"Greer, what's happening?"

"Someone is talking to me. They're asking me to join them because they have something to show me."

"Greer, who is talking to you?"

"I can't see them yet. I'm out of the pool and wiping my eyes. Oh my God!" Greer's face rapidly drained of color as he jumped off the couch and yelled in terror. "What is that? Help me!"

Beverly responded, "Greer, relax. Remember, you are safe and cannot be harmed. Do you understand?"

Soothed by her words, he immediately calmed down, and laid his torso back on the sofa. "Yes."

Beverly continued to take detailed notes. "Are you able to continue?"

"Yes."

"What do you see, Greer?"

He continued much more objective. "A very tall, uh, birdlike creature is staring at me."

"Can you describe it in detail, Greer? Is this the alien that was talking to you?"

The color slowly returned to his face as he spoke. "It looks like a bird, maybe an eagle, in the face, with a pointed beak and small eyes. It's very tall, at least eight feet, thin and pale. The body is more human, though. And yes, it's speaking to me, by sending thoughts and pictures to my mind; it's how they communicate." Feeling much more relaxed, he added, "Did I mention it's super creepy?"

Having done countless alleged abductee regressions over the years, Beverly had often heard that alien beings favored a telepathic method of conversing. "You're doing great, Greer. What is the being communicating to you?"

"It wants to explain the mission. Greer stopped talking for a second, and then continued, "It gave me a thin towel to wrap around myself."

"What is the mission, Greer?"

Greer paused as he recalled the information given to him in his memory. "They're from Earth! Well, kind of. It's dumping a ton of info into my brain! It's hard to sort it out."

"I can help, Greer, don't get overwhelmed. We will sort it out together, are you up for that?"

"Yes."

"Great, relay the information as you receive it."

Greer began, "It's a story...no...it's their story." Greer paused, before speaking again, "No freakin' way!"

Beverly broke character, just slightly. "Want to clue me in, Greer?"

He chuckled, almost in disbelief. "It starts in Egypt. Ancient Egypt, to be exact. The aliens procreated with humans beginning with..." Greer fell silent.

Beverly's expression displayed a clear recall of a triggered memory. Making a connection, she flipped through Greer's file until she found the regression session where he recalled his incarnation as the half-alien, half-human Pharaoh. Burdened with the responsibility of cross-breeding with very early homo-sapiens, he'd seeded meta-human potential via his other-worldly DNA.

Incredulously, she read the name in the notes. "Merkharu."

"Merkharu!" Greer exclaimed, in unison with Beverly, as he sprang up off the sofa, once again recalling his personality in Egypt, a very, long time ago.

Beverly, a bit startled, clutched her chest with her left hand. Quickly, she composed herself and asked him how he was feeling.

"Good and I can remember so much more about that lifetime now!"

She took a moment to sift through the notes, refreshing her memory while Greer resumed his position on the sofa.

Merkharu sat motionless, one hand resting on the arm of his golden throne, the other holding a staff topped with an ankh, the Egyptian symbol of enduring life. Adorned with a royal beard fashioned of gold attached to his imperial mask, he appeared stoic and menacing. He was shirtless, wearing a white skirt while two gold arm bands weaved themselves around his muscular arms.

Masked guards stood erect and silent on either side of him. He was the first born of the eight of his kind. A half-breed, revered as a miracle by the Egyptian people due to the union of alien and human physiology.

His seven younger brothers and sister, all half-breeds themselves, practiced magic as high priests.

Merkharu's task was clear: He would remain on Earth and procreate with the indigenous females to continue the new line of more intelligent, capable humans. His offspring were only one-quarter alien, but their abilities were in the DNA; the very goal of his now departed superiors.

Having finished reading her own notes, she asked Greer to begin. Her client excitedly relayed his newfound memories, given to him by the extra-terrestrial being.

Merkharu stood motionless, his golden crocodile mask gleaming in the sunlight, ready to receive his visitors. It had been ten years since the sky people left Egypt, when Merkharu had reached physical maturity and they were confident that he was clear on his task.

He was born of a human mother, who had been impregnated by an alien male. His space family had raised him, denying his birth parent any contact, and programmed him with the knowledge of the stars and the secular primary duty of procreation. And, then they left.

He was, at the same time, unique and alone. His seven, half-breed brothers and sister, each born of a different human mother, lived and flourished together as high priests in the royal temple while he sat isolated, shouldering the heavy burden of a leader with a singular mission.

His relatives from the sky were back to assess his progress; they would be pleased. Merkharu had seeded over three thousand offspring during his ten-year regime, with a seventy percent survival rate.

The quarter-breed children were gathered and presented to the visiting foreigners. Infants were held by their human mothers while the older children stood with perfect posture and looked straight ahead, avoiding eye contact with their ancestors. Merkharu patiently stood to the side, characteristically stoic, as an elder walked the line, his line, of children, in silent observance.

Finally, a telepathic assessment was delivered. "Well done, Merkharu."

He accepted the approval of the tall, avian-headed visitor he knew by the name of Kapherus. "Gather your priests and priestess in the royal chamber at once."

Merkharu and the ancient magicians sat respectively quiet in a circle while Kapherus conveyed to them, through thoughts and mental images, the importance of their new mission.

Greer opened his eyes, the trance broken, as his excitement over this vivid memory eclipsed his relaxed state.

Beverly's fingers cramped as she feverishly completed the last entry as relayed, verbatim, by her client, enabling her to take a much needed break.

Greer was, again, off of the sofa and pacing the floor with his right hand flat on his forehead and his left on his waist. "The alien that showed me these memories of Egypt is the same race." Beverly resumed her note-taking and nodded affirmatively, prompting him to continue. "They're the same bird-race as Merkharu's ancestors!"

A bell chimed softly from Beverly's desk. "We're almost out of time for today."

Relieved to put down her note-taking tools and rest her hands, she replied, "You did great. I think we covered a lot of ground today." The last sentence was Beverly's go to platitude designed to wrap up a session. She said goodbye to her client and walked him to the door. Greer hardly noticed her sense of hurry as he possessed the same haste in seeing his beautiful Ashley.

On the way home, Greer picked up the ingredients for a spaghetti dinner at the grocery store. Something told him to cook anything, except chicken.

By seven o'clock the dining room table was set with a "guy's version" of nice china.

"Some store in the mall." Would be his reply when asked where he had purchased the attractive white, gold etched dinnerware.

Their meal would begin with cool, crisp Caesar salads. But it was the spaghetti sauce, angel hair pasta and warmed bread in the center of the table that was responsible for the mouth-watering aroma permeating the house. Ending the meal would be a delicious Tiramisu, specially purchased from a local bakery, for his Ashley. She would find his gesture as sweet as the dessert.

Abduction III

"Are the croutons homemade?" Ashley asked, enjoying her salad.

Greer stared blankly. *Is she serious?*

She put down her fork and covered her mouth with her napkin while laughing. "I'm sorry, they're really good, Sweetie." She realized then that the only thing that she had ever known him to make from scratch was a protein smoothie.

His expression changed from shock to mildly hurt.

Blue eyes and warm, appreciative smile, you're up. Ashley thought to herself.

"Thank you for making this wonderful meal for me, G, it's delicious."

Greer lost himself in her beauty and, as his face lightened, he suggested, "Try the meatballs, I made them with turkey!"

Of course you did, Sweetie.

She had learned to save her burger runs for meals with her friends; lovingly accommodating her boyfriend's, mostly, healthy, eating habits.

As they enjoyed their main course, Sobek ambled into the room. While his thick, wagging tail swung his hind end to and fro, he flashed his big, brown Lab eyes at Ashley.

Ashley smiled at the big, loveable dog. "Hey, Sobeky."

Bek made his way to Greer's feet and laid down. His eyes locked on his provider, he patiently awaiting his "prize" from the table that, tonight, would come in the form of a turkey meatball.

Greer grinned from ear to ear as he glanced between Ashley and Sobek.

His infectious delight forced her to laugh and she asked, "Wow, what's got you all giddy?"

He took a drink of his water, still beaming. "Just happy, I guess. It's been a crazy couple of weeks and I really enjoy it when I get the time to relax with you."

Greer had allowed himself a very candid, spontaneous moment. Surprised as she was by his uncharacteristic sentiment, Ashley played it cool as to not dissuade him in the future. "So, what's new? You said you had lots to tell me?"

Greer froze amid an internal thought. *Ruin a moment much, Ash?*

"Tell you after dinner?" He responded, casually.

"Sure." She had come to understand that he would surely tell her of his most recent adventures, but in his own way and in his own time. Switching topics, she asked, "I'm thinking of going home for a visit. Want to come?"

Greer was flattered. "Yeah, I would love to visit Chicago with you."

Her face beamed with delight as she told him of the places she would take him. "I'll show you around Deerfield, where I grew up. Then we'll take a walk on Michigan Avenue and see the Buckingham Fountain…"

As she lamented about her friends and family back in The Windy City and how much she missed them, Greer struggled to maintain his smile as he recalled Charles and Julia's fateful motorcycle ride.

The couple finished their meal, but chatted another fifteen minutes, before finding their way to the corner of the couch where Greer's outstretched arm created an irresistible invitation for Ashley to snuggle next to him. Sobek assumed the opposite end of the sofa and curled into a shiny, albeit large, black ball.

"Ready for dessert, Ash? I picked up tiramisu from that bakery you like."

Ashley put her hand to her stomach. "I couldn't eat another bite. Maybe later." She turned and kissed him. "You're so sweet."

"Hey, enough with the profanity."

Ashley rolled her eyes. "I won't tell anyone, tough guy." She wrapped his arms around her and was embraced in pure contentment. They sat in comfortable, secure silence. She caressed his muscled arms while he inhaled the sweet, strawberry scent of her silky, light brown hair. Before long, they both drifted to sleep.

It was after ten o'clock when Ashley woke up her boyfriend. "Sweetie, I have to get going. I have another early morning."

Greer stretched and looked at his watch. "I can't believe I slept that long. I must have eaten too much bread and slipped into a carb coma."

He really thinks that's a thing. Ashley later told her friend.

She finished gathering her belongings and made her way to the front door where her boyfriend took her hand and escorted her outside. They embraced one more time, leaning on her car, where he gave her a final kiss goodbye.

"What's with the early day? Meetings?" he asked.

"No, I help out at the homeless shelter before work when I can. You know, serve breakfast and help clean up, that kind of stuff."

"How did I not know about this?"

"Because you're self-absorbed, Sweetie."

Greer silently and unobjectionably accepted the honest response.

Ashley laughed, "I'm joking! I've only done it a few times but I'm making an effort to go at least once a week now."

Greer smiled, loving her even more as he recalled the time she forced him to pull over so she could remove a turtle from the road and place it safely in the next pond they happened upon.

"Drive safely, Ash. And text me when you get home."

She rubbed the sleep from her eyes. "Good night, Sweetie."

Greer was met at the door by an anxious, expectant canine. His orders were evident so he grabbed the leash and accommodated the unspoken, yet clearly received, request for a late night walk.

He could still smell the strawberry fragrance of Ashley's hair. As he walked, he felt light, invigorated, and refreshingly content.

"You skipped the gym, dick." Read the text from Sean, interrupting his moment of bliss.

"I told you I had dinner plans, remember?"

Sean's reply was as close to an apology as Greer would ever get. "My bad, G."

Greer's retort ended the exchange. "See you tomorrow, dick."

Sobek's hiked leg baptized several palm trees during the walk back home. The canine's instinctive need to leave his signature in the surrounding area now satiated, Greer was able to shower and clean up. Afterward, he found he was wide awake due to the impromptu nap he had shared with Ashley.

He retrieved a rawhide chew bone from the cabinet to busy his boy until bedtime and then sat back on the couch, with remote in hand, only a moment later. After flipping through a dozen or so of the several hundred channels, he abruptly stopped his search as his fingers froze. He stared, awestruck as the chilling image of a grey alien stared back at him from his television. Dumbstruck, he sat motionless and absorbed the haunting, yet familiar, frightening sight. Its large, round, dark eyes lacked pupils, appearing devoid of emotion.

Greer began to shake. He blinked but the image remained on the screen. The creature's mouth was a tiny slit above a pointed chin. Its enormous head rested, remarkably, on a very small, thin neck.

Greer was trembling with fear. The sudden appearance of the being triggered intense feelings of dread. His hand moved instantly to his neck, feeling a slight tingling as he rubbed a hard knot just beneath the skin.

In that instant, truth revealed the alarming realization that his memories of aliens were not nightmares, but actual recollections of painful and terrifying events. Immobilized by fear, he felt the color drain from his face and his mouth was agape as he stared back at the grim image in undeniable horror.

As if sensing his discomfort, Sobek strutted into the room and rested his head on Greer's knee. The contact breaking him out of his trance, he finally regained control of his faculties. Greer reached out to scratch Bek's thick neck. Upon doing so, he noted all that remained of the chew bone were tiny specs of rawhide clinging to his dog's greying muzzle.

He turned off the television and made his way to the bedroom where he laid for several hours, consumed with the disturbing implications of his abductions, until emotional exhaustion snuffed out consciousness.

Unfortunately, he would soon be witness to more alarming, vivid and revealing encounters.

Hundreds of small grey beings surrounded Merkharu. While they looked up at him with blank stares from their hauntingly deep, dark eyes, their minds, in unison, cried to him, a plea for help.

The half-alien Pharaoh appeared God-like standing over them; any expression on his face was concealed by his golden crocodile headdress.

Merkharu broke his frozen posture slightly when he glanced over to his half-brothers and sister who were assembled just a short distance from the gathering mass of small, grey creatures. The priests and priestess, dressed in dark brown, hooded cloaks, formed a tight circle while holding hands. Their expressions, while not visible, were stoic and focused in a collective trance.

As a result of their coordinated command, rocks from across The Nile River drifted into place, one on top of the other. The granite pieces aligned themselves from foundation to top. As the magicians continued their group meditation commanding the rock fragments in a focused, singular effort, a structure was quickly forming. Going forward, it would be known as a pyramid.

Thus, the mission had begun. He recalled the unfortunate outcome and specific directions given to him and his sorcerers by Kapherus.

"We are pleased with the prolific production of offspring resulting from the human womb. Future generations will transition well with an enhanced intelligence that will enable an accelerated evolvement of the planet."

Merkharu silently nodded. Kapherus' confident demeanor waned slightly as he looked away and slowed his delivery, carefully choosing his words. "The results on our home world were…unexpected."

Merkharu caught the leering eye of the priestess. Having only spoken to the second born, Nookhotep, who led the conclave, he had never interacted with the others. Immediately the half-breed lowered her eyes in reverence. The Pharaoh felt an intense sensation of attraction but quickly regained control of his emotion.

Kapherus had used the lull to determine his next words; they would easily capture the full attention of his audience.

"Your children will prosper having been born of human females. Those we brought to you, those born of Carian females, will not fare as well." He paused, gesturing for all to sit while he remained upright, then continued. "With normal brain functions customary to our kind, they are intelligent and seem self-aware. Sadly, their reproductive organs are not fully developed leaving them unable to procreate. They are born with many muscular and neurological conditions and do not survive for long. Furthermore, their prodigious heads often prove fatal to their progenitor at the time of birth."

Merkharu telepathically asked, "What is to become of them?"

"They are to remain here, in the newly constructed pyramid."

The Pharaoh noticed the head of the female magician once again turn to eye him. A mixture of concern and confusion colored his voice as he asked, "Kapherus, I assumed the structure would be their home, but are they to be confined there?"

He ended their exchange with a curt, dismissive reply, "With no ability to reproduce and a significantly short life span, this problem will not endure." He turned to leave but abruptly stopped to field an unsolicited comment; this time from the female priestess.

"We will care for them."

Kapherus' head swung around at the remark and he eyed the priestess. She quickly bowed her head. His gaze shifted to Merkharu. With squinted eyes he spoke in a restrained tone. "They are aberrations."

The Pharaoh stared at the brave female, but this time she would not look up. Nookhotep mentally assured his ruler that he would address the inappropriate behavior.

Greer stood staring at what he now understood to be a Carian whose presence along with the hum of the ship around him, alerted him that the dream was over.

"It was not a dream; we showed you the past to help you understand the future." The thought successfully planted in Greer's mind, he understood that he had been abducted, again.

Panic set in.

Was this really happening? Was he on the sofa in Beverly's office? Could this be some sort of lucid dream?

Sensing his inability to focus and accept this explanation, the alien moved toward him, lifted his long arm, and touched Greer on the neck. Greer screamed as he felt a rush of painful heat wash over him.

The next thing he knew he was lying perpendicular on his bed, holding his breath. He exhaled loudly, startling Sobek and prompting his dog to jump down off the bed in favor of the floor. His mind blown, he laid there, recalling the scene from Egypt until he realized he was holding his neck. Painful to the touch, he felt something small just beneath the skin.

A nodule? A mosquito bite? A pimple, maybe? His considerations were suddenly halted by the piercing shriek of his alarm clock, scaring an already on-edge human being.

I didn't need that heartbeat anyway.

An early morning walk around the neighborhood with his canine companion gave him some time to clear his mind. After that, a shower helped him relax and collect himself. Between entries of his experiences in his journal, he sucked down a protein shake. Smiling, he anticipated the proud expression on Beverly's face; finding his journal account of the recent abduction, before his memory faded, a prudent decision.

Arriving to work at seven a.m. required a double hit of coffee to get him through the morning. He remained fairly alert through lunch and afterward.

I stayed away from the carbs. He would later tell Sean.

By three o'clock, he was, once again, in Beverly's office. Pacing the room, he waited as she silently read his journal entries of the events that involved Kapherus, the grey aliens, the priestess and his abductor's comments.

Abduction IV

Beverly finished reading his journal entries, paused and read them again while transcribing select passages into her client file. Greer felt edgy and was becoming overwhelmed. Finally, tired of pacing, he sat down on the edge of her sofa.

Still writing and without looking up, Beverly suggested, "Why don't you lie down and relax, Greer."

Relax?

A switch inside of him flipped as he allowed his fear and annoyance verbal expression and shouted, "You mean like I normally do? It's just another day of couches and aliens, right? Sure, that's normal!" He pointed to his journal while asking, "Does anything that you're reading in there seem normal to you?"

In an attempt to discourage the rising volume of his voice, she put down his journal and her file, gave him her full attention and calmly asked, "What is normal, exactly?"

Greer raised his left eyebrow. "What? Are you kidding me?"

She remained silent and displayed a patient, yet expectant look.

He was now officially annoyed. "Let's see, synonyms for normal would include usual or typical." He put his hand to his chin, mock thinking. "Are little grey aliens usual or typical?" Turning to Beverly, he blurted, "The judges say no!"

Beverly had experienced her share of outbursts during her years performing regressions and this client's moderate tantrum would be easily contained.

She was firm. "Greer, please sit down." He complied, still agitated.

She was confident. "I'm going to help you. My intention is not to upset you. It's important that you understand that in order to move past the trauma of your experiences, you must first accept them. Not just that they occurred, but that you truly understand how the events affect you regardless of how abnormal they may seem."

Greer let go of his building anger and relaxed his posture, signaling at least a partial acceptance of her alternative perspective.

She was reassuring. "Things happen for a reason, Greer, and you possess the courage to unearth, so to speak, the truth."

Greer felt a new determination envelope his emotional state as he lifted his head and locked eyes with Beverly. With a warm smile, she asked, "Shall we dig?"

He assumed his position on the sofa and began his breathing exercises.

Beverly retrieved her electronic pad and instructed Greer to continue the relaxation process. "Clear your mind and focus on the sound of my voice."

Greer allowed his tension to dissipate while breathing deeply and denied any intrusive thoughts entrance to his mind.

A few moments later he felt a tingling, much stronger than usual, that began in his toes and shot up through his entire body to the top of his head. He could no longer hear Beverly's instructions. In an instant, he had reached a tranquil state under the hum of a soft vibration that rendered every limb listless. To his shock, he felt himself begin to rise. Slowly, he felt himself float upward. Fear stepped forward and he opened his eyes at the sensation of falling back. He sprang upright, almost knocking Beverly's pad out of her hand.

"Greer, what is it?"

Wide-eyed and disoriented, he replied, "I was really relaxed and, it was like, well, like I was floating up."

Beverly smiled and waved off, literally, his explanation. "Oh, you must have reached a deeper state of relaxation and were going to astral project."

Befuddled, he just looked at her.

Several seconds of silence coupled with very uncomfortable staring prompted her to elaborate. "Astral projection or an out-of-body experience is when your spirit leaves your physical body. It occurs often when you are sleeping."

Crickets.

Beverly made a mental note to circle back on what she called, OBE's, then returned to the task at hand. "Lie back down and let's try this again. Remember, stay focused on my voice as it will ground you in your physical body."

Greer slowly laid himself back down on the sofa, shooting one last glare of disbelief at Beverly. She was patient as he worked to remove the startling effects of the recent, unnerving experience. Eventually, she helped him reach a calm state…this side of astral projection.

"Concentrate on the sound of my voice and stay with me, Greer. Let's move forward to the next abduction in your memory. Remember, you are safe. Describe to me what you see."

In his mind's eye, images formed; he recounted another close encounter to Beverly.

The tall alien hovered just above the floor of the ship, gliding through the air as he led Greer down a narrow passage. The interior of the craft was dark. Soft illumination appeared when triggered by movement or telepathic instruction. A low but palpable hum resonated throughout the vessel. The hum was accompanied by a vibration which entered through Greer's feet as he walked. The sensation instilled an odd sense of calm as it extended upward, reaching to the crown of his head.

A quick right turn revealed a white, circular room filled with very small, grey alien beings. Greer noted they were barely a foot tall, much shorter than the ones he had encountered up to this point. Many were sitting and interacting with individual view screens that continuously changed images; not as a result of touch, but rather, their thoughts. Others were running and squealing like happy, well, alien children he supposed.

Greer's thoughts were detected by the large extra-terrestrial; therefore his conclusion, while not spoken, was heard.

"This is what you would term, a nursery."

Greer was temporarily distracted by one of the adolescents who brushed up against his leg while running past, playfully chasing another of its kind. Its skin was slimy, leaving a residue on Greer's leg. Following the young creature was an older alien that stopped and bowed; then made its way past Greer.

Aliens have manners?

In that moment, he remembered Kapherus explaining their inability to reproduce which begged an obvious question: Where had all of these alien children come from?

Greer received a response, or at least the beginning of one, as a vivid scene suddenly unfolded in his mind; the content of this telepathic transmission so intense and fantastic, it challenged the preconceived notions held in regards to ancient Egyptian history.

Merkharu waited as the magicians removed the loosely placed rock, which obstructed the entrance to a secret door, and rolled it aside. The hidden entryway that they stood before was located some three hundred feet up, on the north side of the five hundred foot tall, symmetrical pyramid.

It had been a hundred days since the departure of Kapherus. Surely the undesirable offspring he left behind were now dead, having been sealed inside the structure for over three months.

The Pharaoh obeyed Kapherus' commands, but he had never stopped considering alternatives to their abandonment; it pained him that they had been imprisoned and left to perish.

With the clandestine entry revealed, the magicians returned to their chambers while the brave, vocal priestess, though hooded, glared at her king in disgust. He could just make out the hot tears streaming down her face, as she passed him by.

Feeling ashamed, Merkharu stomped down the spiral, stone stairway with a heavy heart.

My mission, indeed my very purpose, is to produce life, not destroy it.

"Despite the unfortunate circumstances, these measures are necessary." Kapherus had offered, prior to his departure, in hopes of consoling the half-breed Pharaoh.

Merkharu struggled to retain his composure as he braced himself for the inevitable scene at the bottom of the stone stairs. His heart pounded harder, accelerating with every guilty step downward. He gripped the lit torch in his hand tighter, wondering when the inevitable stench of decay would engulf his senses completely.

With the lengthy descent concluded, he raised his head to witness the aftermath of tragedy. But, to his surprise, his eyes fell upon a sight that prompted a relieved smile to replace the pained expression upon his face and lighten the heaviness upon his heart. Bypassing the empty tomb, he hurried to inspect a gaping hole in the floor. Unable to suppress a hearty sigh of relief, it echoed back to him as he peered down into the hastily dug deep, escape tunnel.

The images in Greer's mind had stopped. He glanced up to discover that the alien was clearly distracted and looking away.

One last thought was placed in his mind while the extra-terrestrial's long arm reached out for Greer's nape. "It is time for your treatment."

Greer sprang from Beverly's sofa, and touched the slightly bruised spot on his neck; the small hard lump he'd noticed before remained just beneath the skin.

"What is this?"

Beverly, who had been feverishly documenting Greer's account while he'd been under light hypnosis used this opportunity to take a break.

"What is it, Greer?"

He stepped toward her and lowered his body, placing his neck adjacent to her shoulder. "What does this feel like to you?"

Beverly, not a particularly big fan of "personal space invasion", smiled politely as she felt the hard spot and then quickly retracted her hand.

Greer took a few steps back, still very much engrossed in his mystery, and didn't notice that she'd doused her hand in sanitizer while asking, "Have you been to see a doctor yet, Greer?"

He shook his head. "No, not yet."

She retrieved her notes, documented her suggestion, and recorded his reply.

"Greer, how are you feeling?"

"I'm alright." He sat back down on the sofa with his hands on his knees. "The alien is giving me portions of memories each time I'm with it. It's careful not to overwhelm my mind as I don't communicate in their fashion."

Beverly nodded as she wrote. "Did the being tell you that?"

"It's hard to explain but, yeah, I got that impression, in my mind, anyway." He continued. "What's crazy is that I almost got the feeling that they're helping me in some way. I mean, it's still terrifying and all but...I don't know." Just then he felt a tingle in his neck. "Unless, of course, I've got some kind of implant embedded in me." He paused to consider, only half-joking, he asked, "But what if it gives me alien powers?"

Beverly, quite intentionally, did not acknowledge his final comment but reminded him to seek medical attention as soon as possible. She then smiled and said, "I think we made some good progress today."

Realizing she was wrapping things up, his thoughts shifted to a more enjoyable pursuit: a workout. As he made his way out of her office, he replied, "See you tomorrow, Beverly."

Sean was doing dumbbell curls to loosen up when Greer found his way to the gym floor, just after a quick change of clothes in the locker room.

"What's up, G?"

The guys shook hands as Greer responded, "Not much."

Lie.

"What's new with you, big man?"

Sean motioned for his buddy to walk over to a bench close to the window, and away from the growing crowd of members. He wore an uncharacteristically solemn expression upon his face.

Sean's serious face occurs only once every year; it's kind of like the Winter Solstice, and, it rarely ends well. He would later explain to Ashley.

Greer remained quiet; more than a little curious as to what Sean had to say.

"I saw the Native American ghost again."

Greer stood quietly with his arms folded and gave his friend his full attention thus allowing him to elaborate.

"Last night, I woke up around three a.m. to piss, and he was, just there, man." His words carried a tone of discomfort as he continued, "I thought I was dreaming, or seeing things, so I closed my eyes. When I opened them again, the Chief was still there."

Sean stopped talking. His expression mirrored a combination of worry and disbelief.

Greer never quite learned how, exactly, to handle a serious, concerned Sean; he had to get the specifics out of him while he was willing to talk.

"What was the Indian doing?"

"He was just standing at the end of my bed."

Greer smiled. "Help me out, buddy. Was he staring at you? Did he look angry? Did he look happy? Was he wearing a toga? What, man?"

Sean relayed the uncomfortable details to his buddy. "He was standing with his back to me. I could see his arms were folded." Sean's expression went to full-on confusion. "A toga?"

Greer grimaced. "It was a joke. Did you talk to him?"

"I wanted to but was too freaked out. I just sat up in my bed staring at him. Then, this...thing came at him."

Puzzled, Greer asked, "Thing?"

Sean explained, "Yeah, this black figure came out of nowhere and, like, flew right at him. He held up his hand and then this white light flashed for less than a second and then they were both gone."

Exasperated, Sean ran a hand through his short, blond hair and clearly needed some levity.

Greer decided that an intense workout would be just the thing to help them both to shake off some of the insanity produced by their recent, metaphysical events.

"Let's get a hit, brother." Greer slapped Sean on the shoulder as they made their way back to the weights.

Abduction V

The guys finished stretching and focused their energy on Wednesday's scheduled arm hit. Their efforts resulted in fifteen sets of triceps and biceps exercises, with conversation limited to proper form and the Buc's upcoming season.

With the workout complete and neither expressing the slightest interest in doing cardio, they headed out to their respective trucks.

"Great hit, G. Thanks, man."

"I'm already sore."

"That's because you're a girl."

Greer rolled his eyes. While it was obvious his friend was acting more like himself, he wasn't sure if he would be willing to revisit their earlier conversation.

He decided to tread lightly. Leaning against the door of his truck, he asked, "Do you want to talk, Sean?"

"I gotta roll but yeah, we'll talk, man." He slapped Greer on the shoulder.

"Thanks, G. Beers, Friday night?"

"Sounds good, Sean. Later."

Greer arrived home fifteen minutes later and ran through the evening routine of Sobek's walk through the neighborhood, a hot shower and then the usual chicken and vegetable dinner.

Routine is next to Godliness. He'd once joked to Ashley.

You're rigid and inflexible, Sweetie. She'd retorted, only half-jesting.

Settling down, exhausted, with an early morning ahead of him, he texted his girlfriend. His face displayed a doting smile the second he picked up his iPhone and would remain during their short text exchange.

"Hey Ash, how was your day?"

"Hi Sweetie! Long, but good. Helped out at the shelter, had two meetings that went well, got in a run and missed you. ☺ How was yours?"

"All good."

She read his reply and mused, *He's a plethora of detail.*

"I miss you too, Ash. Sorry I've been so busy."

"We've both been busy so I understand, Sweetie. I was about to take a shower and go to bed."

"Me too, I'll call you tomorrow."

"Sounds good. Good night, Greer."

"Good night, Ash."

Greer lost himself in thoughts of Ashley. He truly did miss her, and wondered what it would be like to have her around more often.

"Is it too soon to move in together?" He asked aloud, looking at Sobek. As if dismissing the idea, Bek hopped off the couch and barely glanced at his provider. With droopy eyes, he turned to make his way to the bedroom, signaling his intention to assume his spot at the end of the bed.

Amused and weary, Greer followed him. "We'll talk about it later, boy."

Greer's head hit the pillow, heavy with the usual stresses and worries compliments of the day's events. But this time, fatigue delivered an uncommon first round knockout, allowing him to fall asleep much sooner rather than later.

Greer could see his reflection in the empty, dark eyes of the grey alien just inches from his face. Unable to move, he lay flat on his bed with a sensation of tingling in his neck. The being turned its head left to right as if studying Greer's face. High pitched whines emanated from behind the small creature which, he deduced, were the cries of a similarly paralyzed Sobek.

For all of Greer's strength, he was completely powerless to escape and terror consumed his emotional state.

As he considered his time, unharmed and engaged in conversation on the alien ship, this new experience left him frightened and confused.

At the thought of the alien craft, the slimy entity reached out and grabbed Greer's neck. In the next instant, he found himself reclined in the same cold, metallic chair he had recalled during his first abduction, still unable to move. The short creature stepped away while a warm, blue light bathed his abductee's head and torso. The sensation was, surprisingly, deeply calming, despite the fact that he was physically frozen. He lost consciousness, only to awaken, naked in the alien gel-like substance.

At least I could move again. He would later tell Sean whose expression would suggest he could have done without that imagery.

Greer heard the familiar voice of the tall Carian from whom he had been receiving history lessons, in Ancient Alien Egypt.

He climbed out of the pool, and was wrapped in a thin towel by one of the small grey beings. The alien bowed then left, leaving Greer even more baffled.

Greer "heard" in his mind, a greeting from the Carion thus establishing a means for dialogue. Greer immediately took full advantage of the opportunity. "What the hell?"

The tall, avian extra-terrestrial rested its elongated arms by its side and squinted at Greer. Only the tilting of its head and subtle changes in its small, beady eyes expressed emotion. It responded to Greer's vague yet poignant query. "Your treatment is complete."

Greer thought for a second. "The thick liquid bath is a treatment? For what?"

The response was sent telepathically. "No, it is a disinfectant. There any micro-organisms aboard our ship, which can be harmful to you. It is a precaution."

"Then, what was the treatment?"

Just then Greer felt a tingling in his neck. He reached up, expecting to rub the lump, but found it missing beneath his skin.

"It's gone!"

"The device has been removed."

Growing impatient, Greer suddenly understood some of Ashley's frustrations.

"And it was there...why?"

"It enabled us to bring you aboard our ship. Once you closed the portal we required an alternate mode of transport."

The implications of the statement hit Greer in the gut as he recalled the presence of the grey alien in his bedroom, just before he destroyed the Ouija Board. Feeling violated, he quickly grew angry. "How long have you been abducting me?"

"We were attracted to the open portal and found you bore the mark. Our first exam revealed abnormal cell division in your neck. Through several treatments, it has been corrected."

Stunned, Greer repeated the words. "Exam? Abnormal cell division? As in cancer?"

"The very early stages of a cancer, yes."

He experienced a rush of several successive emotions at the onerous diagnosis: First, he was dumfounded, then scared, which morphed into relief, and eventually landed on appreciation. However, the overall emotion remained confusion. "Uh, thank you?" Greer's mind raced with questions.

The Carian explained, "This will be our final visit as the answers you seek have already been revealed. We have had many conversations during your time with us. It was necessary to suppress your memory in the beginning but you will recall them during your sessions."

The alien host extended a long hand out to his guest. Greer held his own hand out in response, while something was placed in his palm. Precisely at the moment of their touch, Greer awoke in his bed.

Slightly disoriented, he reviewed the conversation and his just revealed health scare. He lifted his hand to his head to wipe his brow, but discovered something hard and small in his palm. Curiosity forced him out of the bed, as he made his way across the room and turned on the light. A tiny, black metallic object, no larger than a housefly, sat in his hand. While he could feel tiny ridges on its surface, it was too small to visualize any detail.

Sobek, still on the edge of the bed, awoke and wagged his tail.

Greer walked over and sat down next to his big pup. Bek rolled on his side, with his legs slightly bent. His big, expectant, brown eyes were fixed on his human pal while he enjoyed the loving interaction. Scratching Bek's neck, Greer observed his grey muzzle and quipped, "You're getting old buddy and I'm going crazy. We're a helluva team."

Sobek lifted his head and lathered the left side of Greer's face with his tongue which prompted a much needed heartfelt laugh.

The alarm clock displayed the time of three fifteen a.m. when he finally allowed himself to lay back down on the bed. His head reeled with the startling information that the Carian had placed inside. But his body eventually defeated his heavy thoughts and collected its prize of slumber.

Sean tossed and turned in his bed while moans and slurred words emanated from his mouth. The nightmare vividly unfolded in his subconscious mind.

He was being chased. Barefoot, he ran through a thick growth of dense, overgrown woods. Behind him, he could hear the angered cries of his assailants as they closed in. They cursed him while calling out, "Betrayer!"

His feet stung as they sunk into thorns and sharp rocks on the hot ground.

He had been running fast, but he began to grow weary and slowed. Arrows landed to each side of him as the attackers shouts intensified, signaling their close proximity.

Out of breath, his body overcome with fatigue, he desperately searched for the strength to keep moving. But his effort would prove to be a futile endeavor.

The arrow entered between his shoulder blades, inserting itself deep into his back. His arms flailed outward with the forward momentum of the shot, forcing him, face-down, upon the growth-covered ground. The pain, so overwhelming, he barely noticed the thorns cutting into his chest and face from the ground cover hidden beneath his dying body.

Helpless and with a bittersweet sense of relief that he no longer needed to run, he felt his warm blood drain from the wound on his back.

Quickly losing consciousness, he heard the cascade of voices escalate as his enemy was almost upon him. Through a hazy vision he detected movement directly ahead. Calling on the very last remnants of his energy and resolve, he somehow mustered the strength to gaze upward, at the final thing he would envision as he gasped his dying breath. Standing before him, at his moment of death, was the Native American Chief.

Sean woke up, startled, and looked around his bedroom. The familiar setting helped him, quickly, reach the conclusion that he had been dreaming. But what unsettled him the most, was the fact that he'd experienced this exact nightmare the previous three nights.

Abduction VI

Thursday arrived and Greer made his way through most of the work day without incident. He was leaving to make his three o'clock appointment with Beverly, when he was pulled into the break room to "celebrate" someone's something-day. He signed the card, never asking for any additional information.

With a vague, insincere sentiment delivered and a slice of store bought cake devoured, he'd managed to escape and achieve a punctual arrival for his unconventional brand of therapy.

Sitting on her sofa, Greer told Beverly of his recent, and apparently, last, abduction.

She listened intently while simultaneously taking notes.

When he'd finished, Greer stretched himself along the sofa and began his familiar breathing regiment. Beverly verbally guided him to the memory of an unrecalled previous abduction.

Pictures began to take shape in Greer's mind, delivered telepathically by the towering Carian. As the E.T. approached him, his movement triggered the soft, overhead lighting. An extra-terrestrial with a head resembling an eagle, unremarkably tall, relayed the continuing story to the human passenger.

Merkharu stood at the entrance to the secret civilization. His usual hard, stoic expression was concealed behind the golden crocodile headdress he wore. Beyond his intimidating, cold stare, the menacing reptilian head cover instilled fear in anyone that was brave enough to gaze upon it.

However, on this day, unknown to anyone but him, the elaborate mask hid a smile.

He thought back to the day he entered the pyramid expecting to find the remains of his half alien relatives, only to discover they had tunneled out and were surviving, barely, in the desert.

His guilty conscience granted a chance at redemption, he set a series of events in motion.

First, he had a subterranean compound dug with a tunnel which connected to the very pyramid that was originally their prison.

Second, he ordered the construction of underground homes for the several hundred half Carian, half human beings.

He then called upon his sacred priests. To address the many birth defects, the magicians introduced their genetically challenged brothers and sisters to the healing power of crystals in an effort to extend their short lives.

While physically limited and ailing, the small grey creatures were intelligent and possessed the same mental capabilities as their Carian mothers.

Their strong survival instinct was undeniable; within seven years they had constructed several crystal powered generators.

They used astrologically aligned pyramids covered in tufa limestone coupled with crystals within, to generate electrical power. They improved and lengthened their lives, however there was still loss. In another three years, they numbered only two hundred and fifty. They weren't thriving, but many were surviving, a while longer.

Merkharu, distracted from his memory, looked to the sky as several shiny discs soared above him, then landed nearby. Kapherus had arrived.

Merkharu had received no correspondence since his last visit when Kapherus had left the grey offspring behind. The half-breed Pharaoh was quite unsure if he would be commended or disciplined for disobedient actions.

The visiting Carian said nothing as the half-human king walked him through the underground community, boasting of the grey creatures' accomplishments.

When the tour ended, Kapherus immediately assembled the king and his priests in the royal chamber.

Kapherus directed his words to Merkharu, but allowed them to be audible to the priests who sat silent with lowered, reverent heads.

"As Pharaoh, you are responsible."

The priestess looked up; her motion caused a distraction that interrupted their conversation, but when they turned to her, she remained quiet.

Kapherus continued, "You were given clear instructions and you disobeyed them."

Abandoning all reverence, the priestess shouted in defense of her leader, "He helped save them!"

Nookhotep commanded her to silence.

Kapherus heard the mental message. "No, allow her to share her thoughts."

The brave, vocal priestess stood. Donned in her royal robe, her face was obscured by the attached hood. Fueled by her compassion, she spoke, "We can help them. We should help them."

Merkharu and Nookhotep exchanged glances, both fearing the worst.

"What course of action do you propose?" Kapherus asked, as he stared down his Carian, beak shaped nose, awaiting her response.

Her head remained lowered, her face hidden, as she spoke. "Leave behind a ship. We can transport them to an unpopulated area where we will colonize them, as we have here, but above ground, where they can truly utilize the resources under our sun."

Kapherus' demeanor remained unchanged. "To what end?"

She continued, "We are working to enhance their DNA. But we lack the necessary tools for genetic duplication. We will need your assistance with that endeavor."

"Explain." Said their now slightly, intrigued, alien ancestor.

"We may be able to save them if we can create hybrids with functioning reproductive organs. But, again, we will need your help."

Kapherus paced the chamber and considered the possibilities. Indeed, the very reason they joined with the human race was to enhance their innate human abilities and help them ascend. And certainly, their compassion stemmed from their human side.

Telepathically adept, he allowed only Merkharu to hear his thoughts. "Is this your desire as well?"

Merkharu replied, "Yes."

Kapherus then addressed the conclave of magicians. "Are you all so committed to their survival?"

To which he received seven hooded nods to the affirmative.

Kapherus paused then smiled. "Then show me the brave faces that would save their ailing siblings."

One by one, they slowly reached up with both hands, and pulled back their concealing hoods, to reveal their faces.

Greer sat up on the sofa. Beverly stopped writing to address his incredulous expression. "Are you alright, Greer?"

He spoke slowly, astonished at his realization. "Ashley. The Priestess is Ashley. And Nookhotep…is Sean."

Intrigued but not overly surprised, Beverly resumed her dictation and entered her client's words into her notes before responding. "As you know, Greer, we often reincarnate with those closest to us."

Greer was silent and at a loss for words. He raised his arms and placed his hands on the back of his head.

Beverly noticed his body ink peeking out from beneath his shirt and made a connection. "Greer, can I see your tattoo?"

While he was slightly surprised at her request, he pulled up his short, black sleeve.

Beverly smiled as she observed the artwork. Before her, on his muscled arm, was a depiction of Sobek, the crocodile headed God of ancient Egypt. He was adorned in a full headdress and his long snout boasted sharp teeth. The deity held a staff topped with the magical ankh, a symbol of his mighty power. It crossed a band that spelled his name and was fully connected by tiny ankhs around his arm.

Greer noted Beverly's smile and asked, proudly, "Nice, eh?"

Sensing he was more proud of his unnecessarily flexed arm muscles, she stated, quite matter of fact, "Your tattoo is the mark."

As Greer relaxed his arm and pulled his sleeve back down, he was suddenly embracing several new considerations. "The mark. The Carian said I bore the mark."

Beverly sat down to take notes and allow Greer the opportunity to find his own enlightenment.

Growing more excited, Greer continued. "Merkharu wore a crocodile headed mask! But, what's the connection with Sobek?"

Beverly looked up, "What does Sobek represent to ancient Egypt?"

"Sobek was worshipped for power and protection. He was kind of a badass."

Beverly nodded. "Anything else?"

Greer pulled out his iPhone. "I'll ask Dude-Siri."

"Dude-Siri?"

"Yeah, I changed the voice response to a guy."

Beverly struggled to find fault in his logic.

After his phone had powered up, he asked, "Who was Sobek?"

A few seconds later, he received, "Here's what I found."

He read, aloud, the first link, "Sobek-The God of Fertility."

Beverly smiled and continued to make notes.

Greer was silent for a moment before admitting, "Yeah, I'm going to need you to connect some dots for me, Bev."

"It's Beverly." She finished scribing her notes and looked at Greer. "Why did you choose to get that tattoo?"

"I got it when I adopted my dog, Sobek."

Beverly took a second swing. "OK, why did you choose to name your dog Sobek?"

Smiling at the mere mention of his big pup, he told her the story. "Before I got Bek I was having all these dreams about crocodiles. Sometimes, they were just swimming around me. Other times, I would see them off in the distance. In one dream I was standing on the edge of an indoor pool as a giant croc talked to me, but I don't remember what it said. Anyway, when I adopted Bek he had a tiny collar with little crocodiles on it. I looked up their meaning, found the reference to Sobek in Egypt, and it all clicked together." He paused before adding, "Did I mention he was also a badass?"

Ignoring his last comment, as a matter of course, she asked, "What do crocodiles represent to you, Greer?"

He thought for a second, then listed; "Consistency, perseverance, and strength. They're impressive if you think about it. They've stood the test of time. Hell, they've been around since the dinosaurs. They haven't changed much because they didn't need to. In their environment, they're the apex predator."

Beverly grinned while choosing a word from his vernacular. "So, they're badasses?"

Greer sat back down on the sofa and reciprocated. "Indeed."

He paused and nodded while fitting a big piece of the puzzle together. "Fertility."

Beverly elaborated, "It's plausible that the stories of Merkharu became somewhat of a legend in the Egyptian culture. He would be depicted as a man with a crocodile head, having always worn his mask outside of his royal temple. No doubt he chose the guise of a crocodile as they were either feared or revered as great monsters infesting The Nile. Therefore history would recall him as a reptilian God from the stars that fathered thousands of children."

Beverly did a quick search on her tablet as Greer finished her explanation. "Hence, the God of Fertility." She continued. "Tales, as well as names, change throughout history as they are passed down through each generation. Merkharu becomes Sobek, which changed to Unas in the twenty-third century BC, among many other names in between."

Beverly's session bell rang, ending the appointment. With so much to digest, little was said as Greer made his way out of the office except, "Thanks, Beverly. See you tomorrow."

Needing a caffeinated crutch, Greer drove straight to the Starbucks near his home. The line in the drive thru was seven cars deep so he opted to go inside. The familiar baristas greeted him a-la-Norm entering

Cheers. At his sight, they began preparing his "usual" while he waited to pay.

A male skateboarder in line in front of him had several obvious tats. Greer admired the colorful, intricate artwork, especially a barcode on the back of his neck.

"Does that scan?" Greer blurted out.

Having heard the questions many times, the younger guy replied, "Yeah, man."

Greer was intrigued, and asked the familiar counter worker if he could scan the tattoo with his register gun.

"Sure."

As if bored with the process, the skater turned and allowed the employee to scan his neck.

The computer system displayed a series of, seemingly random, ones and zeros across the screen. Greer raised his left eyebrow, impressed, considering the level of detail and perfectly straight line work necessary for a tattoo to be scanned.

"It's binary, dude." said the young man, as he walked off with his drink.

Somewhat defensively, Greer replied, "Yeah, I know."

He didn't know.

Greer remembered the small piece of alien technology, formerly in his neck that he had put in his pocket, but forgot to show Beverly. He pulled it out, looked at it and had a hunch.

"Can you scan this?"

The barista handed him his iced coffee and glanced at his hand. "I can try, it's tiny. What is it?"

Greer didn't answer and allowed him to scan the alien object. Again, a series of ones and zeros read across the screen.

"Can you print that?"

After a minute the clerk, handed him a receipt with the following series of numbers:

01110011 01101111 01100010 01100101 01101011

"Are you going to translate it?" asked the coffee maker. "There's an app for that."

Even more defensively, he retorted, "Yeah, I know."

He didn't know.

Greer got back into his truck and made his way home. Upon arrival, he was thrilled to see Ashley waiting for him in his driveway.

"How long have you been here, Ash?" he asked as he grabbed her and spun her around.

She laughed, saying, "I just got here, and was about to call you."

Wanting, and very much needing, to shake off the day, he scooped her up in his strong arms and carried her to the door. The gesture lost a little of its impact when he had to put her down and retrieve his keys, but she continued to display a loving smile of contentment anyway. The two rushed inside and straight to the bedroom, having missed each other terribly over the past few days.

After some very intimate time together they shared a meal and a short chat. To Greer's dismay, Ashley had to go home for another early day on Friday, which left Greer to retire to bed, alone, and characteristically early.

Sean couldn't get the nightmare out of his mind. He searched the internet for an explanation of dreams in which you are being chased.

One website recommended a lucid dreaming technique that allowed you to turn and face your fears.

Lucid?

Another site suggested that the dream represents guilt for the people you've turned your back on, and that you should go to confession.

That's not gonna happen.

Then he remembered something Greer had said about recurring dreams being a past memory, and even a past-life memory.

Why not?

He texted his buddy, "G, do you still have that past life regression CD?"

"Yeah, why?"

"Fill you in tomorrow. Later."

Surprisingly, that exchange wasn't the shortest conversation they'd ever had.

Abduction VII

Friday morning arrived, and Greer took Sobek on a very long, early walk to compensate for the prior evening's skipped exercise.

A quick shower, and a second cup of coffee, en route, enabled him to make it to the office by seven a.m. where he discovered a series of vocational trials awaited him.

Staying awake during the three back-to-back, hour long, conference calls was the first Herculean task accomplished…barely.

Next, he fielded a complaint from an associate who felt underappreciated and just wanted a "thank-you."

Thank you.

The rolling of Greer's eyes occurred, luckily, after the employee turned to leave his office.

Their biweekly paycheck is an implied "thank-you"; guess it should come with a hug? He would later quip to Sean.

He thought he was in the clear after lunch until someone collecting money for somebody else, for some reason, cornered him in his office.

He put his hands in his pockets and feigned disappointment, while he delivered his standard response, "I don't have any cash on me."

Having grown wise to this tactic, the seasoned, self-appointed office collector replied, "No problem, I'll come back tomorrow."

Two o'clock arrived, and he boss-smiled his way past the overly enthusiastic shouts of "Have a good weekend!" and "TGIF!"

He chose to ignore the not-whispered-low-enough remark, "Must be nice to leave early whenever you want."

Blue skies and bright sun above, he drove out of the parking lot and headed to Beverly's office. Somewhat belated, he mused, "Yeah, it is."

Appreciating his punctuality, Beverly smiled while greeting her client as he walked through her office door.

Within minutes, they were positioned in their usual places. Beverly guided him back to an unrecalled memory of abduction, while Greer lay relaxed and breathing in cadence; his focused mind finally was primed to reveal previously learned, but forgotten truths.

Greer faced the bird-alien, while the hum of the spaceship vibrated softly throughout his body. A scene in his mind, compliments of his otherworldly host, depicted the fate of the small grey aliens as they fought for survival in ancient Egypt.

For years the priests assisted their struggling grey relatives in the creation of an impressive civilization located on a Mediterranean island. Supported by advanced, alien technology, they boasted powerful devices used in scientific and genetic experimentation. The small alien beings worked tirelessly to achieve their singular goal of reproduction.

Sadly, their efforts remained unrewarded as they helplessly watched their population dwindle to less than one hundred. Sensing their impending doom, with little hope in sight, the priestess petitioned the help of her fellow magicians to perform powerful magic.

"The risk is too great," Nookhotep explained, in response to her request.

She begged him. "Please, what other choice do we have?"

Nookhotep sighed as he answered, "None".

The magicians gathered in the center of the island, where the power was the greatest. Holding hands in a tight circle, in their ceremonial robes, they chanted. Inside the human ring lay a massive piece of selenite adjacent to thin lines of copper, which stretched to each one of the priests. The giant ore of selenite glowed intensely in conjunction with their repetitive and impassioned chanting.

They called upon the very magic of the Earth herself. If they stopped the ritual too soon, they would yield nothing.

Alternatively, they could generate too much power that would prove disastrous. They relied on intuition alone as they asked Mother Earth to heal their brothers and sisters.

Perhaps, it was their overwhelming compassion. Or maybe their intense, unwavering desire. It could have been simple miscalculation. Regardless of the reason, they failed. The island began to implode. The selenite, bursting with a staggering amount of energy, collapsed into itself; the resulting folding of space created a vacuum, and pulled everything around it inside.

The priests, exhausted, fell into the collapsing ground beneath them. All, except one.

The priestess called telepathically to the tiny grey beings and implored them, to assemble in the smallest of the powered pyramids.

There, they found the alien ship that had brought them to their island home. Less than fifty were aboard when the ground ceased to exist. The disc-shaped transport soared up and out to space, leaving no survivors below them.

Greer looked at his Carian narrator with watery eyes. "She died trying to save them." He smiled through the sadness, shaking his head at Ashley's unrelenting desire to help others. A trait that was so deeply ingrained that it traversed lifetimes.

The avian alien motioned for Greer to follow, and returned him to the nursery where the adolescent aliens were playing. Greer was unsure if it was his own determination or a thought inserted by the Carian, but he now understood that the young aliens were a result of cloning. He also grasped their need for human abductions. "You need to fill in the DNA gaps."

"We regret the discomfort of the process, but we offer healing in exchange for the genetic material."

"Given that we don't have much of a choice in the matter, I guess that's something."

The Carian bowed its head and Greer understood the meeting to be over. The last thought received was the name of the once powerful, alien civilization that had folded in on itself: Atlantis.

Greer opened his eyes but remained flat on the sofa. Without looking, he knew Beverly was feverishly working to record the final details of his recall and, of course, add her own commentary.

Instinctively, he felt he had recalled the full story told to him by the Carian alien and felt lighter at having purged the suppressed memories of his abductions.

Greer sat up and looked over at Beverly.

She stopped writing, smiled and asked, "How do you feel, Greer?"

"Good. It's a lot to absorb, but I do feel better."

Beverly was genuinely pleased and leaned forward to say, "I'm very proud of you, Greer. You did great."

Greer smiled and nodded in silence.

"You can release the experience now. I know that sounds difficult, and it will take time, but that is part of the healing process. And, remember, I am here to help you."

Greer took a deep breath and stood up to thank Beverly for her assistance. "You've been awesome. Thank you."

"You are very welcome."

He left her office and climbed into his truck. Craving a non-alien, more secular experience, he headed home just after sending Sean a text.

"Beer?"

A half-hour later, the guys were sitting on Greer's deck enjoying a cold Miller Lite. Sobek rested beneath them, just one of the guys.

For the next hour or so, Greer told Sean of the abduction recall he experienced during the light hypnosis administered by Beverly. Sean was surprisingly quiet as he listened to the failed alien agenda in ancient Egypt, which ended in the fateful demise of Atlantis and was accumulating countless questions and comments as his disbelief gave way to consideration.

It wasn't until Greer revealed yet another incarnation with Ashley, the compassionate priestess that his buddy was prompted to converse, but his thoughts fell to his recurring nightmare.

"Speaking of past lives, do you have that disc?"

Greer was shocked when Sean had asked about the CD in his last text and truly taken back at his second request. But, he withheld his comments and went inside to retrieve it for him, with Sobek in tow.

A moment later, Sean heard the doorbell and Greer's subsequent greeting of his girlfriend.

That's my exit cue. He grumbled to himself.

Sean went inside to greet Ashley, who was scratching the back end of an overly excited black Lab. "Hey, Ashley."

"Hi, Sean." Ashley was genuinely concerned when she asked, "Did I interrupt guy's night?"

Sean looked at Greer. "Naw, I was just leaving."

Ashley excused herself. "It was nice seeing you, Sean." She turned to Greer and whispered, "I'm going to use the little girl's room."

Greer handed Sean the past life regression disc. "Man, you don't have to leave."

Sean waved him off. "Spend some time with your girlfriend, G." He paused and looked at the CD. "Besides, I got something I need to do."

He shook Greer's hand and then pointed at him, "Gym in the morning, don't be late."

Greer stared suspiciously and replied, "Eight o'clock, big man."

Ashley returned, still concerned, as she eyed Sean drive away, "Sweetie, did I interrupt you guys hanging out?"

Greer smiled reassuringly, "We had a beer and chatted, but he's got some stuff to do so it's all good."

Relieved, she smiled. "How about dinner and a movie?"

The week behind him melting away from memory in the presence of his beautiful Ashley, Greer beamed. "Sounds great! I'll feed Bek and then we'll leave."

After finding a comfortable and quiet spot on his living room couch, Sean followed the guided meditation. Breathing in through his mouth and out of his nose, he began to relax.

He recalled his recurring nightmare of being chased and the sight of the Native American ghost at his moment of death. The soft, female voice on the disc began a backward count from ten to one. At the countdown's completion, Sean began to witness events of another lifetime.

Pahana turned his horse and observed his little brother draw back his bow. He felt a sense of pride seeing him participate in his first attack since having been deemed a warrior by their father, the Chief. He followed his sibling's line of sight to see a young girl, the target of his arrow, coming out from beneath the blanket. At first, she didn't notice the weapon fixed on her position as she surveyed the death of her family and friends.

The natives had come out of nowhere. Her mother told her to hide just before she was shot off of the wagon. The little girl stared at her mother's bloody and lifeless body on the ground as tears poured from her eyes. Then, looking back up, she engaged her fate as she stared at an arrow aimed directly at her.

A moment later, Pahana watched while his young brother slowly lowered his weapon. His hung head told him that he could not bring himself to take the life of another pale-face, at least not this young female.

He called to his sibling, "You must find the strength, brother."

To which came the reply, "Then leave me to my task." The bow was again raised.

Pahana returned to camp. He gathered some of the tribe and scouted for dinner, arriving home just before dark to find his brother returned. "Well done, young one. Father will be pleased."

His sibling looked up at him with tears and pleaded, "I need your help."

He led his older brother to his hut where Pahana found the terrified, young girl, bound and gagged.

Pahana's eyes enlarged, only to squint in anger a second later. "What have you done?"

Tears fell in lieu of words. A boy of thirteen, having killed his first man this morning, could not bring himself to murder this young female. He panicked, and brought her to the camp. In desperation, he found his words, "What do I do, Pahana?"

With little time to think, Pahana grabbed the pale girl and carried her to his hut. But he was spotted before he could make entry. Within seconds, the tribe had gathered around him. They made their assumptions which labeled him a traitor, or worse, as weak, for feeling sympathy for the pale skinned girl.

Seeing the display, his younger brother ran to confess to the hostile mob, but Pahana saw him and stopped his approach. "Say nothing, young brother! Go, get father, now!"

The angry tribesman attacked Pahana, taking the young girl from his grasp and ultimately chasing him into the woods. He ran for his life, dodging the flying spears and arrows as they grazed his head and shoulders. To his left, he saw his father on horseback, rushing to catch up to him, shouting at the tribe to retreat. But, fueled by their mob mentality, they could not hear him above their own cries and screams for justice.

Sean's familiar nightmare played out, this time during his regression, of the arrow sinking deep between his shoulder blades. His dying body was sprawled out on the thick ground cover, as life seeped out of him. He looked up with hazy, weary eyes to witness his father, the Chief, crying over him.

Slightly disoriented, Sean opened his eyes and sat up on the couch. He understood Greer and Ashley's incarnation with him and, more profoundly, the identity of the protective Native American ghost.

I think I'll grab that second beer now.

Sean reviewed his experiences with the Native American apparition. Indeed, the Chief's materialization in the backseat was enough to stall his entry into that intersection, saving him from an imminent crash.

He wasn't sure what the ominous, advancing, black form which had vanished into the white light was, but he assumed the Chief's place at the foot of his bed was a measure of protection.

Despite his considerations, he was still not a hundred percent willing to accept these events as fact, but he would admit there was some solace in the contemplation. One thing, not up for debate, was that the subject matter of tomorrow morning's gym conversation had certainly been chosen.

It was just past midnight when Greer rolled Ashley off his shoulder. After dinner they decided to watch a movie at his house, of which she would enjoy for just under an hour, before falling asleep on the couch.

Greer reached for his phone to check for messages. As he did, he remembered the barista's comment about the app for binary decryption. He did a search and to his surprise, there was a free install. He downloaded the program, and then retrieved the receipt with the series of ones and zeros from his wallet. He carefully punched in the numbers and hit submit to which the program revealed the name, SOBEK.

He smiled at another instance of the significance of the name. It also helped explain the nods and bows of the small aliens as they observed his Sobek tattoo, granting another reason to accept the recalled metaphysical events as reality.

The long week over, he retrieved his sleeping beauty from the couch and carried her to the bedroom. She fell fast asleep, assuming she had even woken up.

I don't even remember going to bed. She would say the next morning of her fatigue.

Greer laid flat and achieved a relaxed state very quickly. He felt a tingling in his feet that shot up, through his body, to the top of his head.

Recalling the incident in Beverly's office, he quickly opened his eyes.

He was stunned by what he saw: As if hovering, he, unbelievably, gazed down upon both his and Ashley's motionless bodies.

The story continues in 7 Projections-Book 5 in The 7 Novellas Series.

7

Projections

by

Gare Allen

The 7 Novellas Series by Gare Allen

Dedicated to Dane

Projection I

Am I dead?

Greer hovered high over his bed as he incredulously stared down at his motionless body. Ashley, ever the heavy sleeper, was turned on her side and facing the opposite direction.

Despite the precarious sensation of being suspended in mid-air, coupled with the terrifying possibility that he had died, he tried, nevertheless, to left-brain his situation.

I must be dreaming.

His determination provided little comfort when, suddenly, he recalled his very brief flirtation with an out-of-body experience, when he had entered a hypnotic state, in Beverly's office.

A numbing, tingling feeling had moved from his toes to the top of his head and increased until he felt himself rising off of her sofa, only to immediately fall back.

Feeling secular again, he composed himself and described the involuntary ability to his regression therapist. She causally explained that it was a common occurrence for your spirit, or soul, to project when the physical body is deeply relaxed, especially during sleep.

Greer glared closer at his stationary, physical body lying on the bed and observed the slight rise and fall of his chest while it breathed in and out. He was, understandably, quite relieved to determine that he had not passed away.

Two points for Bev. He would later enter the recognition into his journal.

Acceptance of the extremely comforting conclusion that he was still alive allowed his attention to shift to the rest of his surroundings.

The bedroom walls, the floor and every piece of furniture emitted a soft, white glow, while a very low hum emanated from seemingly everywhere.

Suspended, he found that, surprisingly, the more he absorbed the meta-environment, the more at ease he became. It was quiet, not eerie, but serene.

He knew nothing about out-of-body experiences. When Beverly had previously suggested that he had triggered one during his relaxation exercise, his skeptical reaction and subsequent dismissal of the notion suggested to her that he had found his paranormal line in the sand.

His eyes shifted to the penetrating beam of crystal moonlight entering through the window. He admired a brilliant display of tiny, sparkling, diamonds frantically circling one another; each contained and gloriously shimmering in a dazzling cone of lunar illumination.

The moon.

At the very thought of the heavenly body, he felt a rush of force against his face and body and then found himself transported high above his home.

The Earth's satellite was nothing short of brilliant in the night sky as it showered him with its radiance.

In a moment of breath-taking awe, he was bathed in the beauty of the orb's reflected light as it shared a celestial stage with millions of bright, twinkling stars. Suspended and absorbing the full effect of the

244

spectacular, heavenly display, Greer was amazed at the warmth of their glow. The sensation nudged the left side of his brain back into the game.

The spirit body feels heat?

Greer looked up at the intense moonlight and somehow understood that the warm feeling was that of energy, specifically, spiritual energy.

Not pausing to consider how or from where he had obtained the enlightening clarification, his thoughts turned to a single goal of going to the moon.

He braced himself for the rush of movement.

Nothing happened. He remained stationary.

Tapping into his inner-supervisor, he mentally commanded, *go to the moon.*

Again, nothing happened.

Confused, he looked down to see a long, thin, silver cord stretching from behind him, ending at his house. He reached back with his hand and followed the cord as it entered the back of his neck.

I'm on a leash?

This time, he mentally received the answer to his query from the soft voice of a woman.

"The string of energy binds your spiritual body to your physical."

Who are you?

Greer felt the rush of extreme movement and a fraction of a second later he found himself, no longer floating, but standing in what appeared to be the ruins of an old, abandoned castle.

The ancient stone walls had suffered the effects of time. Long cracks stretched from the floor to the ceiling and overlapped each other like the lines on a map. Invasive vines and weeds surfaced between the gaps in the foundation in search of sunlight. Similar to the physical objects in his bedroom, every single thing was bathed in a colorful hue, resonating with the murmur of a faint hum.

Where am I?

To which he received the retort, "Where...or when?"

Greer gasped as a blinding white light instantly filled every corner of the castle and then dissipated just as quickly to reveal the enchanting beauty he knew to be named, Selene.

His Spirit Guide was exactly as he recalled her. Standing only a few feet away, he lost himself in her presence. Her waist-length, straight, jet-black hair shimmered, much like the diamond effect of the moonlight. Selene's piercing dark eyes would have intimidated him, if it were not for her unconditional, loving smile that accentuated her impossibly high cheek bones. The moonlight sneaking through the breaks in the roof reflected off of the garnet she wore around her neck and held in place by a thin, silver chain. Her form fitting, ivory white gown stretched down to the castle's foundation as she coupled her hands loosely at her waist, emitting the pure elegance of an angel.

She repeated herself. "Where...or when?"

Greer took his eyes off of her figure and resumed an ocular connection before responding. "I'm not sure what you mean."

Her patient, loving expression never changed as she explained. "The plane of existence in which your spiritual body is currently focused is known as the astral. Among all the planes, the astral frequency is closest to the physical plane, where your body resides. On this level, time is not restricted by the laws governing physical reality." She then glanced to her right.

Greer followed her gaze to his left to see a corridor. An assumption of her direction and a growing curiosity prompted him to enter. Once through, he beheld an impressive stone, spiral staircase.

While their presence is not uncommon in European castles, this particular spiraling walkway's attributes were certainly remarkable for it had remained intact, clean and free of cracks and foliage, while the once grand fortress around it had aged and deteriorated.

Greer walked over, peered up at the twisting stairs and saw a thick, swirling mist.

He looked over to Selene. "What's up there?"

Still radiant and smiling, she replied, "The staircase is a portal." Anticipating his obvious follow-up question, she continued. "As you continue climbing upward, you move forward into time's future. Each step is a doorway to a different reality."

Greer raised his left eyebrow. "A different reality?"

She continued. "Yes. Each day a reality is shaped based on decisions made out of free will. For every possible outcome, that reality exists."

Greer was able to grasp the concept, albeit superficially. "So, there's a reality where I had turkey instead of chicken for lunch?"

Selene's words were unwaveringly patient as she answered his question. "The realities of the individual weave in and out of each other driven by the choices that do not directly impact the masses."

Greer looked around as if wondering if the rest of the class was lost too.

She quickly offered an example. "Today, you choose to go a restaurant, eat a turkey lunch and then see a movie. That aligns with what we will call Reality A. But just before ordering, you change your mind and choose the chicken meal instead which aligns you with Reality B. Afterward, you proceed to see a movie where you are, once again, in alignment with Reality A. You are consciously unaware that you shifted between different realities although you, indeed, changed, or more accurately, determined the outcome with each of your decisions. These subtle realities are available to you through choices." She looked at the stone spiral staircase. "Alternative global realities, some far different than the one in which you currently reside, are accessible through portals."

He deduced that his angel must have held him back from his trip to the moon in favor of, well, moving him to the castle and delivering a lesson in realities.

Greer followed her line of sight, looked over the staircase and characteristically simplified her explanation.

"So, each step is a doorway to a different future of Earth?"

The enchanting woman turned her gaze back on Greer and smiled at his understanding.

Greer felt a tug at his neck. Then, another. The next one almost yanked him off his feet. He looked at Selene who simply stood silent as her image began to fade. The familiar rush of movement overtook his sense of being.

Only a second later it was gone and he opened his eyes to find that he was, once again, lying flat on his bed and next to his sleeping beauty, Ashley. She was curled up against him, with her arm outstretched across his muscular chest.

For a moment, he struggled to retain the fading images of what he assumed to be an elaborate dream involving stars, stairs and an angel. The visuals were unable to sustain themselves in his short-term memory and they quickly dissipated as did his consciousness, until his alarm sounded for his early, Saturday morning gym hit.

Greer prepared an egg-white omelet while Ashley cracked open a "real egg" for herself. After breakfast she accompanied him on Sobek's walk around the neighborhood. She wrapped herself around his left arm while his right was tethered to a big black dog that appeared to be on a mission to mark every palm tree and at least, every other, mailbox in sight.

Greer lost himself in the bliss of the moment and pulled his girlfriend closer. The sweet smell of strawberries wafting from her long, light brown hair made him almost dizzy with delight. They barely spoke, but words weren't required on their perfect, morning walk.

Once back to the house, the couple said goodbye while standing beside Ashley's car and made plans to meet for dinner.

"Have a good workout, Sweetie. Tell Sean I said, hello."

Greer smiled, remembering that Sean had some explaining to do after having borrowed his past life regression disc. "Will do. See you tonight."

Twenty minutes later and ten minutes late, Greer found Sean doing bicep curls with dumbbells in their surprisingly, mostly empty, gym.

"You're late."

Greer ignored his curt greeting and grabbed thirty pound dumbbells and began curling. "So, what's up?"

Sean's mind was still reeling from the vivid imagery of the past life recall where he had been brutally attacked and killed by his own tribe of Native Americans while trying to protect his younger brother.

Greer finished his set and then turned to address his workout partner. He was shocked to see an unusually stern expression had fallen upon Sean's face. This was the second incident of "serious-face" in less than two weeks.

Its occurrence is foretold in Revelations as a sign of the apocalypse. He would later joke to Ashley of his buddy's unusual demeanor.

Hearing this, Ashley wondered if her eyes would ever get stuck in the back of her head if she continued to roll them so frequently.

Greer shot his bud a serious look of his own. "Talk to me, buddy."

Sean looked around. Observing only two other gym rats on the other side of the facility and therefor confident that their conversation would be private, he shared his recalled memory of the Native American incarnation with his best friend.

Greer was initially stunned at the synchronicity of the shared dreams but the shock faded to an emerging acceptance as he recalled Beverly's karmic comment: "We often incarnate with those closest to us to continue working through our karmic paths together."

Greer then identified their dynamic in that particular lifetime. "So, we were brothers? And, you protected me?"

Sean nodded and replied, "You tried to protect Ashley, I tried to protect you and the Chief tried to protect me."

The heavy content became too much for Sean as it breached his non-secular comfort level and he put on the brakes. "Those discs should come with a warning label."

He picked up his dumbbells and resumed his workout while switching subjects to the Saturday morning fishing show on one of the gym television monitors.

Greer allowed his buddy to dictate the topic of discussion for the remainder of the bicep hit and silently wondered if Sean realized that he had opened a door that he might not be able to close.

Projection II

The guys finished their bicep workout routine which consisted of fifteen sets of various curls and then, as a matter of course, treated the cardio area as a dark alley to be avoided.

Greer complained about his work week while they downed a post-exercise protein drink from the gym's smoothie bar. He paused, mid-rant, realizing that Sean had never talked about his job.

"What exactly do you do?" Greer asked, sincerely unaware of his vocation.

Sean just grinned. "Ready to go, G?"

Walking to their trucks, Greer offered, one more time, to talk about Sean's regression. "You sure you're good, man?"

Sean waved off the question. "All good, man."

"Call me if ya wanna chat." Greer offered.

"Will do. Later, G."

Twenty minutes later, Greer arrived home and leashed up an expectant big, black dog for the day's second walk through the neighborhood.

They weren't five houses away when Sobek squatted and left a sizable deposit on a neighbor's lawn. Having forgotten a waste bag, Greer walked to the closest doggie-poop station, retrieved a plastic bag and returned to the scene of the crime.

The owner of the home happened to walk out to get his mail as Greer was returning and asked, "Did your dog do that?"

In classic deadpan Greer style, he replied, "Well, it wasn't me."

Not waiting or even worried about a response, Greer cleaned up the waste and continued on his way, leaving the neighbor standing, staring and speechless. Greer grinned as he tossed the waste in the next trash can that they encountered.

He made his way back home with his, slightly lighter, canine companion. He tossed Sobek a treat and then took a hot shower before finally relaxing on his super comfortable, brown couch.

As any red blooded American would do when faced with any amount of downtime, he pulled out his iPhone to text.

"Hey, Ash. Whatcha doin?"

Her response was almost immediate. "Hey, Sweetie. I'm out with some friends. How was your workout?"

"It was good." He chose to be respectful of her time with her girlfriends, so kept the exchange short and asked, "See you tonight, for dinner?"

"Yup, see you later, Sweetie."

Greer typed in a colon and parenthesis to send a smile, but then deleted it in favor of, "Cool. See you tonight."

He looked over at Sobek who had found his corner of the sofa and explained his deletion of the emoticon. "I don't want to be too mushy, Bek."

Sobek barely lifted his head in response to his name and then sighed out of his greying muzzle. The return of his square, Lab head back down on the cushion clearly indicated his disinterest in the subject matter.

"Good idea, Bek. I could use a short nap, too."

Greer laid flat on the couch with his toes just shy of Sobek's curled shiny-coated body and contemplated the night's meal.

I could go to the store and get everything I need to make a really nice dinner.

He decided to employ the relaxation techniques used during his regressions with Beverly to help him fall asleep more quickly. He breathed in to the count of six.

I could make chicken and rice.

He breathed out to the same count.

Salmon would be good too.

The tingling sensation started at his feet and spread throughout his body, ending at the top of his head, inducing total relaxation.

We'll go out to eat.

Greer lost consciousness when the tingling sensation that was accompanied by a humming in his ears had grown steadily louder, until he was completely out...of his body.

For a brief second he stood beside his couch and looked down on his sleeping body. Sobek lifted his head and glanced in his general direction.

Can Bek see me?

Suddenly, a strong, unseen force swirled around him and when it subsided, he was back in the abandoned castle.

Greer looked up, with astral eyes, at the spiral, grey, stone staircase. While conscious, he had retained only a vague recollection of his "dream" of the stairs. Back on the astral plane, he experienced a full recall of the spiral portal and his conversation with Selene.

Each step leads to a different future.

He recalled his determination as he looked up to the swirling mist just above his head and wondered why his Spirit Guide was not present.

Keeping in character by favoring curiosity over caution, he stepped onto the first step and the blinding fog surrounded him. He stood, unable to see through the haze, and waited.

Nothing.

Is there some sort of command or something?

In conjunction with his musing, the step beneath him disappeared and he felt himself propelled, by the rush of an extreme, unseen force.

He wasn't sure if his eyes had been forced shut or if he was simply not aware of the passing time during his projection into one of Earth's futures, but they were certainly open now and absorbing a startling reality in the year 2026.

Greer found himself standing in the driveway of a two-story brick home, in what appeared to be a middle class neighborhood. The sky was dark. If it were not for the low, abundant, heavy cloud cover blocking the sunlight, he might have assumed it was nighttime.

But the cloudy display lost its audience to giant, silver, saucer-shaped crafts hovering just off the ground. Approaching them were a dozen lines of hundreds of men that, one by one, were transported, via a beam of light, inside the ships.

They seem to be going willingly.

Greer moved toward one of the men in line and asked, "Where are you going?"

The man, with a solemn, intent expression either ignored the query or was unaware of Greer's presence.

But, to Greer's surprise, he could hear the thoughts of the man, battling his fear.

I'll be back soon. Stay calm. Don't look scared.

Greer reached out to console him only to see his hand disappear though the man's shoulder.

Astral body...got it.

Eventually, the last of the men were aboard the space ships. In perfect unison, the crafts flew into a circular formation high in the sky and each emitted a stream of light toward the heavens. The sky's response was the vanishing of every cloud which released the once trapped, blazing sunlight.

In the same instant, the remaining neighborhood residents emerged from their homes.

Still undetected, Greer moved toward a woman and daughter, who had walked out to their driveway, in an effort to understand the nature of this particular future.

"Mom, can I go play?"

The young mother smiled, and replied, "Of course. Have fun, but don't go far."

The mother's smile faded as the daughter ran off to play with her friends.

A slightly older woman and her two twin sons, came out of their neighboring home. After similarly permitting her children to indulge in the afternoon light, she walked over, with her arms crossed, and stood next to the younger mother.

The two glared with folded arms and clenched jaws, watching their oblivious, playing children.

Greer moved directly beside them and would learn much from their exchange. The older neighbor woman tugged at her dark, brown, braid and asked, "How long do you think we'll get today?"

"I don't know. Hopefully long enough to charge the panels and get us through the week." The younger woman delivered her sardonic reply while still staring at the growing mass of excited kids.

Greer surveyed the surrounding houses to see that every home's roof was equipped with large, black panels that he now deduced were solar.

The younger woman continued. "The kids are starting to ask questions." She looked up at the sky to see extraterrestrial crafts crossing the high sky. Her black, shoulder length, hair, flew back in a gust of wind. "How am I supposed to explain... this?"

The neighbor responded with carefully chosen words that were clearly, and intentionally laced with detest. "The devil you know."

Her friend turned sharply at her response which prompted her to elaborate, but not soften her wry delivery. "It's simple survival. One alien race came to destroy us and the other came to save us. This is the cost of protection."

The younger woman became emotional but forced back her tears. "Our husbands are slaves. We don't see them for months and when they return, they're, well, not the same."

"But we survive. That was the deal. And, of course, they unblock the sun."

Her anger returned in lieu of her sadness and she replied, "Which we wouldn't be so dependent upon had they not taken away our ability to generate electricity."

Startling Greer, another, much older, woman came scurrying up to the two women, waving a bible above her head. She was almost out of breath from yelling, as she approached with cries of, "Revelations, Revelations 13:2!"

Both women stood silently, anticipating, but not entirely welcoming the subsequent scripture. "In 13:2, John describes the Beast as a leopard, a bear and a lion!"

Instantly understanding the biblical connection, the women recalled this timeline's most recent, disturbing history as Greer read their thoughts.

The much televised, first contact of the hostile extraterrestrial race intent on human destruction was the image of three black, stadium-sized, triangle ships that landed in Egypt.

From the crafts emerged three giant beasts. One displayed the form of a leopard, another a bear and the third, a lion. The trio of intimidating creatures stood silent as our defenses arrived that consisted of countless tanks, helicopters, planes and armies of thousands of soldiers. Earth's repeated requests for an explanation of their presence were met with silence. Finally, the visiting aliens returned to the inner of their ships.

The crafts hovered for a short time and then formed a triangular formation in the sky. In perfect unison, each emitted a beam of energy that surged outward and destroyed everyone and everything within a thousand mile radius.

The enemy crafts performed the same atrocity in Australia and China which ultimately resulted in the loss of millions of lives.

Military artillery proved ineffective and access to nuclear weapons was restricted with some kind of alien force field. With Earth's missles useless, the world braced for extinction.

Hope had been certainly lost until the Reptilian's ships arrived with hundreds of heavily armed and more advanced space crafts. The stronger, more advanced alien race easily neutralized the attacking triangular ships. With their superior technology, they assumed the role of protector, in exchange for our labor. The human race was hardly in a position to decline the cold blooded, lizard-like race.

The older woman wet her fingertips continuously, while excitedly flipping through the Book of Revelations. Her focus on the prophetic scripture never wavered as she somehow saw through her intrusive, long, white hair dancing on her face in the gusty breeze.

Having found the relevant passage, she released an impassioned shriek while making another biblical connection.

"It's all here! The Beast is said to have ten horns which are the ten future kings!"

The women hardly heard the elder, frantic lady recite the remainder of the verse as they both considered the ten leaders.

It was a short conversation when the intervening aliens and human leaders agreed to their "arrangement" of manual labor on their distant planet in exchange for Earth's protection. They further determined that the world would be divided into ten sections; each with an appointed leader, who would be the liaison between the protectors, as they called themselves, and the humans.

The areas were assigned as Australia, Canada, The United States, South America, Africa, Antarctica, Europe, Northern and Southern Asia and Greenland.

The suspicious isolation of Greenland had given credibility to a conspiracy theory that the aliens had long inhabited the core of the planet, using interior access points at polar north.

Each area's ruler was chosen by the other-worldly visitors, which was nothing short of damaging evidence to those citing conspiracy with their previous presence and involvement.

The women's thoughts grew softer. Greer strained to hear them better but their volume quickly decreased to mute.

Suddenly, a rush of energy swept him away and he found himself, briefly on the first stone step. The familiar, if not jarring, wave of movement struck again and removed him from the stone castle.

Greer opened his eyes and immediately took solace in the familiar surroundings of his living room. Sitting up on his brown couch he looked over at Sobek, who also was coming to life after enjoying what Greer would soon determine was an hour and a half nap.

He recalled the stone steps and this time, he brought back with him the full memory of the events of that particular timeline in Earth's future.

He grabbed his journal and quickly logged the specifics of the potential, unpleasant forecast, but never questioned the implications of the vision.

Projection III

As the hazy fog cleared from his eyes, Greer tapped the specifics of his astral experience into his iPad.

His buddy, Sean, unbeknownst to him, had also chosen a post-workout recovery nap. To his surprise, it would result in the recall of his presence in a lifetime that he had, previously, only heard about.

Johnny knocked on Charles' door. He waited a moment to allow Charles ample time to move himself to the front door.

There was no response, so he knocked again.

Despite his ear pressed to the door, he heard no movement inside the apartment. Finally, he reached down and turned the doorknob to find it unlocked and decided to enter.

Once inside he was overtaken by the stale smell of cigarettes and whisky. He looked down to see a slightly overweight tabby cat present him with a typical friendly, feline greeting of brushing up against his pant bottoms. The behavior almost tripped him but he was more concerned with the amount of tiny grey and black hairs that now clung to his best pair of dress pants.

His frustration was compounded with the sight of his brother, who was passed out in his wheelchair in the living room of the small, cluttered, one bedroom apartment.

A last, not-so-comical moment occurred, when he took another step, lost his balance and crushed an empty, yellow, cat food bowl.

Johnny regained his composure and, looking at his younger sibling, easily dismissed his annoyance in favor of support on this very, sad day.

The vigorous shaking of his shoulders forced Charles to open his eyes. Slowly, he came to life and his sleepy vision revealed the hazy sight of his older brother, looking down at him.

His temporary, alcohol-fueled, descent into unconsciousness that allowed a brief release from the agonizing pain of heartbreak had ended. Now, he would endure the conscious, inescapable return of his excruciating reality of loss.

Johnny's heart broke at the sight of his grieving kin. Remaining silent, he removed the empty bottle of booze from his brother's lap with one hand and administered a comforting squeeze on his shoulder with the other.

Charles' eyes, now clear of their initial fog, observed Johnny in a plain, black suit with matching tie.

With his slicked back, dark hair, he looked like a secret government agent.

Before he could rib his sibling, the crushing reason for his attire was realized, and his heart sank heavy in his chest, rendering him speechless.

Johnny spoke softly as he fought back his own tears of sorrow for his brother's current state. "Let's get you cleaned up, buddy. The funeral starts in an hour."

Johnny retrieved a bowl of warm water, soap and a clean bath sponge and then helped undress his brother so he could clean himself.

Charles stared, with watery eyes, but at nothing in particular, and tried to hide his embarrassment as his brother dressed his legs in dark suit pants, socks and shoes.

Charles was forced to break his trance when Johnny handed him the wet sponge to clean his face and underarms. Giving him some space for his quick clean-up, he went to the closet to retrieve a white dress shirt and dark tie.

Being cognizant of his little brother's discomfort at being dressed, Johnny assisted as little as possible. However, the high wall mirror demanded his assistance with a splash of tonic and a comb through Charles' thick, black hair.

Finally presentable, the two brothers had just made their way out of the apartment and into the hallway when Charles realized that he had forgotten something. "Be right back."

Johnny waited patiently as Charles returned from the bedroom, and never asked what he had retrieved.

Out of pride, Charles demanded he tie his own neckwear, which took the majority of the drive time to the funeral home to accomplish.

They arrived just as the service began. Johnny retrieved the chair from the bed of his pickup truck and helped his younger brother out of the passenger seat.

Charles insisted on pushing himself up to the entry and Johnny adjusted his pace, to remain, by his side.

As they approached the entrance to the home, Charles choked back his sadness long enough to say, "Thank you for being here, Johnny. I know it's a long drive from Florida and I appreciate it, brother."

In response, he gave his burdened brother's shoulder another affectionate squeeze and simply explained, "We're family."

Every tear-filled eye focused on Charles as he entered. His older brother's protective instinct shifted into gear. "It wasn't your fault. It was an accident."

Charles had not met Julia's parents during the few short months that they had been a couple. But the glare from the faces of a devastated, grieving couple standing beside the open casket certainly told him who they were.

Charles recalled the horror of the fateful motorcycle accident. He had swerved to miss a patch of spilled oil only to land his front tire in a pothole. He was thrown from the bike and landed on the hard road that crushed his spine. Sadistically, he was the lucky one.

Julia was dragged beneath the bike as it skidded along the hot asphalt. In shock, a paralyzed Charles looked up helplessly as his love's cries for help abruptly ceased. His memory was truly evil. No matter how much he drank, he would recall, in horrific detail, the devastating accident. Ingrained within his mind were the images of twisted metal, her lifeless body beneath the wreckage and a bloodied, pink scarf dancing on a gust of wind.

Charles pulled a pink scarf from his pocket and began sobbing.

His brother leaned down until he was eye to eye with his little brother. "I'm so sorry, Chuckie."

Charles cried for another minute and then regained control of his emotions long enough to make his way toward the casket. Johnny helped raise his chair over two steps of the elevated platform so that his proud brother was now able to proceed on his own, toward Julia.

Charles could just see her from his seated position.

It doesn't even look like her.

His tears easily broke through their restraint and began to pour.

Just then he felt the light touch of a small hand on his shoulder. He turned to see the pained face of the woman whom he had correctly identified as Jules' mother. She gave him, through her overwhelming grief, a smile of condolence. Her eyes were filled with a drowning compassion. But her mouth protested words as insufficient and deeply insulting to the staggering, crushing emotion surrounding the loss of a loved one.

Charles drew strength from her gesture. He managed a few words between the manifesting, physical, painful anguish of both a cramping stomach and an aching chest.

He held up the pink scarf. "This was her favorite." He had barely spoken the last word when he succumb to overwhelming grief and covered his face with his hands and sobbed uncontrollably.

Julia's mother took the scarf and then walked to the casket. She paused, staring at her young, beautiful daughter and then carefully wrapped her signature trademark accessory around her daughter's neck. The mother walked back to her husband who then nodded to Charles.

Johnny, having observed the exchange, walked over to his little brother and gave him another, comforting squeeze on his shoulder.

Smiling, he hoped to remove some of Charles' guilt. "See, my brother, they don't blame you."

Sean woke up from his nap with the vivid memory of another shared lifetime still very much active in his mind. The left hemisphere of his brain sent out warnings of disbelief while the right side catered to sympathy and compassion.

However, both were interrupted by a phone call that easily directed his full attention to his upcoming date.

Later that night, Sean enjoyed a night out with a bright, confident and beautiful woman.

She was totally into me. He would later tell Greer.

I wasn't into him. The woman would later tell her friend.

Greer treated Ashley to dinner and then a trip to the beach, where, to her surprise, he pulled out a blanket that he had packed. They sat for over an hour, embraced, on the sandy shore and listened to the crashing waves.

In a feeble attempt to be charming, Greer tried to identify the stars in the sky. It wasn't until he pointed out the "Monster Truck Constellation" that she laughed and called him out on his nonsense.

She enjoyed his infrequent, silly moments and found them to be a pleasant contrast to the pensive brooding of his default nature.

It was when Ashley began to yawn that they called the evening. They would arrive back to Greer's house just before midnight.

"Are you staying over?" Greer asked, incredibly hopeful.

Ashley reached her arms out and pulled her boyfriend toward her while speaking seductively. "Only if you promise tuck me in."

Greer said nothing, took her by the hand and led her down the hall to his bedroom.

Just before they reached the bedroom, Ashley added, "And pancakes. I want pancakes for breakfast." She continued, in a playfully serious tone, while pointing her finger at him.

Greer laughed but, truth be told, even in this intimate fun, light moment, he still had to fight back his urge to comment on the carb count in a typical pancake.

The couple made love and then fell fast asleep just after thanking each other for a wonderful evening together.

Ashley fell into what Greer called a light coma and would wake only when the morning sun intruded through the window. She would then report that she experienced a very restful night that was free of dreams and nightmares.

Alternatively, Greer would wake with the memory of his next venture into one of Earth's potential futures after an involuntary astral projection and the choice of the second step, on the stone staircase, of the castle's spiral portal.

After the now familiar, but still jarring, whirling sense of rapid movement, Greer, again, stood in the driveway of the same home where he had found himself during his last projection.

Thinking, "same place, different time", he struggled to make any kind of headway regarding the specifics of temporal mechanics.

Coincidence or not, it took a backseat to the loud barks of several dogs in the distance. Ever the slave to his curiosity, he mentally chose to find them.

Immediately, Greer found himself standing in a vast, open, grassy area that was adjacent to a small pond. He turned to his right at the movement of an eclectic pack of dogs.

Several different breeds ran together across the field and towards the water. Leading the charge was a light brown, Chow Chow mix that was followed by a mix of Labs, both black and brown. Large Shepherds and Pit Bulls bounced and strutted behind the retrievers while a small Yorkshire Terrier brought up the rear.

He marveled at their speed and agility as they enjoyed their "leash-freedom" and continued to charge toward the water. Upon arrival, most of the canine brigade drank from the edge of the water line. He laughed as the water-loving retrievers immediately indulged their breeding by paddling across the pond and back.

Greer imagined his own black pup, Sobek, running and swimming with the impressive group, until another consideration stole his attention.

Where are the owners?

As he mentally thought the question, he was thrust back to the same street and driveway of the young woman's home. It took only a second to orient himself to his surroundings. And, with that clarity, came the deafening howling, crying, barking and growling of countless dogs, from inside the neighborhood homes.

Needing to investigate, he walked up the driveway to the front door. Remembering the instance where his hand went through the man's shoulder, he walked, literally, through the front door.

That was...different.

Inside, he turned back to see the family dog, a large mix of a Hound Dog and a Rottweiler, clawing at the bottom of the entry door. The canine whined as his raw paw painted the door with its blood which clearly demonstrated its unrelenting desire to be outside.

Greer turned his head back around and saw, down a short hallway, the silhouette of a woman sitting at a kitchen table. He moved toward her and his astral sense of smell overwhelmed him with the pungent aroma of death.

Upon closer inspection he observed that this young mother was, sadly, dead. A large portion of her bloodied neck missing, he easily deduced the cause of death. The lifeless lady's hands hung down at her sides and her terrified eyes remained open.

Greer could not endure the grim sight any longer. He moved from room to room until he found a young girl, the woman's daughter, dead on the floor, beside her bed. Her throat, similarly, had been savagely ripped out and the pooled blood had darkened the once light carpet.

Greer noticed several bite marks on the little girl's hands and imagined her fighting for her life after being dragged out from underneath her bed, where she had been hiding.

How long had she fought before the final moment?

Greer could still hear the howling and whining of the large dog that was clawing at the front door and began to put two and two together.

Greer moved from house to house and found the same canine serial killing in each along with at least one agitated dog that was hell-bent on escape.

He wandered in and out of stranger's homes and tried to make sense of what he observed.

But his morbid contemplation was interrupted by more barking and the shouts of a man and a woman outside the home.

He moved outside to see that the same pack of mixed dogs that he had watched in the open field were now in pursuit of a terrified, young couple. The man and woman fled down the street as the dogs quickly closed in.

Greer merely thought to be closer to the chase and he found himself just a few feet away from the pursuing pack. Reaching his prey, the Chow Chow nipped the ankle of the man and brought him crashing down on the asphalt.

A herding dog, the Shepherd instinctively employed the same tactic to stop the young woman. Within seconds every dog in the attacking pack descended upon the bodies. Clothes, skin and blood flung about as a corrupted symphony of snarls and growls signaled the predatory achievement of their kill.

Dumfounded, Greer simply stood and watched the wild display until the sound disappeared and the sensation of movement embraced him.

The very instant before his astral consciousness was rushed back into this physical body; he looked up to see a shiny, round disc, flying through the air.

Projection IV

Greer sprang upright in his bed. While still quite alarmed at what he had witnessed, he happily absorbed the familiar sight of his bedroom, the comfortable feel of his bed sheets and the soft background noise of the ever-so-slight snoring of his Ashley.

With his senses stimulated, he was fully awake and the images from the potential future dimension were not soon to be forgotten.

Greer looked at the alarm clock to see the time of eight fifteen on a gym-less Sunday morning. Just then his regimented dog entered his bedroom to request that the big guy with the necessary opposable thumb fill his unacceptably empty, food bowl.

I'm coming, Bek, don't eat me. Greer joked, admittedly, in poor taste.

Sobek's tail whipped horizontally at the sight of Greer getting out of bed.

A few minutes later after Bek had devoured his breakfast and Greer had brushed his teeth, early morning inspiration struck and he made a quick run to the local grocery store.

Forty-five minutes later, Ashley woke to the smell of something wonderful. She sleepily stumbled to the kitchen to see a plate piled high with blueberry pancakes and topped with a generous dollop of whipped cream.

Greer took a pan of warmed syrup from the stove and began to pour it over the stack while stating, "Tell me when."

Surprised and smiling ear to ear, she allowed him to pour until the syrup reached the edges of the plate.

Greer raised his left eyebrow and put the pan on the table, next to her. "I'll just leave this for you."

She sat down, still smiling as she took her first bite.

"These are good!"

Greer tilted his head as if he had performed this miracle countless times in the past.

"Did you make these from scratch, Sweetie?"

Greer couldn't help but laugh at the idea. "No way. Last time I tried to make something from scratch I conjured a demon." He pointed to the box of pancake mix on the counter. "I used that."

Suddenly, he felt as if he hadn't truly owned his gesture and added, "But I had to mix it all and cook it!"

Ashley laughed. "Thank you, Greer. They're delicious."

He watched as she enjoyed her breakfast and marveled at her natural beauty.

Just out of bed and stuffing her face with carbs and she was still stunning. He would later tell his best friend. Sean would assume his intended compliment was much more loving than the words he chose would suggest.

The couple would spend the entire day together. After breakfast they returned to the bedroom behind a closed door, for some intimate time together.

Next, they spent a few hours by the pool, cooling off under the hot, Florida sun.

By mid-afternoon, Ashley brought up the subject of lunch.

Greer spoke before thinking. "Are you hungry? Even after eating…"

She glared, stopping his anti-carb rant dead in its tracks.

He switched gears. "Is Mexican good?"

She smiled and replied, "Perfect."

Think…then talk, G. Sean had often reminded his buddy.

After the late lunch they took Sobek to the nearby dog park. Once off leash, the large breed monster sped off and became lost in a cluster of canine playdates.

The scene reminded Greer of his astral experience and he wondered, again, about the circumstances that would lead to those events.

Dogs hunting humans? They didn't seem rabid. And, I swear I saw a disc in the sky…

Ashley noticed his pensive expression and, as she had done countless times before, nudged him out of his mental retreat.

"Still with me, Sweetie?"

Greer snapped back to current events. "Yeah, just thinking."

She smiled and waited.

Oblivious, Greer turned his attention to the antics of Sobek and found that he had chosen a small white Maltese to chase. Embarrassingly for Bek, the small pocket-dog was, literally, running circles around him.

He chuckled and then looked over to see that Ashley was staring at him expectantly.

"Hey, Ash." He said sheepishly.

She played along, only slightly annoyed. "Hey, G."

He chose this moment to mentally review their relationship status. Ashley was a confident woman with a strong sense of who she was. He loved that she allowed him to be true to his character. She often called him out on his nonsense; not as a criticism, but in an effort to strengthen their bond and grow closer.

Her physical beauty notwithstanding, she was a beautiful person. He felt blessed, honored and even lucky that she felt an intimate connection with him.

The look on Greer's face didn't tell Ashley what he was thinking, but it certainly expressed his deep affection. And, that was enough for her to abandon all curiosity regarding Greer's thoughts. He reached out and squeezed her hand, all the while staring into her warm, blue eyes.

He leaned in, intimately close to her. She closed her eyes and slightly tilted her head, awaiting the warmth of his lips. His eyes now closed, their lips moved closer and closer until…

Greer nearly fell to the ground when Sobek clipped his knee as he ran between the couple, in focused pursuit of the little white dog.

Ashley, untouched, couldn't contain her laughter.

Greer's annoyance at his dog's accidental interruption quickly dissipated at the sound of his girlfriend's joyful giggling.

The roadblocks continued as a hyper Toy Poodle ran up to Ashley. She beamed with delight at, what she felt, was an adorable dog, and bent down to say hello.

"Aw, aren't you sweet?"

Greer grimaced. "It's kinda small."

A young, attractive man came trotting over to retrieve his puppy. He looked directly at Ashley as he spoke.

"Sorry about that, she doesn't listen to me, yet." He watched Ashley interact with his puppy. "Wow, she really likes you."

Ashley was engaged in the hyper playfulness of the young poodle as she spoke. "She's so sweet."

Greer glared at the young man who either didn't notice him or didn't care.

The attractive young man never took his eyes off of Ashley. "I'm Rick, and that's…"

Greer interrupted, loudly, "I'm Greer."

Ashley looked up in response to her boyfriend's elevated tone and saw him "staring down" the man now known as Rick.

Rick was now very aware of Greer and couldn't help but notice that the hardly concealed muscles behind his tight, black t-shirt, far surpassed his own. He reached down and picked up his tiny poodle. "Nice meeting you."

As he walked away, Greer jabbed, "Get a real dog."

Ashley turned to her boyfriend and rolled her eyes. "What was that all about?"

Greer, still watching Rick walk away, replied. "Nothing." He turned back to Ashley, smiled, and then asked, "Ready to go?"

"Sure." While she appreciated his protective spirit, she couldn't help but poke at the metaphoric pounding of his chest. "He's gone. You can stop flexing now, Sweetie."

Greer ignored the jab while taking one last glance to ensure Rick had continued on his way.

Wisely, he had.

Greer managed to get Sobek away from his little buddy and then they all went back to the house.

Ashley gathered her things to head home and prepare for the upcoming work week, while her boyfriend asked, in a not-so-masked whine, "Are you sure you can't stay over?"

She smiled, genuinely feeling loved. "Sweetie, all of my things are at my place. My computer, my clothes, my cat…"

Greer couldn't believe what he said next. "Then bring them all over here."

Ashley stopped packing and looked, wide-eyed, at her boyfriend. "What?"

Trying to keep it from becoming awkward, he tried to back pedal. "I mean, you could bring some of those things, ya know, clothes and stuff, here, ya know? I mean, not the cat. I like that cat, but, ya know, not the cat."

It was now awkward.

Ashley, characteristically direct, asked him, "Were you asking me to move in?"

Greer fumbled. "No, no, I mean…no." He wanted nothing more than to end the conversation and offered what he thought was a simple explanation via a casual delivery. "I just thought you could leave some stuff here, ya know, so you would…have…stuff…here."

Smooth.

Proving that someone, somewhere is looking out for him, Ashley's phone rang.

Thank God.

Ashley saw that her mom was calling. Having finished packing her overnight bag, she kissed Greer on the lips and said, "Thank you for an awesome day, Sweetie."

"Bye, Ash." Greer smiled and walked her to the door and wished he could suck the ill-chosen words that he had recently uttered, back into his mouth.

As he closed the door behind her, he heard her answer her mother's call.

Greer looked down to see Sobek's big brown eyes looking up at him while he wagged his black tail. "Let's get you some dinner, boy." Insecurity reared its ugly head and Greer felt painfully, concerned that he had screwed up with Ashley. "And, get me a beer."

That one beer became two and then three. In his worried state, he would empty three more bottles while half-watching the Buc's game.

It was sometime during the fourth quarter that Greer "fell asleep".

Light weight. Sean would later designate his friend.

Greer awoke standing, once again, on the concrete foundation of the stone castle, adjacent to the spiraling stairs.

The astral glow permeated every corner. He thought to move up the staircase to continue his exploration of Earth's potential future timelines. And in that consideration, he found himself standing on the third step.

A sensation similar to an engulfing whirling wind and the force of rapid movement ended as quickly as they began. Quickly oriented, his astral senses revealed, again, the same driveway of the same house in the same neighborhood that he had explored during his previous projections. However, the inhabitants were experiencing, rather, enduring, a very different, reality.

Greer stood motionless as he surveyed the horrific demons around him. Crawling across the ground were thousands of tiny brown, spiderlike creatures. They moved quickly, on eight legs, and their long antennas waved high above them as they moved across dead grass. Behaving like scavengers, the rapid moving bottom feeders picked the remains off of the skeletons of both man and animal that were strewn across the brown, dead grounds.

Countless flying beasts swarmed the skies and blocked the sun's illumination thus bringing darkness to the Earth. The black, aerial beings breathed fire like the mythical dragon but were more avian in appearance with their long beaks and sharp talons. Their high pitched screeches drowned out the sounds of whatever indigenous Earth animals remained.

He looked up at the swarming mass of soaring beasts to see several space ships hovering just above the horizon. He counted five in all, as each released a stream of white light. As the beams stretched across the sky, he could just make out the image, behind the black, flying demons, of a pentagram.

Greer's focus shifted to the home where he had found the mutilated young woman and her daughter.

At the thought, he was inside their home. Huddled at the kitchen table were the, thankfully alive, mother, daughter, the much older neighbor woman holding her bible and a growling family dog.

Uh-oh.

Greer quickly realized at what the protective pup was directing his warning growls. A few feet from the table, circling the women, were several ghostly forms.

A corpse of a woman, with razor cuts covering every inch of her decaying skin, shrieked as she leaned in to grab the child, only to pull back as if burned with fire.

Two short, bald men, both in straight-jackets laughed wildly as they jumped around the gathered humans. Their puffy, pale faces displayed the unabashed delight of a child but their insanity fueled a lust for painful expressions of rape and torture.

Able to hear their evil thoughts, Greer winced at the sickness inside of them.

One of the men reached out to grab the older woman and screamed in agony when his foot crossed a white threshold on the floor.

Greer moved closer to inspect the circular boundary to find it was salt. He had watched enough paranormal shows to understand its cleansing effects on negative energies and he, per Beverly's direction, had even used sea salt when he had disposed of the Ouija Board.

Closer to the table, he could hear the older woman, once again, referring to a passage in her bible. "It's Hell on Earth!"

The young mother simply replied, "With the veil down, I can't argue that."

Greer pondered her words.

The veil? Between dimensions?

As if on cue, one of the moaning, crazy men leapt toward Greer.

He can see me!

His fear a catalyst, he was immediately thrust back to the stone castle staircase and then whirled back to his house where he awoke on his couch.

Projection V

Greer stood up and checked his phone to see the displayed time of ten o'clock p.m. At his movement, Sobek sprang to life and moved toward the front door, to signal his readiness, for a walk.

Give me a second, buddy.

Logging into his phone he found that he had received a text from Ashley that read:

Sorry I had to leave so fast but wanted to catch up with my mom. I had a great weekend with you! Have a good night, Sweetie. ☺

While he still intended to revisit the conversation with her, her text made him feel a lot better; his beer headache notwithstanding. He breathed a sigh of relief at his determination that he hadn't done any major damage.

In hindsight, my worry was a slight overreaction. He would later determine in a very superficial self-aware moment.

Sobek's rear end swung back and forth as his tail whipped the air. Greer grabbed the leash and complied with his demand.

Sorry to keep you waiting, Bek. I know you have a busy schedule.

Once back, Greer drank several glasses of water in a concerted effort to rehydrate, recorded the astral events into his journal and then took a shower before going to bed, just a little after midnight.

Surprisingly, he slept well.

He was unusually alert for a Monday morning which helped him navigate through the continued neediness of the office staff. Ever the approachable boss, Greer often chose to employ the use of several effective platitudes, throughout the day, to defuse, confuse and refuse.

When his boss asked how he was going to increase productivity, he explained that he had developed an action plan to "raise the bar" and "remove the low hanging fruit".

Defused.

When a subordinate complained that their performance expectations were too high, he told them that "we all have to work together as a team to reach our common goal" and to "prioritize the priorities, appropriately".

Confused.

A particularly brazen associate inquired about an increase in their salary. Greer explained that "the company" was unable to approve such a request by casting a wordy, wide net of economic ambiguity citing an "ongoing recession" and a "tough economy".

Refused.

"At the end of the day", the empty words magically mollified them and left Greer with a false sense of inspired leadership.

By five-thirty, the details of the work day were fleeting from his mind as he and Sean chest-pressed dumbbells on a flat bench in their gym.

About halfway through the workout, Greer told Sean all about his great weekend with Ashley.

Although he kept it to himself, Sean was happy for his friend. Instead, per character, he kept it real. "So, how did you screw it up?"

The question initially annoyed Greer until he accepted the truth in the assumption. "I think I asked her to move in."

Sean finished his dumbbell flies and sat up. "You think?"

Greer relayed the short and painful conversation he had with Ashley.

Sean brushed off his concern. "So, have her leave some stuff at your place. She's there a few nights a week already, anyway."

"What about when she's not at my house?"

Sean replied, "Uh, she's at her place?"

Greer became silent.

Sean sensed insecurity. "Are you freaked out because that dude at the park hit on her?"

Greer remained quiet while Sean became genuinely confused. "G, I've never known you to be insecure. Where's this coming from?"

His workout partner was equally as befuddled and chose to end the discussion. They finished their last few sets and then chugged post-workout drinks on the way to their respective trucks.

"Later, Sean. Thanks for the hit."

"No problem, G. Taking tomorrow off, so catch ya back here the day after tomorrow."

Greer drove home and began a typical evening with dinner and a shower. Per Sobek's insistence, they also took a lengthy walk on what turned out to be an unusually cool, September, Florida night.

Later, while relaxing on his big, brown couch, he sent Ashley a text that he was thinking of her and asked how her day had been.

Her reply arrived only seconds later. "I just got home. Long day. How was yours?"

"Typical day at work. Good chest hit. So, all good." Greer was hopeful and extended an invitation when he asked, "See you tomorrow night?"

"Sorry, Sweetie. I have another long day tomorrow."

Greer's stomach felt like it was twisting into a knot. "Ok, have a good day tomorrow."

"You too, Greer! Good night."

"Good night, Ash."

His confidence taking a hit, he now assumed the worst.

"You're reading way too much into that, G." Sean determined after reading his buddy's text that he thought he had gotten blown off.

For the first time, an unusual sense of insecurity had planted itself inside him. He found the feeling confusing, unsettling and unpleasant.

That guy, Rick, at the park, was totally hitting on her. He rationalized of his jealousy and overprotective behavior. But, he still found his lack of confidence in their relationship ridiculous and he was sure Ashley found it unattractive.

He drained himself, mentally, while reviewing his actions until he called the day and climbed into bed, with Sobek at the foot of the mattress.

He struggled, unsuccessfully, to remove the intrusive and confusing emotions so he employed the relaxation technique that often yielded journal-worthy results.

Tonight, would be no exception.

Greer stood beside his bed overlooking his sleeping body. Sobek lifted a heavy head and with half-closed eyes looked in his general direction. He thought he saw his tail begin to wag just before the extreme rush of motion swept him away, instantly, to the stone stairs of the aged castle.

He looked around the timeworn fortress and wondered why he hadn't seen Selene recently. Secretly, he had hoped the mere thought of his spirit guide would summon her, but he remained alone.

He turned back toward the staircase.

Number four it is, then.

A brief second on the fourth step resulted in the forward thrust to the driveway of the home of the young woman and her daughter. Same place, same year, but a much different timeline.

Greer watched as molten rock fell from the night sky. The homes, the streets, the cars, almost everything was being pelted and melted.

He looked up to the sky and saw what was left of Earth's moon. To his horror, barely one-quarter of the orbiting satellite remained intact.

He wondered about the young mother and her child. His concern moved him into their empty house and he hoped that they had evacuated to safety.

But where is it safe to go when the moon blows up?

Greer assumed the worst. He went back outside and stared at the unusual sky. A celestial ring was forming from the moon fragments that were caught in the planet's orbit. He elevated himself to survey the area, from a higher perspective.

His tearful eyes were witness to the complete destruction of entire cities as massive pieces of the moon had crushed areas, many miles wide.

More destruction reigned down as the much smaller orb no longer deflected asteroids and meteors on a collision course with Earth.

He moved himself back to the ground to feel it shake as the planet continued to circle the sun without the stabilizing balance of the moon's pull, in a wobbly, unstable orbit.

Suddenly, a large rock crashed right in front of Greer, startling him directly back to the castle steps and then, immediately, back to his body.

He sprang upright, still very much saddened by the unfortunate possible future. Sobek briefly lifted his head, glanced over and then rested it back on the bed as if he had become accustomed to his provider's mid-night activities.

Greer took a few minutes to journal the apocalyptic memories while they were still fresh in his mind and then fell back to sleep.

At the same time, his buddy Sean, asleep in his own bed, was about to remember his role in another lifetime. His use of Greer's regression disc had triggered his subconscious to reveal the key events of another incarnation. But unlike Greer's future timeline, Sean's was in the past, indeed, a very ancient past.

Nookhotep gave in to the priestess' plea. He called on her to join him in the underground chamber. Torches hung on rock walls but casted more shadow than light. He wore his brown, ceremonial robe and kept his face concealed with the attached hood.

The priestess watched in silence as he demonstrated the use of crystals and copper to harness the massive power of Earth's, core energy.

It was dangerous magic, but she would not relent. She argued that their deformed, dying siblings deserved a chance at survival. And the conclave had agreed.

The magicians assembled, holding hands, in the center of the island and called upon the very essence of life from within the planet.

A huge piece of selenite glowed in the center of their ritualistic circle while copper connected each of them to the charging crystal. As the gem pulled energy from the Earth, immense power moved through the priests and priestess, intensifying and growing stronger, with each syllable of their chant.

Nookhotep monitored the increasingly, dangerous surges of energy and was prepared to break the circle when he received a telepathic message from the priestess to continue.

We're almost there. We just need to stabilize the…

Just then the crystal imploded and created a fold in space that pulled five of the priests into a black hole of nothingness.

Nookhotep mentally told the priestess to run and save their ailing, alien siblings. She ran, desperate to save them and implored them, telepathically, to join her, immediately, at the smallest pyramid.

The ground beneath Nookhotep disappeared to reveal an abyss of empty space. Luckily, he stood close enough to the edge of the massive hole to grab an exposed, thick root. Desperate to complete the mission, he sent his own telepathic message to Merkharu and informed him of their catastrophic blunder. Unselfishly, he asked for his assistance in saving, not himself, but the priestess and the small, grey beings.

The priestess arrived to the pyramid and boarded the small disc-shaped craft to help as many of her brothers and sisters inside until the ground beneath them began to crack. Feeling the very foundation weakening, she programmed the craft to ascend to the sky, having only had time to send about half of the population to safety.

Merkharu arrived as the ship propelled itself into the sky. He stared, still connected mentally to Nookhotep, who was being pulled downward and hanging by a weakening root on the side of the newly formed crater.

The dirt and debris cleared to reveal the priestess. Merkharu took one step forward but she vanished as the ground collapsed beneath her.

The Pharaoh fell to his knees, unconcerned with the continued danger around him, and wept.

Nookhotep cried out, "No!", as he witnessed the death of the priestess through the eyes of his king.

Fate delivered its final blow when the remaining ground around the root to which he had so desperately clung, finally gave out and cast Nookhotep deep, down, inside the Earth.

Sean's alarm sounded but he just lay there, contemplating his ongoing dynamic with his friends. His head and heart worked to process the stunning realization that Ashley had been the priestess and Greer had once lived as Merkharu.

Projection VI

Greer's early morning alarm sounded and jolted his consciousness back into physical reality. He began the day by feeding Sobek and then mixing a fruit protein shake for himself.

He grabbed Sobek's leash and had started down the street with his best buddy when his phone signaled an appointment reminder.

I totally forgot about my session with Beverly.

She had previously explained that weekly follow-up meetings were a vital part of the healing process for abductees who had recalled their experiences. For many, the recall is traumatic and nothing short of disruptive, to their daily lives. Unfortunately, the often hurtful ridicule from both friends and family only impedes their progress while on their road to recovery.

I'm good. I started time-traveling in my sleep to take my mind off the abductions. He later quipped to Beverly.

With an afternoon appointment, he would still get in a decent day's work. Being the boss, no one would question him anyway, at least not to his face.

He was characteristically punctual when he arrived just minutes before the scheduled time of three o'clock.

Beverly greeted him with a firm handshake but displayed a genuine, warm smile. She wore her dark hair back, pulled tight into a bun and wore a black pant suit that was, curiously, accessorized with a gold scarab, broach.

Greer, out of habit, found his way to her sofa.

Beverly, out of process, took out her note-taking device and opened his file to document his state of mind, post-extra-terrestrial abduction.

She was pleased to hear him speak of the matter with confidence rather than fear. She was thrilled that he had accepted the reality of the experience and was truly, letting it go. But above all, she was relieved that he had no longer been experiencing abductions, which enabled him to enjoy everyday life.

"Before you get too excited, let me fill you in on the astral thing."

Without missing a beat, she created a new section in his file.

Greer told Beverly of his involuntary out-of-body projections. He described the glowing hue surrounding everyday objects while on the astral plane. And, the instant, rapid movement to different locations and times, triggered by only a thought. Lastly, he told her of the castle.

She found his conversation with Selene and the use of the stone staircase, portal, intriguing, to say the least. Beverly feverishly documented his description of each potential future of Earth.

When he had finished, she had a few follow-up questions. "Was every future timeline that you visited in the year, 2026?"

Greer nodded, "Yup."

"Where is the castle?"

He shook his head, "Not sure. I just think of it and I'm there." He paused then asked, "Is that important?"

She didn't respond and finished her current entry regarding the castle.

Seeing an opportunity to gain insight to Greer's metaphysical endeavors on the astral plane, she leaned forward and asked, "Greer, would you be willing to astral project now, with my guidance?"

He was somewhat surprised but agreeable, to her request. "Sure."

His responses make for easy note-taking. She fought back the urge to put that in his file.

Greer assumed a comfortable position on her sofa, as he had done multiple times before.

Beverly accessed a wave file on her iPad and explained its application. "You will reach the theta stage of sleep, where out-of-body experiences occur." She paused and pressed 'play'. "The audio is binaural beats at a frequency of 6.3 Hz that will help induce astral projection."

Not even gonna ask.

Greer relaxed and cleared his mind. He felt the tingling begin in his toes. The sound waves ignited the tingly vibration until his entire body felt electrified. The increasing resonance rang inside his ears with the hum of the pulsating sensation. He felt pressure building in his head, almost painfully, between his eyes until…he was out.

Greer stood in Beverly's office and looked down at the familiar site of his sleeping body. His regression, abduction and now astral projection therapist made intermittent notes of his subtle, physical reactions while he was out. He observed the glow of the sofa, the chairs and the office desk.

But the aura around Beverly was different. The energy danced, almost playfully, around her physical body. He felt warmth emanating from her. Similarly, the pathos plant hanging in the corner behind her displayed the same, lively energy.

Greer suddenly remembered the castle and it's time traveling stone staircase and before he could form the image in his mind, he was standing beside the portal. He climbed up to the fifth step. The white mist was accompanied by a rapid force of movement that propelled him into yet another possible future outcome, in the year of 2026.

Greer, hardly surprised, found himself in the driveway of the young woman's home and at first glance, this particular dimension seemed promising.

It was a beautiful, sunny day with high, blue skies. The air carried the laughter of countless, young children as they played together, at the end of the block. Some older teenage boys were throwing a football and slowly recruiting more players to create a match.

A shiny disc-shaped craft flew overhead. The children waved and shouted greetings at the ship. The aerial machine now gone from sight, the kids resumed their games.

That's new…

Greer entered the young mother's house to find her standing in front of a large bay window. She wore a cheerful expression and watched her young daughter play outside with her neighborhood friends. Her contented smile widened when her husband walked up behind her, wrapped his arms around her small waist and whispered in her ear.

"The world is safe now."

Yeah, I'm going to need some back story.

Greer moved toward the couple to read their thoughts; one at a time. He focused on the memories of the man to obtain an explanation of his statement, which he found, would be from the perspective of an informed, former, military officer.

Threats of worldwide destruction transmitted to every nuclear capable country, simultaneously, from an unknown source.

Panic and confusion ran through every government body as they found their outgoing communication abilities inoperable; presumably sabotaged.

The repeating message of impending attacks continued as tensions turned to accusations and assumptions with each country poised to attack their most hated enemy.

Then, at the height of paranoia, the message stopped. War rooms fell silent as military and defense men and women stood frozen, stared at one another and braced themselves for the inevitable.

For what seemed like an eternity, was actually only thirty seconds before every defense radar screen in every military base displayed the images of nuclear missiles on a direct course for every major city in the world.

Every targeted country's immediate response was the deployment of their defensive rockets. Within minutes, every radar and tracking screen was saturated with the tiny images of the harrowing, delivery instruments of death.

Military and government officials held their breaths. The rest of the world went on with their day, except for the few on their lunch break or mowing the lawn, who happen to look up and, understandably, question what objects had filled the sky.

Indeed, they did, as thousands of disc-shaped space crafts hovered above each major city in the world. In a vast, coordinated effort, they each emitted an energy pulse that neutralized the nuclear warheads and left the harmless rockets to fall to the ground.

The ships landed and convened with each governing body. In one extraordinary afternoon, the world became graciously aware of the existence of extra-terrestrials. Moreover, human beings understood that they had saved mankind from their own extinction. Humans, globally, joined together to nourish their relationship with the birdlike creatures that they came to know, as Carians.

Greer severed his connection from the thoughts of the man, who had been in one of those war rooms, and had felt the intense fear, firsthand.

Shaking off the residual fear, Greer smiled at the influential presence of the Carian race, both in Earth's past and future, or at least potential future.

After another moment he shifted his focus to the young woman's thoughts and uncovered that she had chosen a complete acceptance of their new, other-worldly friends and moreover, their teachings.

Having seeded ancient humans with their alien DNA, the Carions were very aware of Earth people's hidden potential. Given their longtime influence, they were anxious to develop the unused capabilities and transition them into a more evolved species.

They taught men and women how to heal themselves by using crystals which reduced the need for medications.

Telepathic abilities were increased using mental exercises which resulted in more open communication and understanding of another's thoughts and feelings. The more intimate connection fostered stronger relationships and enduring peaceful, alliances.

Perhaps most importantly was the profound global acceptance of the visiting extra-terrestrials. The once dividing diversity among the human beings paled in comparison to the physical and cultural differences of the Carians. Mankind finally was beginning to see itself as one unified entity.

Greer smiled and disconnected from the woman's mind.

He wasn't known for his faith in the world and always assumed we would eventually obliterate the planet, or at least each other.

His pessimism challenged, Greer began to reconsider his doubt in mankind. The secular musing triggered the return of his astral spirit to the stone steps and then back into his physical body, where he lay on Beverly's sofa.

Greer excitedly described the events of this particular future timeline to Beverly who logged every word into his file.

She shared his enthusiasm at their mutual understanding of the Carian presence and the transition that Kapherus had alluded to during Greer's previous recall of that lifetime in very ancient, Egypt.

"It seems there is an alien influence in all the future timelines." She determined.

He made an appointment for the following week and thanked Beverly for her ongoing support before leaving her office for home.

He thought about the different potential futures and Beverly's comment of alien involvement as he drove through the streets of Tampa.

An alien takeover? Not good.

Killer dogs? Again, not good.

Crumbling veil between dimensions? Definitely, not good.

Destroyed moon? Anything, but good.

Aliens saving us from…us? Way good.

He pulled up to his house and all thoughts and considerations vanished as his surprised eyes beheld the image of his beloved Ashley.

She stood with her phone to her ear, smiling at him.

His phone rang. He smiled at the silliness as he answered. "Hey."

"Hey, Sweetie. Can I come over?"

He watched as she giggled, illuminated by his truck headlights, in his driveway.

He jumped out of his truck and scooped her up in his arms. "It's great to see you. I thought you were mad at me."

She smiled, knowingly. "I know, Sweetie, that's why I'm here.

Projection VII

The couple made their way into the house where Ashley endured several sloppy licks from a very excited, black Labrador Retriever.

Sobek rolled over on his back and, per their unspoken agreement, Ashley scratched his belly with her long nails. She had surely found "the spot" when Bek's big brown eyes rolled back into his head and his left foot repeatedly kicked at the air.

Greer smiled as he watched the playful interaction. "Are you hungry, Ash?"

"Yes, I'm starved!"

Greer initially pulled the leftover chicken out of the refrigerator and then thought better of it.

Thirty minutes or so later, the pizza arrived.

Ashley had switched to a game of fetch but the big black pup lost his interest when the doorbell rang. His deep, base barks alerted the household, and, surely, several close neighbors, that someone was at the door.

Greer managed to pay an intimidated delivery man and retrieve dinner while using his right leg to keep his canine beast at bay.

Ashley kissed Greer on the cheek. "Thank you, G. I know this is hardly protein enriched."

"All good, Ash. I'll just move my cheat day from Saturday to today."

Ashley found his, slight, accommodation amusing. "You're nothing if not flexible, Sweetie."

The couple ate their slices while they sat together on his couch and chatted about their work day. Greer ignored any intrusive thought that had anything to do aliens, projections or the past. The future, however, would feature itself as serious subject matter.

Ashley suddenly displayed "serious-face". "So, do you really want me to move some of my stuff here?"

Greer took a deep breath and delivered a well-rehearsed answer. "I love spending time with you, Ash. And I love when you spend the night here. And I love you."

Ashley blushed.

He was earnest and passionate as he spoke. "And, I love the guy you bring out in me. I feel good about moving things forward." He held up his right hand as if testifying. "Those are my honest feelings."

Ashley's eyes watered at the refreshing display of emotional honesty.

Greer adopted a more cavalier delivery and asked, "So, are you gonna move in or what?"

She lunged forward and passionately kissed her Greer. She took him by the hand and led him to the bedroom. "Thank you for being so open and honest, Greer."

It was exhausting. He later told Sean.

You're a girl. He replied, but delivered a proud, squeeze on his buddy's shoulder.

The couple made love and then held each other until Ashley noted the late hour and tomorrow's impending, early workday.

He had always hated when she had to leave. Standing next to her car, he kissed her goodbye.

Greer was about to turn back toward the house when she smiled and said, "By the way, I love you, too."

His elated smile expressed his joy in a way that his words never could. Standing in his driveway, he felt the familiar sadness of her departure. Then, returning to his moment of pure bliss, he realized that soon, he would never have to endure the sight of her going home, again.

Once back inside he found Sobek was sound asleep. It appeared that his playtime with Ashley had worn him out.

He sent Sean an excited text. The words explained that Ashley was moving in with him but the energy and emotion behind them celebrated the continued development of their romance.

"Cool." Was his buddy's response, which, in Sean-speak, loosely translated to, "I'm happy for you, buddy."

Greer took a shower and retired to bed. He lay there, still boasting a content, fulfilled, smile, until he finally fell asleep.

Greer found himself standing next to his bed where his physical body breathed securely in what was, according to Beverly, theta level sleep.

At some point in the night, Sobek had made his way up on the bed and was sprawled out with his head and feet hanging off the edge of the mattress.

He noted the difference in the glowing aura around his dog. They moved like harmless flames all around him, seemingly alive and jubilant.

The castle...

Consumed and released by unseen propulsion, he suddenly found himself adjacent to the dimensional, stone staircase. Recalling his previous journeys into tomorrow, he stopped his climb at the sixth step and waited, only briefly, to be transported forward in time, to another 2026.

Greer stood outside the same house on the same street as he had in his previous visits.

What's the deal with this house?

At the query, he was moved inside. The house was currently empty but inhabited, as evident by the dishes in the kitchen sink and the wandering, and seemingly unaggressive, family dog. He looked around the downstairs living area for clues as to why he would always arrive near this home during his astral journeys.

It wasn't until he decided to go upstairs to further his investigation that the answer presented itself.

How could I have missed this?

To the immediate right of the front door and, already behind his line of sight once he entered, was a wooden, spiral staircase. Tapping into his inner sci-fi geek, he determined, "The other end of the wormhole."

Is it me or do they resemble a DNA strand? Is every spiral staircase a portal?

His mind logged these and other inquiries that, he decided, he would later ask Selene. That is, assuming he ever saw her again and, of course, recalled the questions.

A pensive Greer paced, heavy with his considerations. A moment later, a needed distraction occurred when his eyes fell upon the family photos that hung on the wall. He smiled when he observed that the family dog appeared in every group picture.

I'll do that too when…

He abruptly traded his current thought in for a fantastic realization.

It's 2026 and I should still be alive!

For less than half a second, his ears filled with a whisper of wind and he was instantaneously moved to another house, which he quickly understood, to be his. Greer stood and gaped, wide-eyed and with a dropped jaw. He stared in amazement and tried to process what his eyes beheld.

A young girl, just eight years old, with light brown hair, tied in pig tails, laughed as she hopped in and out of the lawn's sprinkler system. Her younger, dark haired brother of six years of age duplicated her actions while laughing and calling out for his daddy to watch.

Future Greer was shirtless and busy washing his truck but happily paused for a moment to acknowledge his boy.

I'm bigger and I have more tats. I look awesome. He later told Sean of his future physique.

All I heard was his ego was bigger and he had more tats. Sean later quipped to Ashley.

"Astral-Greer" was overwhelmed with joy while watching his two future children, happily running and playing. To his delight, his bliss heightened as Future Ashley, came out of the front door of their home, to join her family.

She was still breathtakingly beautiful. His astral heart pounded fast at her sight; twelve years in the future and she was just as stunning.

Proving she had retained her playful demeanor even in parenthood, Ashley grabbed the hose from her husband and chased him around his half-washed truck. The wet children joined their parents in the silliness of the chase until the water weapon changed hands and their mom was playfully soaked, from head to toe.

Greer's thoughts fell to his current Ashley and fondly recalled the strawberry scent of her hair.

That was enough to propel him back to the young woman's house and wooden staircase. From there he was whisked back to the castle's stone steps until finally waking up, back in his physical body, in his bed.

Best...future...ever.

Greer had woken up wearing the same smile that his face displayed when he fell asleep. The alarm clock read the time of three forty-five in the morning and would not sound for another couple of hours. He eventually drifted back to sleep, but not before he replayed the images of the recently viewed and happy, potential future repeatedly, in his mind.

Ashley was finally asleep. Like Greer, she had replayed their loving exchange in her mind, in lieu of sleeping, until fatigue finally triumphed.

Beverly would later surmise that her heightened emotional state had exhumed, within her subconscious, a very old memory of love which found its expression, as a dream.

The priestess, unaware and uncaring of the very late hour, continued to charge the impressive array of crystals. She captured the energy of the sky's full moon as she displayed the bloodstone and quartz gems beneath its glow. In only a day, they would be fully charged and provide much needed healing power to her dying siblings.

Bloodstone would assist with their blood and energy circulation and quartz would alleviate some of their relentless, physical pain.

Nookhotep walked up behind her and yawned. "You need rest, Sekhmet. We all do."

Without turning around and with a weary voice, she asked, "How can we rest when they are dying?"

The fatigued priest smiled at her relentless compassion and dedication before silently returned to his chambers.

Sekhmet cleaned the remaining gems with sea salt and water to remove any residual energy, before placing them under the moon's beam.

Several hours later, hundreds of crystals were soaking in the powerful lunar light, compliments of a very ancient, Egyptian sky.

She warily made her way through a back entrance into the royal chambers to avoid detection by the guards. Climbing into bed, she pulled the soft, silk sheets over her tired body and closed her eyes, welcoming a recuperative slumber.

Sekhmet was quickly losing consciousness when she felt a strong, muscular arm reach across her torso and hold her lovingly.

She smiled in contentment and just before she would succumb to sleep, she whispered, "Goodnight, Merkharu."

Sean stood, in frozen confusion, next to his bed, and stared at his physical body. His mind reeled with several, but one important, implication until he observed the slight rise and fall of his chest.

At least I can scratch being dead off the list.

He surveyed his surroundings. A hazy glow emanated off of every object, as well as the walls and floor of his bedroom.

What the hell?

He felt a soft vibration running through his entire being. A sense of calm struggled to inhabit his state of being as he began to panic.

But, before his emotions could root themselves, the room filled with a blinding, white light. Instantly, he felt safety and security from the warmth of the bathing illumination.

The white brilliance faded to reveal the proud image of the Native American Chief. Sean stood in his presence and, somehow, understood him to be his protector, his mentor, but more accurately, his Spirit Guide.

He balanced the uncanny experience with a completely natural acceptance.

The Chief stood easily over six feet and even taller as his impressive feathered headdress reached for the ceiling. His worn face displayed the deep lines of a leader. A few stubborn, black strands peaked from beneath his long white hair and provided a contrast to his dark, aged skin that personified experience, endurance and wisdom.

Sean didn't yet understand that he had projected onto the astral plane and would receive important teachings from his spiritual mentor that would be placed into his subconscious and surface when needed.

Additionally, many of his memories of these astral events would be interpreted as dreams; some of them very elaborate and involved.

The Chief broke his silence. "I want to show you something."

Sean, open but still unclear as to what exactly was happening, asked, "What is it?"

His Guide broke his stoic expression by raising his left eyebrow and replied, "A castle."

The story continues in 7 Predictions-Book 6 in The 7 Novellas Series

By Gare Allen

7
Predictions

by

Gare Allen

The 7 Novellas Series by Gare Allen

Book One- 7 Sessions

Book Two- 7 Regressions

Book Three- 7 Apparitions

Book Four- 7 Abductions

Book Five- 7 Projections

Book Six- 7 Predictions

Book Seven- 7 Reflections

Prediction I

Greer softly kissed Ashley on the forehead and then turned to leave. The morning sun began its climb into the sky and cast a radiant glow on her angelic face that forced him to pause and absorb her natural beauty. Her long, blond hair cascaded down past her shoulders. He found her soft, alluring lips and small, turned up nose to be irresistibly adorable. In this moment, he longed to gaze upon the hidden treasures behind her slightly quivering lids; her loving, astounding, blue eyes.

Lost in her elegance, he allowed the reality of today to sink in. It was one year ago, this day, that Ashley moved in with him. The last twelve months, while not perfect, brought growth and balance to the union of two strong personalities as they learned to live together.

Greer had learned to compromise on their lazy Sundays when he favored football over Ashley's recorded episode of Downton Abbey. He also came to understand that the gym was actually not a church and God was quite unconcerned with his attendance record.

Ashley learned that while her pink towels and scented soaps had slipped through security, her frilly, lace curtains had failed to make it past customs. Additionally, Sobek was allowed to reclaim his nightly spot at the foot of the bed and, to everyone's surprise, Greer opened his home to her cat, Jewel, with minimal resistance.

I scored major points when I agreed to the cat. Greer later bragged to Sean.

He actually thought it was up for debate. Ashley laughed while telling her best friend.

Greer smiled as the memories of the previous year filled his mind. His smile grew broader as he pondered a happy future with Ashley and he felt that they were ready to take things to the next level.

Today, on the anniversary of the day that they chose to live together, Greer would ask Ashley to marry him.

He glanced once more at his sleeping beauty before he left and guessed that she wouldn't come to life until well after ten o'clock.

She doesn't do Sunday mornings. Greer once joked. Rather, always joked.

It was almost nine o'clock when Greer pulled into Sean's driveway. He honked and watched his blond, bulked buddy waddle toward the truck. Wearing his signature backwards ball cap and form-fitting Under Armor blue, short sleeved shirt, he climbed into the passenger seat which prompted Greer to begin the "countdown to comment".

Sean wasn't big on customary greetings of "hello" or "good morning". Instead, he opted for a less than subtle "current thought on my mind" remark.

One, one-thousand, two…

"Tell me again why we're going to the mall instead of the gym." Sean rolled his eyes at the mention of the mall.

Greer was in a good mood but still dangerously under-caffeinated. "You know that I have to pick up the ring. Don't be a dick."

Sean switched gears when he heard the familiar tone of "Stressed-Greer". "Just joking, G."

Greer began the drive toward the mall and after a few minutes Sean motioned to the right. "Hit that Starbucks and I'll buy you a coffee, G."

Without hesitation Greer pulled into the drive-thru. The barista's voice asked, way too cheerily, what he would like to order.

Greer weaved a tapestry of words in his response that would leave Sean, unusually, speechless. "I'll have a venti, iced, quad, hazelnut macchiato, upside down." He looked over at Sean. "Do you want anything?"

Sean's silence was accompanied by a dumfounded stare mixed with confusion and annoyance.

Greer swung his head back to the left. "And, a bottled water."

As he pulled up to the window, Greer could feel Sean's piercing glare as he waited for the inevitable.

Sean handed him his credit card. "A man should always pay for a lady's drink."

And there it was.

Greer paid and received their beverages. He gave Sean his credit card back and retorted, "Joke's on you, man. This is a six-dollar coffee."

"You need a cheaper habit, then. For what you paid for that ring, you could buy a Starbucks."

Greer smirked. "Yeah, but it's awesome."

Sean was genuinely happy for his buddy and gave him a supportive shoulder squeeze. "She's gonna love it, G."

Fifteen minutes later they pulled into a mall parking space and Greer, loudly, slurped the last of his coffee concoction through the straw.

Sean arched his left eyebrow. "That went down fast."

Greer's demeanor was two equal parts of an expresso-fueled kick-start and delirious yet happy anticipation of asking Ashley the "big question".

The guys got out and headed into the main entrance of the mall which was only a short distance from the high-end jewelry store. Sean worked to keep up with Greer as he speed-walked his way to their destination.

Greer's excitement would quickly dissipate when he found that the doors to the store were locked. Searching for a sign, he found the opening time of ten o'clock stenciled onto the glass door.

Greer looked at his watch. "We've got about thirty minutes to kill."

With limited options to keep them occupied, the guys wandered through the mostly empty mall. Once Sean found that the sports apparel, sports equipment and sports memorabilia stores were also closed until ten o'clock, his focus shifted to his iPhone.

Just a moment later, he was jolted out of his texting trance when Greer exclaimed, "Oh, hell yeah."

Looking up, Sean tried to follow his friend's line of sight and thought he had found it when he observed the mall's mini version of a Starbucks.

Deadpan, Sean delivered. "I'm not buying you another girl-drink."

Greer ignored the jab and directed his buddy to "look to the right."

Sean read the sign posted at the front of a small store.

Psychic Readings-$15 for 15 Minutes.

Sean took a deep breath before he spoke. "You're not, seriously, going to get a reading, are you?"

Greer was growing even more excited and had already committed to the idea as he walked toward the store. "Come on, man."

Sean began a low but audible rant.

It's either past loves, past lives, past deaths...

Greer was two steps ahead of Sean and chose to ignore the background chatter as they approached the store.

...ghosts, demons, aliens...

He was just about to the sign, when Greer saw a small woman emerge from the store's entry.

...abductions, projections, regressions...

Greer introduced himself and took in the image of the woman. Standing just four feet and ten inches tall, she wore her jet black hair in a tight bob with straight cut bangs. Her black, short sleeve blouse was a forgotten backdrop to her impressive sleeves of tattoos. Intricate, ink portraits of stoic Bouviers adorned her arms with striking contrast to her pale skin.

...Egyptians, spaceships, pentagrams...

Without taking her eyes off of Greer, and in a voice saturated with New Orleans, she asked, "What's wrong with him?"

Greer brushed off her concern and grinned. "The jury's still out." He extended his hand. "I'm Greer."

Her dark eyes widened and she returned the gesture while announcing, "I am Madam Fanna."

315

Greer motioned to his friend who had run out of subject matter and was now quiet and scrolling through his phone. "This is Sean."

He looked up and half-smiled.

Madam Fanna ignored the introduction and asked Greer, "What can I do for you?"

"I'd like a reading."

An audible sigh sounded from behind Greer.

She motioned her head to the front doors. "Please, follow me."

The guys followed the psychic into the store where their senses were met with the formidable aroma of sage. They sat down on two small folding chairs that were positioned opposite Fanna, at a small, round table.

The psychic began shuffling a deck of Tarot cards and with her eyes closed, told Sean, "You may want to remove your hat."

Sean, already focused back into his phone, looked up, confused. "Why?"

She stopped shuffling and opened her eyes. Without turning her head, she shifted her eyes to meet his gaze, spoke evenly and explained, "Because, it is polite."

I swear I heard the sound of a nun slapping his hand with a ruler. Greer later joked to Ashley.

Sean chose, wisely, to remove his hat and remain, mostly, quiet for the duration of the reading.

The bad etiquette-intolerant psychic fanned the deck across the white linen tablecloth and then asked Greer to choose seven cards.

After his random selection was complete, she spaced the cards two inches apart and in a straight line. She reached to turn over the first card but suddenly paused and looked intently at Greer.

"Before I begin, would you like to know everything I see; both good and bad?"

Like most people that opt for a reading, he had not considered that she might have something negative to tell him. "Um, yeah, sure."

As if she only had to ask to appease some sort of disclaimer law, she immediately turned over the first card.

"The Hermit." She held her hands over the card. Seemingly, she received divination through her palms. Greer could see the faded image of an old man, in tattered clothing, on the worn card.

Fanna smiled. "Yes, I see." She opened her eyes and looked at Greer. "Your days of being alone are behind you. And, while that is a positive thing, be careful that you do not abandon your inner guidance."

Greer looked left to right and asked, "Inner guidance?"

Madam Fanna was very much aware of the metaphysical energy surrounding her client. "When we experience time alone, we look inward and encounter ourselves. This makes sense, yes?"

Greer recalled the countless past incarnations that he had viewed. "Yes."

She continued. "Do not turn your back on self-discovery. It is because of your growth from this awareness within, that you will soon marry your soul mate, yes?"

Greer was impressed. "Wow, you're first prediction is spot-on!"

Sean narrowed his eyes and skeptically wondered if she had seen them earlier, coming from the jewelry store and was drawing a conclusion, rather than a psychic prediction.

She accepted his words without a response and turned over the second card. "The Moon."

Greer observed the image of a half-moon on the aged card.

Again, with her eyes closed, she placed her palms above the card and her smile widened. "This is the card of intuition, dreams and the subconscious. As sunlight reflects off of the moon, it illuminates our journey into the unknown. Your guide on this venture is known to you and will give you a sign of her continued presence as there is still much work to be done."

Greer felt a new appreciation for Beverly as he feverishly tapped the notes into his phone and struggled to keep up with her reading.

Sean was texting and only half listening, but at least he was quiet.

Madam Fanna turned over the third Tarot card in the layout. "The High Priestess."

Both guys looked up, simultaneously recalling, from their own perspectives, their Egyptian lifetime together with Ashley, the compassionate priestess.

She continued. "She is the guardian of the subconscious. She teaches spiritual enlightenment and divine knowledge. Her card tells you to listen and trust your inner voice. But most importantly, be honest for she will uncover the unknown."

Greer raised his left eyebrow and asked, "The unknown?"

Completely focused on the divination task before her, as well as the fifteen minute timeframe, Fanna turned over the fourth card. "The Devil." She paused.

Greer curved a lip at the depiction of Satan as a winged monster that was surrounded by fire.

Sean broke his silence. "Well, that doesn't look good."

The psychic woman looked directly at Greer and spoke low and intensely. "This card emerges in the center of the layout. Its effects are widespread and you should heed its warning." The energy in the room became heavy as she spoke. "Your fears and addictions bind you to your subconscious insecurities. Release yourself!"

Greer took the notes and while he had no clue as to what she referred, he was a little concerned, nonetheless.

She concluded the card's warning with, "Temptation waits, nearby. Resist!"

Oh, temptation...that. Yeah, got it.

As if she had merely shared a banana bread recipe, she continued and turned over the fifth card. "The Ace of Pentacles."

Sean looked up from his texting, just briefly, to ask, "What's a pentacle?"

Before she could respond his eyes fell to the card that clearly depicted the image of a pentagram, with which he was gravely familiar.

"Never mind." He lowered his head and buried his attention back into this phone.

Madam Fanna's voice lightened. "This is a card of wealth and prosperity of both financial and emotional new beginnings. A very positive card, it is."

Sean scoffed under his breath. "Positive, my ass."

Greer smiled and looked over the five revealed cards and quipped, "My hand's getting better."

She turned over the sixth card. "The Lovers." The depiction was a simple portrait of a man embracing a woman.

The reader smiled, knowingly at Greer. "You are deeply in love, yes?"

Greer turned a little red and shook his head in lieu of an audible "yes".

Sean was just about to once again, question his buddy's gender when he looked to see Madam Fanna glaring at him, having anticipated his mockery.

Sean submitted and kept his comments to himself.

She placed her hands above the tarot card and smiled. "This love runs deep and through many lifetimes."

Again, as if on cue, both guys looked up from their phones and recalled their respective lifetimes that showcased Ashley and Greer's continued romance.

Ignoring their reactions, Fanna turned her head slightly to the left and casually explained that, "She will say no, but then she will say yes. Do not be concerned."

Greer grimaced. *Concerned is my middle name.*

The fortune teller turned over the final card. "The World."

Greer looked at the image of a woman standing in a large circle and surrounded by animals and asked, "Why is the card upside down?"

Madam Fanna didn't respond. Holding her hands over the reversed card, she, for the first time during the reading, displayed an expression of concern.

Greer noted her look and quickly inquired, "What is it? What do you see?"

Here we go. Sean thought to himself.

Suddenly, a timer rang which signaled the end of the reading.

Relieved, Madam Fanna quickly replied that "something needed closure or to be closed."

She escorted them out of the room and left a befuddled Greer and a skeptic Sean in the center of the mall.

Prediction II

"Next time ya wanna throw away fifteen bucks, just give it to me." Sean jabbed and then noted the time on his phone. "It's a little after ten. Let's go get your ring, G." He lightly slapped Greer on the shoulder and hoped that he would forget about the last fifteen minutes. But, he knew better.

Impressed with and blindly accepting her very first prediction of marriage, Greer read Madam Fanna's second prediction from his notes as they walked back to the jewelry store.

My guide will make her presence known.

Sean pretended that he didn't hear him.

"She predicted my proposal so she obviously has some ability."

"Yeah, she's got the ability to take your money." Sean countered and then, with surprising interest, asked, "And, what kind of dogs were those on her arms, anyway?"

Greer laughed. "Bouviers, man."

"I couldn't see their eyes. I don't know what was scarier; the Cajun psychic or the mean-looking dogs." Sean admitted.

"I wouldn't mess with either of them."

The guys arrived to the jewelry store and were greeted immediately upon entering by a very attractive, young woman with dark brown, shoulder length hair. She smiled and pulled a few of the longer strands behind her left ear and extended her right arm as she greeted them. "Hi, my name is Gisela. How can I help you?"

Sean's inner monologue was highly graphic and he took a step toward the beautiful woman. But, Greer would "block his game" when he quickly stepped forward, shook her hand and resumed a singular focus to get Ashley's ring. "I'm here to pick up my ring."

"What's the last name?"

"King."

"I'll be right back." Gisela turned and disappeared behind the door that was clearly marked, *Office*.

Greer didn't need to look. He could feel his buddy's stare and addressed him without looking up. "Take a day off, Sean."

Disgruntled and now even more bored, Sean wandered over to the glass case that housed the men's watches.

A moment later, Gisela emerged from the office with an overly fake smile on her face and delivered, "Mr. King, your ring isn't here yet, but it should be soon."

Greer was confused. "It isn't here? Where did it go?"

The sales associate carefully explained, "We normally size rings in-house, but we were recently forced to outsource the work."

Greer was not prepared and certainly not receptive to any kind of hiccup in the day's events. "What time will it be here?"

"Soon, Mr. King." Gisela shook her head assuredly.

"Soon isn't a time."

Sean sensed the building storm and stepped in. He squeezed his buddy's shoulder and spoke as casually as possible. "I'm sure it will be here any minute." He turned and smiled at the salesperson. "Right, Gisela?"

She looked at her watch and was a bit more specific this time. "More likely, after lunch."

Oh boy.

Sean bit his lip. "You're not helping me here, Gisela."

Greer put one hand on his waist and rubbed the back of his neck with the other and asked Gisela to, "Please, get your manager."

While she was gone, Sean joked with his buddy, in an effort to calm him down. "Wow, you've got major serious-face, G."

Rather than respond, Greer stared at the office door.

Sean stepped in his line of sight. "Hey, G, relax. We'll get it worked out." Shifting into best friend gear, he leaned in close to his friend. "This is a big day and it's gonna be perfect, man. The ring will get here, you'll pop the question and soon Ashley will be Mrs. King." Sean widened his eyes and looked to his right. "God help her."

Greer couldn't help but smile. He exhaled a sigh of relief and realized how tense he had gotten.

"Mr. King?"

Sean turned and stepped aside to reveal the approaching tall, slender woman. She had long, straight, jet-black hair and big dark eyes with incredibly long lashes. She smiled sweetly through her small lips as she waited for a response.

Greer's eyes fell to her nametag. He was stunned to see that her name was Selene.

"Mr. King?" She repeated.

His shock transformed to wonder and he laughed. "Yeah, but call me Greer."

Selene held up a small box as she responded. "Greer, I apologize for the inconvenience regarding your ring. But, I spoke to the company this morning and they assured me that it would be here today."

She paused to assess his reaction but Greer just nodded. His Type A personality needed more specifics. He stared at the manager and she looked left to right while waiting for some kind of verbal indication that he was satisfied with her response.

Their awkward silence was broken by the schoolgirl giggling of Gisela. They both turned to see her laughing with Sean. She was holding his hand as if they were, well, much more than strangers who had just met.

Selene suddenly remembered the box in her hand. "Oh, but I do have the wrist bracelet that you ordered."

Greer had completely forgotten about the bracelet that Ashley had pointed out to him several months ago. But, it was a birthday gift and she would not receive it for another eight months.

She handed him the box. "She was born in June? So was I."

Greer opened the box and asked, "How did you know that?"

He held up the gorgeous rainbow moonstone bracelet. The stones shimmered under the bright, fluorescent lighting as Selene informed him, "I have the same birthstone."

Greer thought for a second then asked, "I thought June's stone was a pearl?"

Selene smiled and explained, "The month boasts three stones actually; pearl, alexandrite and moonstone."

He noticed her necklace boasted a similar, but much larger moonstone.

She realized that he recognized the stone hanging around her neck. "The stones in the bracelet are rainbow moonstones." She touched the gem suspended on the gold chain that rested on her white, silk blouse and then continued. "This is a champagne moonstone. In fact, Selene is Greek for "moon"." She smiled, fondly. "My father gave this to me."

Greer grinned at the uncanny resemblance of his spirit guide's namesake that was standing before him. He recalled the words of Madam Fanna, complete with the drawl of Louisiana, as she interpreted the Tarot's moon card.

Your guide will give you a sign of her continued presence.

Gisela's laugh interrupted his thoughts and they both turned, again, to witness Sean's continued flirting.

Greer looked at Selene. "I'm sorry about him. I hope he's not bothering her too much."

Just then, Sean called out to Greer while holding up his arm. "Hey, G, check out my new watch!"

Selene smiled, knowingly. "I think she's alright."

Greer raised his left eyebrow as he chuckled.

"I promise that I will call you the minute the ring is delivered, Greer."

"Thank you, Selene." He looked past her and called out to his buddy. "Ready, Sean?"

The guys left the store and before they could decide which way to go, Greer's phone rang.

"It's Ashley."

Sean was holding his arm level to his head and admiring his new Invicta watch when he replied, quite deadpan, "So, answer it."

"I don't want her to know where I am."

Still admiring his new timepiece, he suggested, "Then, don't tell her."

"Hey, Ash."

"Hi, Sweetie. Whatcha doing?"

Wanting his proposal to be a complete surprise, he adopted, what he thought was a suave, casual tone and delivery. "Nothing. Ya know, just hangin' out, checkin' out stuff, ya know."

Smooth. Sean dropped his head at his buddy's inability to remain calm.

Ashley wasn't quite awake enough to question his painfully, obvious deflection and was more concerned with her dying phone battery. "Ok, well, you can fill me in later on that. Do you have an extra phone charger? I think I left mine in your truck."

Unaware that, if anything, he had actually raised suspicion and without thinking, he replied, "Yeah, in my desk drawer."

327

"Thanks. See you soon?"

Greer fumbled, again. "Yeah, definitely. Shouldn't be long, ya know. See you soon."

Ashley held back her chuckle. "Bye, Sweetie."

"Bye, Ash."

"That was painful." Sean looked at his friend in disbelief.

Greer was gleefully oblivious. "What? Ashley doesn't suspect anything, man. She's going to be so surprised!"

Sean, dumfounded and wide-eyed, stood silent, in awe of Greer's naïve confidence.

"Oblivious-Greer" was a nice break from "Worried-Greer". Sean later said to Ashley of the day's events.

Try living with both of them. Ashley retorted.

"Come on, Sean. I'll buy you a smoothie." Said, "Oblivious-Greer".

The guys headed toward the food court that was located in the center of the mall.

Prediction III

Ashley opened the middle drawer of Greer's desk in his home office in search of a phone battery charger. She was surprised to find that the drawer's only contents was a black book with the word "journal" scribed on its front cover.

It's the male equivalent to a diary. Greer would later explain. During his follow up, defensive rant, he opted for the term, "life-experience documentation".

You're a girl. Sean's go-to jab, once again, would punctuate their exchange.

Instinctively, Ashley closed the drawer and opened another. Finding the charger, she removed it, slid the drawer shut and turned to leave the office. Her moral compass must have malfunctioned as she stopped a few steps away from the desk and began an inner, moral debate.

It's his personal journal and I have no business reading it.

But, he shouldn't keep anything from me so I wouldn't be reading anything he hasn't already, or will tell me.

If he wanted me to read it, he would have told me about it.

But, he knew you would find it when he told you to look in his desk for the charger.

Maybe he planned for me to find it and wants me to read it.

Maybe he doesn't.

This could go on all day.

A few minutes later, Ashley was sitting, comfortably on their oversized, brown sofa with a cup of green tea and Greer's journal. She stared at the cover, still unsure if she was going to open it and read its contents.

Sobek ambled over and his big brown, inquisitive eyes looked down at the journal and then back at Ashley. Her increasingly guilty conscience believed that Greer's loyal Lab had delivered a knowing and judgmental glare.

She got up and retrieved a rawhide chew bone for the judgy pup. It would be some time before he could devour the treat and a canine nap would surely follow.

Remove the interference. Greer had often claimed that this direction delivered effective results when working through his vocational tribulations. Ashley felt that she had found its, convenient, application at home.

Now, fully committed to her privacy-breaking misdemeanor, she resumed her seat on the couch and opened the journal.

Greer had, perhaps until now, always found it cute that Ashley read magazines starting with the back page and working her way to the front. And, it appeared that her casual, snooping habits were performed similarly.

Her boyfriend's most recent journal entry would take her by surprise. She would learn that he had the same dream of a Native American atop a horse poised to release an arrow at a young girl. Ashley's dream was from the perspective of the little girl in peril while

Greer's was from the young, attacker's viewpoint. His regression into this incarnation provided some particulars regarding their short interaction.

Pahana turned his horse and observed his little brother draw back his bow. He felt a sense of pride seeing him participate in his first attack since having been deemed a warrior by their father, the Chief.

He followed his line of sight to see the young girl, the target of his sibling's arrow, coming out from beneath the blanket. She didn't notice the weapon fixed on her position as she surveyed the death of her family and friends from atop the wagon.

The attacking tribe had come out of seemingly nowhere. Her mother frantically told her daughter to hide just before she was shot and fell to her death on the ground.

When the little girl climbed out from underneath the blanket that had concealed her, she stared down at her mother's bloodied, lifeless body while tears poured from her eyes.

Pahana watched while his younger brother slowly lowered his bow and arrow. His hung head told him that he could not bring himself to take the life of another pale-face, at least not this young female.

He called to his sibling, "You must do it, Ahote."

To which came the reply, "Then, leave me to my task."

Pahana rode off toward the camp and left his brother to his duty.

Ahote, again, raised his bow and aimed his arrow at the pale skinned girl. The sight of her murdered parents coupled with the hot afternoon sun overwhelmed her emotionally and physically. Dizzy and light-headed, she could just see the young Native American boy atop his horse with his arrow aimed directly at her, as she collapsed.

When she woke, she found her arms bound behind her and tied to a wooden beam in the center of a small hut. A strand of softened leather gagged her mouth and prevented her from screaming for help.

Consumed with fear, tears streamed from her eyes as she searched her surroundings. She painfully recognized piles of clothing and personal effects that once belonged to her friends and family; obviously looted after the bloodshed.

She could see, in the corner atop a large pile of clothing, a yellow straw hat that had belonged to Mr. Wilson. She recalled that he wore it every day as he tended to his crops.

In the opposite corner were guns and rifles that her wagon train companions never got a chance to use to in defense of themselves as the brutal attack was swift and unanticipated.

Her eyes hurt from the constant crying and she wailed into the leather gag as her sight fell upon her mother's favorite pale, yellow dress. Now mostly red, it lay stained on the dirt floor, discarded and seemingly undesirable to the tribe.

She felt the dizziness return and welcomed an unconscious escape from the horror in which she now found herself.

Sadly, when she regained consciousness, she discovered that her situation had not improved. In fact, more fear presented itself as she stared into the eyes of the young boy. Sitting on the dirt floor and just a few feet away, he scrutinized the girl.

The white man is the enemy.

He had repeatedly heard these words. And, until now, he had no reason to question them. Indeed, it was a deep need for revenge that allowed a complete acceptance of the hate.

But, for the first time in his young life, he sat face to face with his devil and saw his own reflection. His heart battled his hatred.

They look like us except that their skin is lighter. She weeps for the loss of her family as we do. She is not an animal that we can use for food or clothing. I've been taught to live in harmony with all things. But, father says the white man attacked us and took our land. So much blood was spilled today...

Guilt-fueled tears fell from his big brown eyes as the captive girl stared in confusion. His curiosity determined his next move and he removed the gag.

"If you scream, I'll put it back on."

She shook her head in an attempt to move her long, soiled strands of hair out of her face. She gasped for air and spit out the residual bitter taste of the leather gag.

Ahote was taken aback by the striking contrast of her deep blue eyes against her pale face.

Able to finally speak and enraged by the discarded belongings of her family and neighbors, she glared in pained anger. "You killed my parents."

His compassion was replaced with anger as he blurted back in his defense, "You killed my mother!"

The fuel for his hatred realized, she sobbed for both of their losses. From the limited perspective of a frightened child, they knew only that they were to hate, fear and fight each another. The murders of their parents provided a personal commitment to the cause but Ahote, still, could not allow himself to release his arrow.

Enslaved to his compassion, he was pained by his betrayal of his tribe, his brother and his father, the Chief. On what was to be a glorious day of transition from a child to a man, would now find him punished for his treacherous actions. At the very least he would be banished; but most likely killed.

For reasons she didn't understand, the little girl offered her name.

"I'm Renee."

Suddenly, Ahote heard the voices of the tribe greeting Pahana as he and several other men returned from a hunt, with the night's feast.

Scared and panicking, Ahote replaced the gag on Renee and promised, "My brother will help us. I will be back."

Pahana greeted his younger brother with a broad, proud smile. But as he read Ahote's expression, he knew something to be wrong.

"What is it, young one?"

Without words, he led his older brother inside the hut. Pahana's sight fell upon the pale-faced girl and his eyes widened as he asked, "What have you done, little brother?"

Ahote began to sob and asked through his blubbering, "What do I do, Pahana?"

With little time to think, Pahana grabbed the pale female and carried her toward his hut. But, he was spotted before he could make entry. Within seconds, the tribe had gathered around him. Without accepting explanation and clinging to their assumptions, they labeled him a traitor, and worse, as weak, for feeling sympathy for the girl.

Seeing the display, Ahote ran to confess to the hostile mob, but Pahana saw him and stopped his approach. "Say nothing, young brother! Go, get father, now!"

The angry tribesman quickly stabbed and killed the "enemy" girl and then chased Pahana into the woods. He ran for his life, dodging the flying spears and arrows as they grazed his head and shoulders.

To his left, he saw his father and younger brother on horseback, rushing to catch up to him and shouting at the tribe to retreat. But, fueled by their mob mentality, they could not hear them above their own cries and screams for justice.

Finally, an arrow sank itself deep between Pahana's shoulder blades and his dying body sprawled out on the thick, ground cover. Life seeped out of him as he looked up with hazy, weary eyes to witness his father, the Chief, crying over him.

The tribe retreated back to their camp and left the Chief to mourn his son. The Chief turned to see, through blurry, tear laden eyes, Ahote on his knees behind him, crying into his hands.

Ashley put down Greer's journal and wiped the tears from her eyes. A whirlwind of considerations flew through her mind as she pondered the implications of continued lifetimes. She was formulating many questions to present to Greer regarding the unknown world of metaphysics.

Prediction IV

Sean and Greer sat at small, square table in the center of the mall's food court. They had finished their smoothies and were spending some quality, best friend time, deeply engaged in their phones.

Greer mumbled under his breath. "What's that about?"

Without looking up from his phone, Sean asked, "What's your issue?"

Rereading the text that he had just received from Ashley, he replied, "Ash wants to talk when I get home." A worried expression blanketed his face. "I wonder, what's up?"

Being all too familiar with his buddy's propensity for excessive and often, unnecessary worry, Sean made light of his concern. "Did you leave the seat up?"

Sean's simple humor wasn't enough to shift his focus and he made a connection.

Greer scrolled back through the notes from his reading. "So, Fanna's next prediction was that the high priestess would uncover the unknown."

Seeing where Greer was going with this, Sean thought for a second. And, while he may have started down the right road, he ended up far off of the reservation. "Maybe Ashley found something that she shouldn't have."

Greer's serious-face returned.

Sean continued with exaggerated concern. "What if she found those Capri pants you said were for men?"

Greer replied, defensively, "They're just long shorts, man."

Sean mimicked his buddy's delivery. "They're just for girls, man."

Sean concluded his fashion criticism with a hearty slice of sarcasm. "But, I'm sure they'll catch on. You're a trendsetter that way."

"Oh my God…Greer?" said the very attractive and dark haired woman who had suddenly appeared beside the guy's table.

With a clearly, confused look, Greer replied, "Uh, yeah." His mind raced through the faces and names of the countless employees on his office floor. Not finding a match, that just left the past girlfriends file. But, before he could begin a very lengthy search through his romantic archives, she blurted out, "It's me, Deanna!"

Greer was floored. Deanna was a "Goth" during their short courting. Her hair was jet black and hung in her face. She wore white makeup that contrasted her blackened eyes and lips. Somehow, she had managed to consistently maintain a forced, sour, and angry expression. But, the girl standing before him boasted an infectious smile against lightly tanned skin. Her hair, while still dark, was pulled back to accentuate her, now revealed, soft, facial features.

Greer finally replied. "Wow. You look amazing!"

Deanna tilted her head and her already brilliant smile widened as she basked in his compliment. "Thank you. So, how are you, Greer?"

"I'm good. Wow, I can't believe how much better you look!"

She looked off to the right, half smiling at the back handed compliment.

Greer explained. "I mean, you were always pretty." He got a little cocky. "That's why I asked you out."

"It was a one night stand with a bonus night and then I didn't hear from you." She corrected, but batted her eyes. "But, I'm available tonight."

Sean inserted himself into the conversation as, well, Sean is accustomed to doing where pretty girls are concerned. "Hi, I'm Sean."

For Greer, it was a very welcomed, interruption.

Quickly recalling the shallow nature of his buddy, she replied, "I know, Sean. We met the same night that Greer and I did."

Sean looked at his friend with genuine confusion and Greer tried to help him out while being uncaringly rude to Deanna. "Dark Dana?"

Sean came alive with recognition. "Oh, I remember now." As if knowing her from another name wasn't rude enough he added, "You left that Ouija Board at Greer's house."

Greer jumped in. "Yeah, but I salted and burned it."

Deanna's mouth was agape at what she was hearing.

Greer, regrettably, added, "No, it's all good. My regression therapist told me to do it."

Deanna's eyebrows couldn't have gotten any higher on her face. Without so much as a word, she walked away with a wide-eyed expression of disbelief.

Greer called out to her, "It was good seeing you."

Sean resumed his interest in his phone. "Smooth, G."

As Greer pondered the surprising visit, but, sadly, not their behavior, he made a connection. He scrolled through the notes in his phone and found Madam Fanna's Tarot card prediction of The Devil.

Temptation waits, nearby. Resist.

"Dana, dammit, Deanna, was the next prediction! She was temptation!"

Sean didn't look up but was in agreement with his buddy on one aspect. "Yeah, she was hot."

Greer lost himself in the consideration and, unfortunately for Sean, his thoughts were audible. "A hot ex shows up on the day I'm going to propose. Man, of all days to be tempted..."

Sean raised an eyebrow at his buddy. "You were tempted?"

Greer clarified. "No, I wasn't, but the opportunity was there."

Sean added, "Yeah, until she walked off."

"That was because of you." Greer jokingly blamed.

Sean rolled his eyes and was clearly bored. "Whatever. Is that ring ready yet?"

"She hasn't called, yet."

"Let's go down there and check." Sean suggested, way too innocently.

Greer smiled. "You mean, so you can see Gisela?"

The guys got up and began walking back to the jewelry store while Sean replied, "Two birds, G. Two birds."

If a chance run-in with Deanna was a surprise than the next encounter would be nothing short of a shock. Halfway to the store, Greer, once again, heard his name being called. He turned and stood, unable to speak, as Karla walked toward him.

Two points for Madam Mean-Dogs. Sean quipped to himself.

"How are you, Greer?" Karla asked.

H was stunned to be standing in front of the only other girl with whom Greer had ever had a relationship that had lasted longer than three months. Panic sent a rush of blood to his face and his chest tightened, but he managed to squeak out, in response, "Good."

He marveled that she was more beautiful than he had recalled. Her brown, curled hair flowed down to the middle of her back. He found it difficult to look into her light, but confident, brown eyes. A range of emotions welled up inside him as he did, so he averted their gaze.

Sean, ever the wingman, provided an assist. "Hi, Karla."

While she was never overly fond of Sean's childish antics and extreme-casual dating mantra, Karla was polite. "Hi, Sean, how are you?

"I'm doing good. I thought you moved to Daytona Beach?"

"I did. I'm in town visiting family. I had to stop by the mall and pick up a birthday gift for my sister." She gestured to a small, pink, gift bag in her hand.

She turned back to Greer. The majority of the redness had left his face and he had managed to resume a normal breathing cadence.

"What's new with you? Are you seeing anyone special?" she asked.

It felt odd to say anything until he had actually proposed but his excitement got the best of him. "Actually, yeah. We've been living together for a year now. And, I'm going to ask her to marry me."

Karla beamed a genuinely proud, and surprised, smile. "I'm so happy for you, Greer!"

Greer blushed and looked down. Awkward silence crept in until Sean stepped in, again, for his buddy. "What about you, Karla? Anyone serious in your life?"

Karla curled her lips playfully. "No, not really." She looked back at Greer and recalled their eight-month relationship. He was a scared young man who would change the subject at the mere mention of taking things to the next level; especially living together. Greer had been selfish and self-centered and unaware of the necessity of compromise and communication. He was sweet, but withdrawn into his own self-concern, thus blocking his ability to maintain healthy dynamics. "Well, look at you all grown up." She smiled, lovingly. "Congratulations, Greer."

Greer simply responded, "Thanks."

She smiled and the silent awkwardness crept back in.

"Well, I should go. It was nice seeing you." Karla extended her arms for a hug.

Greer accepted her invitation. "It was nice seeing you, too."

She walked off in the opposite direction and the guys resumed their short trip to the jewelry store.

"Overdosing on the exes today, aren't ya, G?"

Greer sighed. "When it rains…"

A minute later the guys entered the jewelry store to find both Selene and Gisela on the sales floor. The door chime prompted them both to turn and the ladies delivered much-practiced work-smiles.

Sean walked straight over to Gisela while Greer made his way to Selene. "Is it here, yet?"

She smiled. "I was just about to call you. The delivery just arrived. I'll get it for you."

Greer exhaled as his stress subsided and he rubbed his hands together in excited anticipation. He turned to tell Sean but Gisela's laughs at his stale one-liners told him that his boy was already busy.

Only seconds later, Selene emerged from the office with his ring. Greer opened the box to reveal a stunning, one carat diamond ring. Its center placement was graced on either side by smaller, round diamonds that rested on elegant, white gold.

"It's beautiful." Selene complimented his taste in jewelry.

Greer beamed ear to ear. "I hope she likes it."

Selene offered a supportive reply. "I'm sure she will love it."

Greer allowed worry and fear to permeate the moment.

It is too soon to ask her? Am I ready?

His descent into doubt was abruptly halted by his buddy's announcement.

"G, check out my new chain!" Sean called out and held up a just-purchased, silver necklace.

Greer arched his left eyebrow while addressing Selene. "It's been a good day for Gisela, yes?"

Selene smiled and slightly shrugged her shoulders.

Greer looked past Selene and called out to his friend, "Ready to go, Sean?

Prediction V

With narrow eyes and folded arms, Ashley paced the living room and shot confused glances at Greer's journal that sat on the coffee table.

During the last hour, her emotional state had fluctuated with every paragraph that she had read.

She cried in fear during the passage where Greer wrote that he had been in danger of developing cancer. Thankfully, the Carions performed treatments during his abductions to effectively eradicate the abnormally divided cells.

Angry disbelief was her dominant dual emotion as she read the remaining entries that chronicled his abductions aboard the Carion's ship. He was taken against his will, the cancer cure notwithstanding, and tested upon at their discretion. Grey aliens had entered their bedroom; allowed entry by a pentagram on a Ouija Board that was found under the bed.

Slightly easing her tensions were the mildly entertaining entries that told of his astral projections into several of Earth's futures. She found the future, rather their future, with a big house and children, somewhat presumptuous, but she appreciated his optimism.

It wasn't that she didn't see a future with him; they simply hadn't discussed it...yet.

Ashley consciously used her anger and disappointment in, what she would later call, his "book of secrets" to rationalize her continued invasion of his privacy.

She abandoned her typical reading format in favor of a random search through the pages. As she flipped through the book, the words

"Chicago-Death after Death" instilled a morbid interest to which she indulged.

He titles his journal entries like he's writing a book. Ashley noted.

Ashley knew the story of Charles and Julia's short relationship in the late 1950's. Greer had described their deep, enduring love for each other and the tragic accident that killed Julia and left Charles paralyzed.

She resumed her comfortable spot on the sofa and began to read about Charles' lonely and frightening existence after the loss of Julia.

Charles awoke with Ruby in his lap. Jolted out of his sleep by another vivid nightmare, he wiped the tears from his eyes and slowly gained focus, once again, in the waking world. His sudden movement sent the cat to the floor where it then rubbed its body against the metal wheels of his chair.

Physically, his internal system struggled to process the excessive, daily intake of alcohol, nicotine and mixture of countless medications. Emotionally, lucidity allowed the endless guilt to eat away at his very soul while nightmares plagued his unconscious state.

Mentally, after ten long years, time had burned the chilling images from his recurring dreams and haunting memories into his mind. Despite the brain-deteriorating toxins that continuously attacked his system, Charles maintained the capacity to survive, which, in his case, was not a blessing.

His subconscious torture increased when devastating memories surfaced from a lifetime that occurred a very long time ago.

He watched as Julia, a priestess, performed a ritual with her conclave to harness the inherent power of the planet. Unable to control the immense building energy, the space around them folded in on itself. She escaped and saved many lives despite the devastation around her.

Charles watched as a spaceship of survivors, ascended to the sky. The ship out of sight, a revealed Julia stood, thus far unharmed and smiled at him. But, a second of relief was replaced with lifetime of agony when the Earth fell out from beneath of her.

As if on a torturous loop, he endured the painful nightmare repeatedly.

His morning began as every other had for the last decade. Ruby devoured her tuna out of a very, worn, plastic, yellow bowl while Charles, purely out of habit, downed a handful of pills with no regard for their intended effects, good or bad.

After pouring himself a straight whiskey drink, he lit his first cigarette. He rolled himself to the living room and opened the window in hopes of allowing the stale smell of smoke and alcohol to escape.

He didn't bother to turn on the lamps. The sun shone through the windows and cast just enough light to maneuver throughout the small apartment.

Alone and rarely leaving his chair, he would drift in and out of consciousness throughout the day. Each time he woke, he would guess as to what time or even day it was. And then, without exception, his thoughts would rush to Julia.

His final puff on the day's second cigarette was followed by the last swig of his first dose of whiskey. Before he could refill his glass, his attention turned to a muffled, scratching sound. Following the noise, he wheeled himself into his bedroom.

Ruby, displaying typical feline curiosity, swiped her paw underneath Charles', rarely used, bed. The low-sitting bed prevented the curious cat from crawling beneath it. She relentlessly scratched her claws along something but was unable to catch ahold and drag it out.

Charles moved toward the bed. "What's under there, Ruby?"

Either she simply lost interest or was cleverly showing him where to look. Regardless, she scampered off and out of the bedroom.

Cats. Charles shook his head.

He stretched his arm under the box spring and felt a smooth surface in lieu of carpet. His dry, yellow, nicotine-stained fingertips pulled the flat object forward so that it was partially exposed. And, that was enough to tell him what it was.

The board.

Charles retrieved the Ouija Board as well as the plastic pointer that lay on top and placed it in his lap. He ran his fingers across the smooth surface and traced the letters and numbers as memories of "working" the board with Julia flooded into his mind.

In that brief moment of nostalgia, he then placed his fingers on the pointer and asked, "Is there anyone here that would like to play?" But, the pointer remained still.

"It's hardly a game, C." She had corrected him when he referred to their use of the board as "playing". This occurred when, in response to their invitation, someone, or something, had moved the plastic pointer from letter to letter and provided the particulars of ancient Egyptian, crystal magick.

If his heart sank at the recollection of her nickname for him of "C", then it surely broke at the memory of his failed attempt at crystal magick.

Angrily, he flung the board back under the bed, retreated back to the living room and resumed his fruitless, emotion-numbing regiment. For the next few hours, the whiskey coated his tobacco-charred throat in a ruinous, symbiotic, partnership.

Involuntarily, his mind retrieved images of Julia and their use of the board. He pushed them out one by one and either broke a smile or broke down in tears, contingent on the elicited feeling.

Did you close the board, C?

The words felt inserted into his thoughts rather then pulled from a memory. Furthermore, they were clearly spoken in Julia's voice.

Charles hung his head as the water poured from his eyes.

Simply, he was exhausted. Fatigue resulted from his lack of recuperative sleep. His psychological strength waned with every recollection of the accident, the nightmares, the memories and now, the sound of her voice in his head.

Charles, please hurry and close the board.

This time the words were audible. In response, Ruby ran to a corner of the room and hiked up her back end as her wide eyes stared at Charles.

Brought back from familiar desolation, he allowed the content, rather than the delivery, to motivate his actions. He thought back to when they would work the board together.

They sat with the board resting on their touching knees. She playfully scolded him for his lack of attention but he couldn't help but lose himself in the sweet scent of her jasmine perfume. With all of their fingers still on the pointer, they slid it to goodbye.

Julia had explained that the board was a portal to other planes of existence. Light emanates from the doorway which attracts those living and sometimes, suffering in the darkness.

"Those that came through must now go back. We close this board." He successfully recalled the words she had recited at the end of every session and moved back to the bedroom to perform the task. But, he would stop short of the bed and stare in confusion and disbelief at the sight of the Ouija Board that sat atop his bed.

I know I threw it under the bed. I'm sure of it! Incredulously, he wheeled himself closer to the bed and picked up the board. For a moment, he scrutinized the letters, numbers and various symbols. And, then he saw it. Centered, at the top of the board, was a pentagram.

His sobering realization helped him to focus as he placed the board in his lap. With his stained fingers on the pointer, he moved it to "goodbye".

"Those that came through must now go back. I close-."

Charles shrieked as the board was flung from his lap by an unseen force. It landed across the room along with the plastic pointer. Charles sat, terrified and confused as to what had just happened.

The temperature in the bedroom quickly plummeted and Charles could see his breath hang in the air. His chest tightened in fear while dizziness blurred his vision.

Suddenly, he felt a sharp pain in the middle of his back that snaked down his spine and through his legs.

I can feel my legs?

His feet twitched involuntarily as the increasingly painful sensations inside of him spread throughout his torso. The pressure in his chest paled to the wild pounding of his heart. The surge of restricting pain passed through his neck and into his head. And, that is when he heard it.

You belong to me, now.

A deep, raspy and haunting voice echoed inside his head. He looked down to see his feet and legs quivering and moving in gyrations, yet he was not controlling them. The dizzy, swirling sensation made him sick to his stomach.

The sinister voice in his head laughed. On the verge of passing out, he screamed at his realization that he was being possessed.

Delirious and quickly losing consciousness, he could just hear Julia's voice.

Recite the prayer, Charles.

He recalled the protection prayer she had taught him during their studies of light and dark and good versus evil. Charles fought his erratic breathing and unyielding chest pains and said the prayer, in a battle to save his soul.

Father, close the path inside to demons that crawl in me to hide.

Father, bless me with your light and chase away evil with your light.

Charles chanted the prayer a total of seven times and then concluded with "Amen".

At the declaration of affirmation to God's will, the dark being was thrown out of Charles' body. The force sent Charles to the floor. He could see a deep, black shadow race across the wall and out the window. The high-pitched cries of a burning demon pierced his ears and the pungent smell of sulfur assaulted his nose.

With one last labored beat, his heart stopped.

Ashley closed the journal. Her eyes watered with sadness after reading of Charles' horrific attack and his passing. She wondered why she would be so moved by the story of someone who may or may not have even been real.

Was it her connection to Greer? Was it her potential belief in her incarnation as Julia?

Jarring her out of her considerations, Ashley heard the text notification sound from her phone. With the journal in her hand, she

352

walked to Greer's office to retrieve her, now nearly fully charged phone and read the message from her boyfriend.

Hey Ash, on my way home. See you soon.

She placed his journal back inside his desk drawer and then sat down in the office chair. A chuckle arose as she recalled a mini-lecture she had once delivered to Greer regarding communication and the importance of sharing everything with your significant other.

"I guess there is such a thing as too much information." She said aloud.

Greer and Sean pulled out of the mall parking lot. Sean continued to admire his recently purchased watch while Greer silently rehearsed his proposal to Ashley, in his mind.

They arrived to Sean's house and Greer joked, "Wish me luck!"

Sean got out of the truck and walked over to the driver's side. Leaning on the door he told his best friend through the open window, "You don't need it. She's lucky to have you."

He squeezed Greer on the shoulder, winked and walked toward his front door.

Greer smiled at Sean's rare display of brotherly affection before backing out of his driveway.

About halfway home, the "low fuel" light and accompanying alert interrupted his resumed, mental practice session.

He pulled off the road and into a gas station to fill the tank. After, he feared residual "coffee breath" and went inside to buy a pack of gum. The scratch off cards beneath the glass counter caught his eyes and he recalled Madam Fanna's prediction of pentacles, or wealth and prosperity. While he had assumed that those things were more connected to his long term status, he would roll the dice with fate, nonetheless.

After purchasing a gum that promised "fresh breath" and an animal themed scratch-off lottery card, he climbed back into his truck.

His curiosity still wore the pants in their dynamic so he grabbed a quarter from what was intended to be an ash tray, under his dashboard.

After removing the thin, silver substance over the "winning animal" box, he found the depiction of a cat.

Really?

Less hopeful, he rubbed the coin over the card to reveal the hiding animals. Monkey, that's a loser. Mouse, that's a loser. Dog, that's a loser. Finally, he uncovered a cat. Continued scratching revealed the winning amount of five hundred dollars.

Nice! Points to the New Orleans Nostradamus!

Greer went back inside the station and claimed his prize.

Ten minutes later, he was sitting in his truck while parked in his driveway. He took deep breaths to calm his building anxiety and reviewed his strategy.

I'll just act normal until the perfect moment arrives and then ask her.

He took a quick check of his teeth in the visor mirror and then exited his truck. Simultaneously, he spit out his gum and put his hand on the ring that was hidden but slightly bulging in his pocket and then proceeded through his front door.

Prediction VI

Sobek sprang to life and belted out a bellowing alarm that someone had entered the house. Within seconds, Greer's scent provided positive identification and Bek's wailing turned to happy whining as he danced on all fours playfully, in celebration of his return.

Sobek's penetrating bark was impossible to ignore within a two-hundred yard radius. As such, an alerted Ashley emerged from Greer's home office to greet her recently arrived boyfriend.

Greer was crouched low and scratching both sides of his dog's thick neck while affectionately repeating, "Good boy". Sobek's black tail whipped the air and his big, brown eyes begged a clear message of "don't stop".

Greer looked up to see Ashley approaching him and was intentionally light and casual in his delivery. "Hey, Ash."

Ashley's mind was heavy on his journal. Reading about his metaphysical experiences made her feel left out; especially when they described serious, life threatening content.

Does he not trust me enough to share them with me?

She composed herself and asked, "Hey, Greer. Did you get all of your errands done?"

Greer stood up, quickly recalled the lame reason he had given her for his early morning departure and walked toward his girlfriend.

"Yup, all good." He leaned in and kissed her but felt that her lips were rigid. Pulling back he saw that she had a look of concern in lieu of a smile. "What's wrong, Ash?"

She took the opportunity to start the conversation. "We need to talk."

Uh-oh.

His neck straightened and he spoke quickly. "Good talk or bad talk?"

She replied, "Honest talk."

Bad talk.

Greer's mind reviewed his recent behavior for signs of trouble but his rap sheet was clean.

Confused and growing concerned, he asked, "So, what's up, Ash?"

Ashley was calm and felt the need to apologize for reading his journal. "I read your journal."

Greer waited for her next statement.

She continued. "And, I'm sorry."

He had expected something entirely different and asked, "Is that it?"

Trying to match wavelengths, she asked, "Aren't you mad?"

Greer shrugged his shoulders. "No." He pieced together the events of her afternoon and asked, playfully. "So, you went to get the charger and found my journal? And, then took in some not-so-light reading?"

She smiled sheepishly. "I should've asked you first."

Greer was relieved at the subject matter of their "talk" and immediately put her at ease.

"Ash, the journal was in my desk but it wasn't hidden there. I don't keep anything from you. There isn't anything in that book that I wouldn't share with you."

Ashley felt her anger dissipate at his openness. She still had questions but now there was an open forum where there had seemed to be a secret room.

But then, Greer mistakenly used manager-speak when his inner-supervisor headed straight to conflict resolution's final step of "agreement of future behavior".

"Now, going forward, you can simply come to me with any concerns or questions to avoid any misunderstandings."

Ashley's eyes narrowed and her clenched jaw indicated to Greer that he had stepped in metaphoric dog poop. "So, I have to ask if you may have had a cancer scare?"

His mouth waited patiently as his brain pondered her question, formulated a response and then checked it for tone, content and a recommended demeanor.

My brain isn't always right. He later told Sean.

No shit? Sean had replied.

Greer launched into his response. "Oh, that? Who knows if that was even the case? I went to the doctor and there was no indication of cancer or that it was ever there. I just didn't see any reason to talk about something that may not have even been there."

Ashley began to cry and Greer froze awaiting inner guidance. When none arose, he asked, "What did I say?"

She looked through her watery eyes and explained, "Greer, if that happened to me, would you want to know?"

A rush of sadness washed over him at the mere thought of his Ashley becoming sick.

"Of course." He hung his head. When he looked back at her, his eyes were full of tears. "I'm sorry. I should have told you."

He pulled her close and wrapped his arms around her. They shared a moment wrapped inside their mutual love for each other in a loving embrace.

"I love you, Ash."

"I love you, too, Greer."

Their short dispute ended in a mutual understanding of the importance of openness and honesty. Previous feelings of sadness and hurt were replaced with renewed trust and a stronger love and respect for one another.

Slowly pulling apart, Ashley lightened the mood with a reference to a journal entry. "By the way, I read about the future where we have kids and live in suburbia."

Greer was sure this was the opening to the opportunity he was looking for. "Yeah? Is that such a bad future?"

She smiled. "No, it's not a bad future at all."

Greer pulled her close and kissed her.

Ashley felt the bulge of the ring box in Greer's pocket against her leg. Wiping the remaining tears from her cheeks, she asked, "What is that?"

Greer froze. *Was it the right time?*

Ashley tilted her head slightly. "We kind of just finished talking about not keeping things from each other."

He went for it. With no time to recall his rehearsed proposal, he pulled the ring from his pocket, dropped to one knee and held the open ring box out in front of him.

Ashley's eyes widened and she covered her open mouth with her hands.

Greer spoke from his heart. "I don't know what kind of husband I would make. But I do know that I love the person and the man I am when I'm with you."

She smiled behind her hands and her eyes were once again, glassy with tears.

He continued. "Ashley, will you marry me. In the future?" He smiled, obviously pleased with himself.

"No."

Greer was stunned. He looked up at Ashley in disbelief.

She smiled and reached out to him. Wide-eyed in disbelief, Greer stood up while still holding the ring in front of him.

With the beautiful smile that he had grown to adore, she softly explained. "I will not marry you based on some future you saw in a dream. But, I will marry you as we build our own future, based on *our* dreams."

Well said, Ash.

Greer laughed and she held out her hand. He placed the shimmering ring on her finger and in joyous laughter, they embraced.

Ashley excitedly rushed to her phone and called her mother to announce the big news.

Greer sent Sean a text that simply read, "She said no, then yes."

Sean smiled as he read the text and replied, "Congrats, G." As he put his phone down he added, verbally, "I'm happy for you, buddy."

That evening the couple enjoyed a celebratory meal at Ashley's favorite Thai restaurant. Afterward, they devoured cheesecake on Greer's patio and enjoyed the cool November evening.

Ashley had chosen an expensive, earthy, rich and dry Portuguese red wine for their celebration toast, compliments of the state lottery's scratch-off game. They sat close together by candlelight on the sofa, with Sobek beneath them, and discussed their future together.

The happy evening fell to night and the engaged couple made love to each other before falling asleep in each other's embrace.

Greer awoke standing next to his bed. He observed his sleeping body and noted the slight rise and fall of his chest.

I make it a point to check; just in case.

Ashley had rolled over and was sleeping, quite peacefully, in a cocoon of bed covers which left Greer exposed and cold.

Greer heard the whirling of wind around him and felt the push of an unseen force. The rapid movement propelled him into the familiar, old castle. He found himself adjacent to the grey, stone, and spiral staircase that had previously sent him into several of Earth's potential futures.

Suddenly, the room filled with an intense white light that was accompanied by a high-pitched tone that hurt his astral ears. And, then, both vanished.

Glowing of her own radiant light in front of him stood the angelic image of the spirit being that he knew to be his guide and protector, Selene.

Prediction VII

Greer felt Selene's warmth of love and compassion wash over him in a loving, bathing light. She smiled at him with the understanding of an elevated perspective and the patience of an ascended teacher.

Her long, straight, black hair fell down the front of her ivory white gown that stretched down to the stone floor. Her dark eyes were filled with love and reflected the shimmering, red garnet around her neck.

She broke his stare with a single announcement. "It is time for your mission to begin."

Greer looked from left to right. "My mission?"

"Indeed." Selene motioned to the stone staircase.

He looked up at the stairs. "Another trip to the future?"

She maintained her patient smile as she replied. "Yes, the future through the seventh step."

Greer thought for a moment. "What's so special about the seventh step?"

Selene motioned, once again, toward the staircase. "The seventh step will take you to your future."

Greer quickly understood. "You mean this reality's future?"

"Indeed."

Still riding a high from the last trip to the future in which he was married to Ashley and living in a nice house with their two children, he started walking up the steps.

Then, it hit him. "Wait, if this step takes me to the future of this reality, then I won't have the future I saw with Ashley?"

He looked over to where Selene had been standing but she was gone.

I'll hold my questions until the Q&A portion of this meeting.

Greer reached the seventh step and waited. The step beneath him disappeared and a rush of rapid movement thrust him downward.

A moment later, his eyes beheld a very different Earth, of the future.

Greer stood in the driveway of the house to which the spiral stairs, aka time portal, connected.

"Are you ready, Greer?"

Surprised, he turned around and saw Selene standing behind him.

"Uh, yeah. I mean, for what? And, you're here, why?"

She smiled with a little less patience, yet still playful and sweet. "Is it time for Q&A?"

Greer winced. "You heard that, eh?"

"Indeed. To answer your earlier question, while this is not the particular future to which you referred, do not assume that similar outcomes cannot occur in multiple future timelines."

Greer half smiled. "Vague, but I get what you're saying."

She continued. "To answer your more recent query, I am here to explain to you what has occurred to the planet and its inhabitants, in this particular future."

Greer joked, "You're going to be my guide? Get it? Guide?"

Selene's smile waned. "You may not find many things humorous in this timeline."

Greer adopted a serious perspective and looked around him. He noticed that there were no cars in the driveways and no people. In fact, the neighborhood street seemed deserted. "Where is everyone?"

Selene spoke without turning her head. "Take my hand."

Greer complied and they soared high into the air. When they finally stopped, he guessed that they were over a mile high above the ground. Looking down, he suddenly saw the reason for their sudden elevation. "Is that a tsunami?"

"Yes, but just one of many to come." She explained. "Volcanic eruptions occur continuously and send great walls of water to the land. The coastal areas have already fled in search of safer areas."

"That's why I didn't see any people down there. They've evacuated." Greer determined.

"Indeed. But they are not the only ones to be displaced."

He could hear the roar of the water as it moved onto land and destroyed everything in its path. Homes were easily crushed beneath the intense pressure of the massive water wave.

A bright flash of light surrounded them and in the next instant they were high above North America. Greer's view was that of a giant map of the continent. But, something was wrong. The majority of the southeast was now ocean. Florida, Georgia, Alabama, Tennessee, Louisiana and Texas were essentially, blue. He looked to Selene for an explanation.

"The loss of ice, particularly from the polar caps, has dramatically increased the sea levels. Much of Australia is under water as well. In fact, all of the continents have been drastically and devastatingly affected."

"Was there time to leave? Where did everyone go?" He asked while growing despondent at the amount of loss and suffering that must have occurred.

Without warning, everything went white and he found himself above the African plains. Torrential downpours of rain flooded the region as aggressive storms continuously developed along the coastline.

"I know they could use more rain but I'm guessing this is the other extreme." Greer concluded.

"The ocean temperatures have increased which has caused excessive evaporation. And, that resulted in extreme rainstorms." Selene explained.

He considered the loss of land and vegetation that was vital to the survival of the animals and, of course, people.

They moved to another area of the continent to find that the flooding waters had shown no signs of receding. The tops of small homes barely peaked out from the surrounding, muddy water.

Before Greer could ask as to the cause of what they had witnessed, he saw another flash of white light. And, this time, he had a bird's eye view of west coast of South America.

Still holding hands, they descended down, until the ground was visible. Greer stared, speechless, at the devastation.

The grounds shook violently. Even the structures that were designed and built to withstand the worst of earthquakes had fallen. Their once impressive architecture had now been reduced to unrecognizable rubble.

Greer felt a painful sense of loss as he witnessed the natural disasters destroy Earth's civilization. Weary of the loss of life and unrelenting destruction, he asked, rather pleaded with Selene to, "Please, tell me what happened here."

She squeezed his hand and they found themselves back in the water-filled driveway of the now, demolished home that once housed the spiral staircase.

Greer looked worried and asked. "So, without the staircase, how do we get back?"

Selene explained, "The portal is no longer displayed on the physical plane due to the removal of the stairs. However, it exists, as it always will, on the astral plane. Simply shift your focus inward, see the stone staircase in the castle and with all your will, place yourself there."

Greer concentrated and imagined that he was standing next to the stone steps. Instantly, he felt a dull throb in his head that forced his eyes shut. When he opened them, he was back in the castle.

"Cool."

"Indeed."

He immediately turned to Selene. "So, was what we saw the effects of global warming?"

Selene wore her patient smile and spoke clearly and in an even tone. "Global warming occurs when there is a gradual increase in the overall temperature of the atmosphere." She paused. "In this case, the heat is emanating from the planetary nucleus."

Greer thought for a moment. "So, the core of the planet is overheating?"

"Indeed."

Greer felt helpless. "Is this the end of…the world?"

"Perhaps."

Confused, he asked, "What caused it?"

Selene's smile vanished. "You did."

The story concludes in 7 Reflections-Book 7 of The 7 Novellas Series.

7

Reflections

by

Gare Allen

The 7 Novellas Series by Gare Allen

Book One- 7 Sessions

Book Two- 7 Regressions

Book Three- 7 Apparitions

Book Four- 7 Abductions

Book Five- 7 Projections

Book Six- 7 Predictions

Book Seven- 7 Reflections

Also Available on amazon.com

The Dead: A True Paranormal Story

Dedicated to Selene

Reflection I

"How long is the drive from Tampa to Chicago?" Sean asked as he put his suitcase in the cab of Greer's white, Ford F-150 truck.

"Eighteen hours with stops. Less, if ya piss into a water bottle." Greer, crudely, half-joked.

He opened the door to the cab while motioning to Sobek. "Come on, boy, get in."

Elated to be joining the road crew, the black Lab leapt into the backseat and assumed his spot next to the guy's luggage.

Dressed in blue, cargo shorts and a white, sleeveless, Nike t-shirt, Sean completed his signature look with a backwards ball cap and climbed into the passenger seat.

Once seated, he found Sobek's big, square head resting on the middle console and quipped, "I'm pretty sure you don't have the aim needed for a water bottle." Sobek's big, brown eyes looked upward and displayed his breed's typical, inquisitive expression. "Buckle up for a long ride, Bek."

As if showing appreciation of the nickname, Sobek lifted his head and lathered the left side of Sean's face.

Greer wore blue jeans and a pewter Tampa Bay Buccaneers jersey that would later solicit ridicule from Ashley's father.

Like the Bears are any better. He would later note to Sean.

Greer assumed his spot in the driver's seat just in time to witness his canine's sloppy affection toward his buddy.

Sean laughed but quickly looked for something to remove the doggie drool from his cheek.

"There are napkins in the glove box, Sean." He paused as his best friend endured a few follow-up licks. "Alright, Bek, that's enough." Greer scratched the top of his dog's head and Sobek retreated, for the moment, to his spot on the backseat.

Sean wiped the saliva from his face with a small portion of the obscenely large stash of Starbucks napkins that overflowed from the glove compartment. "Even complimentary napkins have a limit, G."

Greer smirked. "I'm pretty sure I paid the manager's salary in macchiatos last year, so not feeling all that bad about the napkin hoarding."

Sean chuckled as he fastened his seat belt.

Greer put the key in the ignition and caught a glimpse of his canine comrade's slightly panting, grey muzzle in the rear view mirror. His ever happy Lab always brought a smile to his face.

Still gripping the unturned key, he looked to his right at his best friend and felt enveloped in support. "Man, I really appreciate you making this trip with me."

Sean look surprised as he replied. "My best friend is getting married, I'm the best man and there's a road trip…" Sean pointed to the backseat as he spoke, "…with a dog! Of course I'm on board. Best long weekend ever!"

Greer smiled and started his truck. "Ready?"

"Ready, G." Sean felt the warmth of the Florida sun on his arms piercing through the truck windows as Greer backed out of his driveway. "What's the weather like in Chicago in May anyway?"

"Ash said it's a little cool at night but warm during the day. Luckily, there's no rain in the weekend forecast." Greer answered and glanced at Sean's sleeveless shirt. "But, if I was you, I'd go with sleeves this weekend."

Sean looked at each of his muscled arms and sincerely stated, "It's a shame to cover them up."

Greer smiled and headed toward the interstate. Within minutes, Sean's buried attention into his phone fostered a quiet, reflective environment of which Greer took full advantage.

He recalled that Sunday in November, just six months prior, when he and Sean had spent the better part of the day at the mall. The late arrival of his engagement ring created some downtime which, much to Sean's dismay, Greer used to receive a psychic reading. One by one, Madam Fanna's predictions were realized, including Ashley's acceptance of his marriage proposal.

He had agreed to her father's wish, or rather demand, to have the ceremony in their home town of Chicago. Contrary to her dad's assumption, Greer's agreement was not a result of her father's insistence on paying for the wedding; it was to lovingly oblige the desire of his beloved fiancé that she be wed in the city in which she was raised.

It makes sense to have it up north. All of her friends and family are there and there's like, a million of them. All I've got down here is Sean and a dog. He had explained to Beverly after telling her the good news.

Although she didn't say so, Beverly was very proud of his growth. She had determined some time ago that his insecurities were very much a result of the loss of both of his parents.

Sadly, they both passed due to a devastating highway pile-up during Greer's last year of college.

Greer recalled the psychic's final prediction foretold by the Tarot card, "The World". Her vague and concerned message that "something needed closure" would be soon understood when he found himself standing with Selene and adjacent to the castle's stone, spiral staircase.

"You must complete the mission, Greer." Selene's words were clear and the resulting fantastic events were still, if only by him, perfectly remembered in his heart and head.

He had chosen, temporarily, to not share his experiences with Sean and Ashley for only one reason; he needed a break from the paranormal.

I would welcome a few months free of abductions, projections, predictions, regressions and apparitions. He had written in his journal.

Greer shook his head and tried to remove the memories of the other-worldly occurrences that now filled his mind. Successful in his effort, he focused on a more pressing, and indeed, secular, event on the horizon; his marriage to the beautiful Ashley.

Their relationship had flourished to new levels since his proposal. Over the course of their engagement they had both learned to navigate through each other's quirks and insecurities.

Greer adhered to the importance of sharing his thoughts and feelings; those both good and bad. Ashley remembered that his words came from a place of well-intentioned honesty and any defensive response could shut him down and deter future, healthy communication.

She assured him that his overprotective nature could be interpreted as jealousy and for her, was most assuredly, the least attractive of all of the emotions. He worked to understand that his strong reaction to other men who displayed interest in her was actually a perceived indication of his distrust in her fidelity.

Admittedly, he is still working on that one.

Greer put on his black, Ray Ban sunglasses, merged his truck onto the northbound interstate and set the cruise control to ten miles above the speed limit. He was now ready to conquer the twelve hundred miles ahead of them.

"This is it, G." Sean broke his silence and simultaneously put down his iPhone.

With wide, accepting eyes, Greer nodded his head.

"Yup. In two days, I'll be married." After very little consideration, he determined, "Things shouldn't change much, though."

Sean held back a laugh and turned his head to watch the passing traffic outside of his window. Mentally, he prepared himself for an exchange with "Oblivious-Greer".

"You don't think so?" Sean asked.

With a casual delivery, Greer explained. "We've lived together for a year and a half now and we've worked out a lot of the kinks." He paused, confident in his determination and glanced over at his buddy. "It'll be business as usual."

Still observing the passing cars, Sean began to carefully poke holes in his friend's theory and would enjoy the process a lot more than he should have. "Did you get a joint bank account, yet?"

Greer's head turned so quickly that it prompted Sobek to raise his head off of the back seat in attention.

"No." He softened his delivery after a quick consideration. "But, that's not a big deal."

Sean nodded. His visual focus remained on the passing cars as he asked, "When are you guys going house hunting?"

Greer narrowed his eyes behind his glasses. "What's wrong with the house we live in now?"

"Nothing, it's just your house. I figured you two would want to buy a house together is all." Sean briefly paused as Greer pondered the validity of his assertion. That gave Sean time to hit the launch button to release the next bomb.

"Think about it, G. You'll definitely need more room for the kids."

Jarred out of his pensive state, Greer exclaimed, "Kids?"

"Well, yeah. You said you wanted kids, right?"

Greer began to feel overwhelmed. "Yeah, but not tomorrow."

With those four words, "Oblivious-Greer" became "Stressed-Greer".

Sean delivered one last glimpse of his best friend's future. "Relax, G. You make good money so you'll be fine when Ashley stays home to raise the kids." Sean turned from the window and managed to ask one last question before his laughter escaped. "Unless you're gonna stay home and be Mr. Mom and Ash is going to work?"

Greer's hands tightened their grip on the steering wheel at "ten and two". His clenched jaw accompanied the realization that his buddy was intentionally subjecting him to unnecessary worries of the future.

The veins in his extended arms were like a road map as he took a deep breath and in a low voice, responded, "Dick."

Sean laughed and squeezed his friend's shoulder. "Just messing with you, G. That's what best man's do." His laughter waned and was replaced with a tone of sincerity when he assured his best friend, "You two have a great future ahead of you. And, I'm happy for you, buddy."

The future.

Greer recalled the events that transpired through time and space with the help of Selene. The emotion of the experience coupled with Sean's sincere sentiment and of course, the upcoming wedding, compelled him to finally share the events with his best friend.

Looking back at the passing traffic, Sean's voice suddenly carried a clear annoyance. "G, I know you're driving too slow because a cement truck just passed us."

Greer smiled and adjusted his speed to mollify his traveling companion. "Whether I drive eighty or eight-five, it's gonna take the better part of a day to get there, buddy."

Sean shrugged his shoulders but didn't respond.

"Since we got the time, ya wanna hear about the mission?" Greer asked.

Sean raised his left eyebrow and turned his head slightly to his left. "Mission? Is this more dream and past life craziness?"

Greer could only, honestly, respond in one way. "Yeah."

Sean sighed. "Well, we've got a long ride ahead of us so, let's hear it." He looked back at Sobek who had quickly adjusted to the motion of the moving truck and was deep into a nap. "Lucky dog."

Sean was riveted by my story and hung on every word. Greer later told Ashley.

I was locked in his truck for eighteen hours with no escape. Sean later clarified to the new bride.

Greer explained how he had traveled forward in time to the year 2026 via the seventh step of the stone, spiral stairs in the old castle. He suffered the role of a helpless witness as Selene provided aerial perspectives of the devastation in Earth's foreboding future.

The torturous sight of floods, earthquakes and the loss of countless life sickened his stomach so much that he could barely stand. Selene's next words would knock him to his knees.

He immediately turned to Selene. "So, was what we saw the effects of global warming?"

Selene wore her patient smile and spoke clearly and in an even tone. "Global warming occurs when there is a gradual increase in the overall temperature of the atmosphere." She paused. "In this case, the heat is emanating from the planetary nucleus."

Greer thought for a moment. "So, the core of the planet is overheating?"

"Indeed."

Greer felt helpless. "Is this the end of…the world?"

"Perhaps."

Confused, he asked, "What caused it?"

Selene's smile vanished. "You did."

Greer held his head in his hands and stared with unblinking, stunned eyes. Nervously, he waited for his guide to explain her words.

"You must complete the mission, Greer."

That didn't explain her words.

Greer remained silent in confused anticipation.

Before she began to elaborate, Selene moved her left arm upward and above her head. Blinding, white light appeared behind her and quickly softened into an oval-shaped mirror that reflected a mass of indistinguishable, swirling images.

"To understand the future, we must review the past."

Greer's shock and confusion quickly turned to impatience and frustration. He harnessed his building anger to rise off of his knees and stand before the cryptic angel. "I'm gonna need a few more specifics to go along with the desk-top calendar quote, darlin'."

Ignoring his attitude and tone in favor of an explanation, she raised her arm once again. The swirling mass inside the mirror behind her quickly formed into clear images of an unsettling scene.

Greer's eyes were transfixed as he watched himself in Ancient Maya attempting to save an endangered Ashley.

Itzel screamed through the hex bag that was stuffed inside of her mouth. The taste of dirt and the aroma of the crushed, wild flowers inside the gag overpowered her senses. She twisted and contorted herself in an effort to break free of the thick roots that dug into her skin and sadistically secured her to the wooden, ritual platform. The terrified, young woman writhed in agony as priests used obsidian knives to carve ritualistic symbols into her chest, arms, legs and face.

The wreath fashioned of pungent, verbena flowers was now splattered with her blood as it rested in her thick, black hair.

Itzel's body became still and her screams fell silent as she succumbed to the paralyzing effects of intense shock.

The priests continued to carve the language of the Sun Gods into the young virgin as the sacrifice dictated. They believed the sweet scent

383

of wildflowers would lure the Gods down from the heavens. Acceptance of their unspoiled offering would provide a pure source of nourishment for the deities. In return, the skies would provide ample rain for crops and healthy offspring to the women.

Itzel was barely conscious as the priests completed slicing their markings into her body and then bowed beside her.

Six crystal skulls that had been arranged to encircle the woman stared, coldly at Itzel. She felt the air sting into her cuts but she was too weak to react. Suddenly, the warm wind became an intense heat as the sky above her disappeared behind a large, oval spacecraft.

Itzel heard the unified chanting of the priests around her increase in volume. Fear and utter helplessness fueled continuous tears and she prayed, inside her mind, for mercy.

The crystal skulls were now dimly illuminated as if charged by the eerily, quiet, hovering craft. Now, directly above her, it slowed and eventually stopped. The ship emitted a light yellow beam of light that engulfed the bleeding, young woman.

Itzel braced herself for death and called upon the keepers of the underworld to find her upon her crossing.

Tepeu sprinted from the nearby pyramid and prayed that he was not too late. The hood on his dark, brown cloak fell down to his shoulders and exposed his identity to his conclave. Uncaring of his own fate, he remained intent on saving his beloved Itzel.

Tepeu was one of nine priests charged with the creation of their calendars and the integration of the knowledge of the Sun Gods.

Foolishly, he had allowed his heart to be taken by the young and beautiful, Itzel. A chance meeting outside of the pyramid sparked an instant attraction. Their longing for one another resonated on their deepest levels and they fell in love.

Clandestine visits and secret meetings were planned and executed for over a year to simply see one another for sometimes, only minutes. His vow of celibacy denied him a physical relationship and she denied herself those same pleasures in favor of their loving connection.

Tepeu's legs sprinted across the ground. He was almost upon the platform and could now see his bleeding love, bathed in light beneath the suspended spacecraft.

It's my fault. I withheld my love for her and she remained pure and was taken for the ritual.

He mentally berated his actions or, more accurately, inactions for only virgins are used in sacrifices to the Gods.

The chanting of the bowed priests became louder and faster. Intent, yellow light melted away the restraining roots around Itzel's arms and legs. Tepeu was almost to the platform when Itzel's limp body began to ascend upward.

He jumped onto the platform and simultaneously retrieved a dark quartz crystal skull from the pocket of his cloak.

Desperate to save his beloved, he held the crystal skull above his head and under the transporting, yellow beam of light.

The other priests looked up and shrieked in terror at Tepeu's actions.

Their protests would go unheard as the six crystal skulls that had been placed around the platform became fully illuminated. Blinding, white light beamed from the eyes from each of the six skulls and into the skull in Tepeu's hands. Static, buzzing and extreme heat surrounded the priests and platform until they had increased in such intensity that they all fell deaf and dizzy.

Greer stared into the mirror and watched, in horror, as the ground beneath the priests enveloped them and the hovering craft.

As a result, a large crater was formed which concealed the events of the past.

Reflection II

"Maybe I missed something but how did that lifetime cause you to end the world?" Sean asked, genuinely confused.

Greer explained, "It will make sense when I tell you about the other lifetimes."

Sean accepted that he would need to endure the telling of each incarnation. For him, it was now a familiar experience.

You definitely have a structure, G.

Sean thought for a moment and made a connection. "Didn't the same kind of disaster happen in the Egyptian lifetime? I mean, the whole ground caving in on itself and all that?"

Greer smiled and remembered that he sometimes didn't give his friend enough credit. When Sean applied himself, he could be very bright.

Just then, Greer received an incoming call and answered it through the truck's hands-free phone. The caller identification displayed the name of his bride-to-be.

"Hey, Ash."

Excited for the obvious reason, she spoke in a high tone. "Hi, Sweetie! Are you guys on the road, yet?"

"Yeah, we're on our way. How are things up there?"

"Good. Your tuxes were delivered today. They look great but they sent an extra tie for some reason."

"Is mine sleeveless?" Sean interjected.

Ashley laughed. "Hi, Sean. Thanks for making the trip with Greer. I feel better knowing that he isn't driving alone."

"No problem, Ash."

Ashley had come to appreciate Sean for the solid friendship that he provided to Greer and moreover his ability to keep him on this side of searching for Bigfoot. They had also bonded over their mutual ridicule of Greer's rigid "life rules", such as his clear guidelines regarding time-inappropriate food.

No red sauce before eleven a.m. He had once declared.

Ashley very intentionally ate a piece of leftover pizza for breakfast, the very next morning.

Greer slipped into manager-mode. "Are we good with the flowers, Ash?"

"Yes, all good."

"What about the cake?"

Feeling like a subordinate, she struggled to retain her patience. "Yes, I checked on the cake and it's set to be delivered Sunday morning."

As if running through a mental checklist, Greer continued with, "Did you check out the church's reception hall?"

Ashley exclaimed in partial mock frustration, "Sean, help me."

Sean looked over at his friend. "G, unless you want a runaway bride, I'd relax."

All three chuckled and "Oblivious-Greer" asked one last question. "Have you decided where we're going on our honeymoon, Ash?"

"I have and it's a surprise. Don't worry, you're gonna love it."

If Sean knew anything, it was that his buddy wasn't overly fond of surprises. "Really, Ash? Have you met Greer?"

Greer rolled his eyes at Sean and intentionally contradicted his assessment by claiming, "I'm looking forward to it, Ash."

"I am too, Sweetie. Mom and I are going shopping so I'll call you later. Drive safely. I love you!"

"I will and I love you, too. Bye, Ash."

"Bye, Greer. Bye, Sean."

"Bye, Ashley." Sean replied.

With the call ended, Greer's face displayed a goofy but happy smile.

Sean allowed him to bask in the happy anticipation of his big day and withheld his juvenile jab. "So, where do you think Ashley chose to go for your honeymoon? And, by the way, major props for allowing her to choose. That must have been hard for ya."

Greer's goofy smile was replaced with an expression of agreement. "It took everything I had, man."

They both laughed as Greer continued. "But, I trust her and it's not about the where so much, as long as we are together, ya know?"

Sean shook his head and smiled in silent acknowledgment of his buddy's obvious, deep love for his fiancé.

Without segue or warning, Greer abruptly switched topics back to his recent astral field trip. Caught off guard, Sean lacked the time to object and would later describe himself as a seat-belted prisoner.

Greer described an incarnation aboard a boat on the open waters that was reflected to him inside Selene's astral mirror.

Miguel maneuvered his small boat across the choppy waters of the Atlantic Ocean. He tasted the salty air on his lips as the afternoon sun baked his face and darkened his already brown, Spanish skin. His thick, dark beard was coarse from the saltwater splashes and his white, long sleeve shirt clung to his sweaty, sticky body.

Miguel was a man in his thirties but sun weathered lines and a leathery complexion easily added ten years to his actual age.

With only a few hired hands to assist with the sails, they endured long days with little sleep. They had left Puerto Rico twelve days earlier and set course for the keys of Florida. Miguel guessed he was a little more than halfway to their destination.

His small boat moved understandably slower than usual given the hidden cargo. For a handsome sum, Miguel was charged with transporting hundreds of pounds of precious gold, silver and crystals.

He was quite aware that, like most of the merchandise that he had moved across the ocean, it had been stolen. The nature of his cargo dictated the necessity for him to demonstrate discretion and ask very few questions.

Of course, he also had to navigate around the looming presence of eighteenth century piracy. But, today, the danger was to be found beneath the ocean.

The boat and its crew suddenly found itself in a very calm area of water. Vanished winds ceased the boat's movement except for the motion caused by the moving men.

Darkening skies above them filled with mysterious storm clouds; instantly formed from seemingly out of nowhere.

The absent wind returned with a circular veracity that viciously spun the small boat in circles. Beneath them, the sea water moved with the wind to create a dangerous whirlpool. One by one, the men were thrown into the spinning waters and instantly pulled under to a drowning death.

Miguel clung to the mast as he helplessly watched his men being flung into the angry waters. Fearing death, his hands dug themselves into the mast and his thoughts fell to his wife and two children.

While his profession may have lacked morality, it provided ample compensation to clothe, feed and provide for his family.

He wondered if he would ever see them again. Miguel held a vision of his beautiful wife, Antonia, in his mind as the boat began to sink into the swallowing vortex.

His hands were losing their grasp on the mast as his heart was losing hope of his survival. The rapid spin of the boat made him sick and dizzy until it was all over. The murderous waters engulfed the boat and stole Miguel from the world.

Selene motioned her hand to the mirror and only the image of a now calm ocean remained. What eluded Greer was the name of the location where the events that he observed had occurred; the Bermuda Triangle.

Greer tilted his head and forced some humor into his statement to offset the dismal display that he had just witnessed. "Is there a way that I haven't died? Although, it seems getting swallowed by the planet is a popular favorite of mine."

Selene remained angelically patient. "Do you see the continuity and outcome of your past actions?"

Greer paused and considered the two lifetimes. "Well, the incarnation in Maya was similar to the one in Chicago."

"How so, Greer?" Selene asked, softly.

In response to the answer, his upper lip curled. "I blamed myself for the death of Julia and Itzel in both. But, in hindsight, I don't see how it was my fault."

Selene smiled. "And, what of Miguel?"

Greer shrugged his shoulders. "Not sure what that life was all about." He thought for a few seconds before continuing. "I mean, that storm came out of nowhere and what a way to die! But, what does this have to do with me ending the world?"

Sean was more intrigued than he wanted to admit. "Did she answer you?"

"Eventually, but first, she wanted to show me another lifetime."

Sean sighed. "So, there's no fast forward button, is there?"

Greer looked over at him and playfully used his earlier comment against him. "Have you met me?"

Sean held up his hand. "Before we take another ride on the crazy train, can we stop and get some food?"

"That sounds good."

They guys had been on the road for a little over two hours and were battling rumbling stomachs as they both had skipped breakfast.

Greer decided that while on the road, he would uncharacteristically enjoy the pleasures of fast food and stray far off of his healthy reservation.

As if God himself had chosen to send Greer a wedding gift, the next exit boasted both a burger place and a Starbucks.

Thanks, Big Guy.

Utilizing the outside seating of the small restaurant, Sobek was able to join them.

The guys enjoyed their cheeseburgers in guilty silence and vowed to never speak of their diet-destroying day to anyone. They both slipped several fries to Sobek while rationalizing that the more of the greasy, wedges that the dog ate, the less they did.

They would later regret their actions as Sobek's internal system reacted to the greasy treat with formidable, expelled gas. Subsequently, the windows would remain down for the majority of the drive to Illinois.

Sean took Sobek to a grassy area by the road so that he could relieve himself while Greer walked to the neighboring steeple of coffee called Starbucks.

After a few minutes, they were back in the truck and had resumed their sojourn to the north. Sean's hunger was satiated, Sobek's bladder was relieved and Greer was well on his way to being sufficiently caffeinated and alert as they closed in on the Georgia state line.

"I'm gonna check in with Ash." Greer informed his buddy riding shotgun. He pushed the Bluetooth button on the steering wheel and directed it to, "Call Ashley."

Her phone rang through the truck speakers three times before she answered. "Hi, Greer."

"Hi, Ash. How are you?"

"Good. Where are you?"

"About half an hour from Georgia. We stopped for a quick bite."

"And, coffee?" Ashley knew him only too well. She could hear Sean's chuckle from the passenger seat which confirmed her suspicion.

Greer responded casually as if he didn't have a moderate to severe caffeine addiction. "I may have gotten a coffee for the road while we were stopped."

"Is it a venti, Sean?"

"I don't know what you call it but it looks like a half gallon container of milk and coffee with a green straw."

Ashley confirmed, "Yeah, that's a venti."

Greer tried to derail the train of mockery coming into the station with, "I do have a long drive ahead of me so, being alert is a good thing, yes?"

"It has sprinkles, Ashley. Sprinkles!" Sean informed her as he shook his head.

"At least order it as "skinny", Greer. They'll leave out the whipped cream and chocolate shavings." Ashley advised.

Greer clenched his jaw. "Yeah, because adding "skinny" to its name really butches up the drink. And, it doesn't have chocolate shavings, whipped cream or sprinkles!"

"Is his face red, Sean?" Ashley asked, already knowing the answer.

"Yup. But that might be from the extra shot of expresso that he thinks we don't know that he orders."

Greer's initial lack of response was their confirmation of an accurate deduction.

When Sean and Ashley were done laughing, Greer adopted a "good sport" smile while trying to change the subject by asking, "So, what's happening in Chicago?"

Ashley's tone became soft and sweet. "I just picked up my dress."

Greer beamed as he imagined his beautiful Ashley in a white gown and standing across from him as they exchanged vows.

Vows.

Greer had yet to write his.

"I can't wait to see the dress and you, Ash. I'll call you when we're halfway there."

"Sounds good. I love you!"

"I love you, too. Bye, Ash."

"Bye."

Reflection III

Sean retrieved a stick of gum from its small package, removed the wrapper and placed it into his mouth. "I have burger breath."

Greer withheld comment in favor of a swig from his cold, coffee concoction and was surprised when Sean passed up the opportunity to deliver another coffee-addict jab.

Sean leaned his head against the window and marveled at the colorful Sugar Maple trees that lined the sides of the highway. Oval shaped and standing over sixty feet tall, they boasted glorious orange and red coloration that were mixed with brilliant yellows.

Don't see those colors in Tampa. He remarked to himself.

While the sight of the vibrant foliage was a delight to his vision, his sense of smell was assaulted by Sobek's gaseous release.

"Holy Mother of God!" Sean exclaimed and simultaneously covered his nose.

Greer pushed the buttons to bring down all four windows and allow the stench to leave the truck while cursing, "Dammit, Bek!"

It was twenty minutes before they felt it was safe to bring the windows back up.

Greer had finished the last of his iced coffee and felt the rush of caffeine in his system. Needing a release of the energy, he resumed his telling of his time with Selene and the often disturbing reflected events inside the mirror.

Selene raised her arm and once again, the oval mirror behind her displayed a swirling mass of white light. Images quickly took shape and replayed Greer's former lifetime as a significant participant in the historic witch executions in Salem, Massachusetts.

Five women accused of performing witchcraft and sentenced to hanging occupied each of the five, newly created wooden gallows. They were arranged in a large circle while a building crowd of angry, righteous spectators filled the center area.

The mob threw small stones and shouted biblical judgments at the women that denounced their practice of the dark arts. The witch's internal, turbulent anger denied the plebian minded pilgrims any satisfaction of displayed fear or regret.

Eyes narrowed and their heads held high, the sentenced women stood, stoic and unflinching despite the unnerving knot of the noose that rested on the left side of their neck and under their jaw.

Darkness blanketed the area, emancipated by the setting sun. The Salem people responded by catching fire atop their torches.

A moment later, they cleared a wide path for the approaching Magistrate Walcott, in response to his obnoxious announcement of his own arrival.

A tall man, with long, white hair and a permanent stern, accusing expression stared down his long nose. He found the exact center of the circular area formed by the placement of the hanging platforms.

His order to build additional gallows for public hangings was carried out immediately and today's carefully planned spectacle was designed to instill faith in his leadership.

In his limited, self-serving mind, murder was an acceptable price to pay in order to gain favor of the residents of Salem. Holding both lapels of his long, buttoned, black coat, he turned in a continuous and dramatically slow, circular motion as he spoke.

"Good people of Salem. These five women have been found guilty of witchcraft. Their dark practices spit in the face of our purity and they must, therefore, be sent back to their creator; the devil himself."

The crowd roared in agreement and raised their crackling torches above their heads.

One by one, Magistrate Walcott glared at the accused and identified each of the women.

"Mary Proctor. You have been found guilty of performing witchcraft and sentenced to death by hanging."

Mary was short with long, brown hair that almost completely hid her face as it fell down from her head.

Standing below her and holding hands were her husband and two children. Scowls of judgment and hatred were clearly displayed upon their faces, despite the darkened evening.

The youngest daughter had been born with mental and physical disabilities. A father's emotional pain combined with the collective paranoia of the town placed the blame squarely on Mary. The consensus was that her practice of magic bore a curse on the young child and the charges rooted quickly.

The red stone hanging around Mary's soon-to-be broken neck was a garnet. Its power provided physical energy and the will to survive.

The Magistrate turned clockwise and continued his identifications.

"Abigail Warren. You have been found guilty of performing witchcraft and sentenced to death by hanging."

She stared back at him with dark, cold eyes. Her long, black hair fell down upon her pale, bare shoulders and blended with her fitted, black dress. Abigail emitted sensuality even with a noose wrapped around her neck. Just above her inviting cleavage rested orange calcite. The stone increased mental, physical and sexual pleasure.

In truth, Abigail's guilty verdict had nothing to do with the practice of witchcraft. Rather, her impending execution would conceal the affair with the married Magistrate who stood before her in hypocritical judgment.

Her magical abilities were merely an ironic coincidence.

"Alice Toothaker. You have been found guilty of performing witchcraft and sentenced to death by hanging."

Alice was a short, round woman with several missing teeth that created gaps inside her sickening grin. Her white, full length dress was still covered in the blood of the carved pig she had been discovered slaughtering, in mid-sacrifice.

Around her neck she wore a tiger's eye that provided spiritual wisdom and clarity of your place within the universe.

"Ann Easter. You have been found guilty of performing witchcraft and sentenced to death by hanging."

Ann was the oldest of the women and had lived alone, all of her life. She kept mostly to herself but made the mistake of angrily chasing a little girl off of her front step. The young child was drawn to the shiny stones that adorned the bottom of her doorstep. Ann had carefully placed them there as part of a spell. On her best day, Ann possessed little patience for meddling children and her screeching threats succeeded in scaring away the curious, small child.

The young girl returned home full of tears and claims that Ann was a wicked old witch who had placed a curse on her. A frightened child's words sealed the old woman's fate and a few days later, Ann stood atop the wooden platform.

A rose quartz hung down on her chest that helped with her connection to the very nature of life.

Magistrate Walcott turned to face the fifth woman.

"Margaret Mather. You have been found guilty of performing witchcraft and sentenced to death by hanging."

The youngest and most powerful of the five women stared down at the Magistrate. Her soft blond hair was pulled back and accentuated her sky blue eyes that contrasted her almost translucent, pale skin.

She had healed several people with minor ailments in the recent past. With herbs, crystals and chants, she had reduced the fever of a small boy, healed the broken arm of a farm worker and restored the struggling liver of one of the town tavern's regulars. Rather than gratitude, they would repay her with accusations of devil worship and a public death.

Her crystal of choice was clear quartz which strengthened the connection to the crown chakra located atop her head and availed to her the power of the universe.

Magistrate Walcott raised his hand above his head. The masked executioners readied themselves by their wooden levers to release the trap door beneath the women.

All five witches smiled and their individual stones glowed beneath their necks. The angry mob didn't notice as they shouted for justice and damned the women to hell for their partnership with evil.

Magistrate Walcott lowered his arm, thus signaling the executions. One by one, the levers were pulled and the witches fell through the trap doors. Their feet stopped short of the ground by the chafing rope around their necks. Gasps sounded from the crowd at the crack of each snapped neck above the five dangling, twitching bodies.

The witch's crystals beamed brightly and engulfed the dead women in their brilliance. In one final act of sorcery, each crystal emitted a beam of bright, white light toward the other stones. The resulting connections created a five pointed star; otherwise known as a pentagram.

The ground shook and the terrified crowd rallied around Magistrate Walcott for direction. Unable to flee and trapped within the center of the mob, he cowardly froze and prayed for protection.

His prayers, along with the cries of the frightened crowd, were quickly muted as the ground beneath them fell out. The Earth swallowed them whole and left no trace of the attendees or events of the evening. Only a curious crater remained to spark speculation and conjecture as to the origin of its creation.

The raising motion of Selene's arm froze the image of a deep crater that was reflected in the mirror.

Greer was speechless as he struggled to reconcile his role as Magistrate and the atrocities executed under his leadership. He had assumed that at least some of his previous personalities had remained this side of sainthood and were most likely tagged for a "do over". Arguably, his lifetime in Salem certainly fell into that category as the self-serving and murderous Magistrate Walcott.

His mind raced with the moral and karmic implications of taking another's life. He failed to find a pattern of continued evolvement in his incarnations. In fact, he recognized a disturbing pattern of selfish mistakes.

Selene waited patiently for Greer to escape his pensive state and then asked him a question.

"Do you see the continuity of the lifetimes, Greer?"

His head was still reeling from the images in the mirror as he spoke.

"Um, yeah. I mean, I keep dying under supernatural circumstances. And, I'm kind of a dick." He paused and frustration surfaced as an outstretched hand, palm side up, in front of him. "I still don't understand how I eventually cause worldwide devastation and what my mission is!"

Selene delivered a loving, patient smile. "I cannot tell you, Greer. You must come to your own understanding. My role is to guide you, but I cannot take from you the very experience and lessons of karma."

Greer dropped his head in overwhelming confusion.

"Again? Man, if the ground swallows you in this lifetime, I hope I'm not around." Sean said, only half joking.

Greer curled his upper lip and nodded in agreement.

"I thought that they burned witches back then." Sean admitted.

Having googled the Salem witch trials after his past-life lesson from Selene, he was well informed to provide a clarifying response.

"No, that's a misconception. They hanged them. There are some documented European witch burnings, but not in Salem."

Sean accepted the clarification and rubbed his eyes. "I'm gonna grab a power nap, G. Are you good?"

"Yeah, I'm wide awake and still buzzin' from the coffee hit. No worries."

It wasn't long before Sean was asleep.

The fries put me in a carb coma. He would later tell Ashley.

They both think that's a real thing. She would explain to her mom and simultaneously roll her eyes.

Greer drove in silence and used the downtime to mentally work on his vows.

Reflection IV

Greer had driven past the halfway point and was crossing through the state of Tennessee when Sean finally woke up.

He stretched his arms out above his head. "How long was I out, G?"

"It's dinner time, man." Greer replied.

Sean retrieved his phone to check for messages and groggily stated, "No burgers."

"No problem."

Greer drove until he found an exit which boasted an establishment that served a chicken sandwich.

The guys ate their dinner on a wooden picnic table just outside of the small restaurant. They chose to dine outdoors partially due to the beautiful weather but mostly to accommodate their canine companion.

Sobek ate his grain-free, salmon dog food out of a collapsible, travel bowl. When he was done, Greer rinsed it out and filled it with bottled water. Sobek satiated this thirst and then began sniffing the grassy area around them.

Sensing his needs, Greer finished his sandwich and walked his big boy to an open area of grass and trees known to dogs as a bathroom. The guys opted to use the human facilities.

The road crew climbed back into Greer's truck and resumed their course for Chicago.

"What's the timeframe, G?"

Greer looked at the displayed time of eight o'clock on the dashboard. "We should be there early, like five, tomorrow morning."

"I can take over if you need me to. Just let me know, G."

"Thanks, will do."

Greer remembered his promise to Ashley that he would call her when they were at the halfway point.

She picked up on the first ring. "Hi, Greer!"

Ashley's voice induced a happy smile on his face. "Hey, Ash. How's it going?"

"Great, Sweetie. Where are you guys, now?"

"We're making our way through Tennessee and just passed the halfway mark." He informed her.

"I can't wait to see you."

"Same here, Ash."

"How's Sobek doing?"

At the mention of his name, Sobek sat up on the seat and sniffed the air around him. Greer caught sight of his activity in the rear view mirror and chuckled as he replied. "He's good. A little gassy, but good."

"Oh, that doesn't sound good. I'm sorry, Sweetie, but I'm heading out to dinner now with the family. I'll call you tonight before I go to bed, OK?"

"Sounds good. Have a nice dinner and tell your folks I said hello."

"I will. I love you, Greer."

"I love you, too, Ash. Bye."

"Bye."

"Before I hear another story about, well, whatever the hell it is you're telling me, what's the plan for Saturday?" Sean asked.

Greer ignored his comment and answered his question. "Like I said, we should get there in the morning. Ash and I have to run a few errands and tie up some loose ends. At four o'clock we have a quick rehearsal at the church and then dinner and drinks at her parent's house."

Sean interrupted with a quick, "Sweet."

Greer continued, "Sunday afternoon at one o'clock I get married." He let that statement hang in the air for a second while he smiled. He continued, "Ash and I are gonna stay at some high-end resort that her parents got for us until the honeymoon. Then, my super cool, best friend drives my truck back to Tampa with Bek." Greer paused and was sincere in his delivery. "You don't know how much I appreciate this, man."

Sean waved off his gratitude. "Consider it your wedding gift, G." A rare moment consisting of real emotion consumed him as he continued. "It's cool that we got to do this road trip. I might not see you that much, ya know?"

Greer wrinkled his forehead in confusion. "I'm getting married; I'm not moving out of state."

Sean retorted. "You don't know that, man. It's gonna be all about your family, like it should be. I'm just sayin' that it's cool to have some time to hang with you."

Greer was moved by his buddy's sincerity but didn't see any validity in his concern. "Do you need a tissue, man?"

Through his laughter, Sean uttered, "Dick." In an obvious effort to deflect the attention off of his candid display of fondness of his best friend, he asked, "Isn't it time for another installment of The Adventures of Past-Greer?"

Ever one for story-telling, Greer smiled and revisited his continued past life recall that promised to expose the secret to saving world.

"I'm sorry, Selene, but I'm not making any connections here." His voice was wrought with defeat and confusion.

Without response, Selene gestured to the oval mirror behind her and smiled as the swirling images displayed a familiar and disturbing scene.

Ahote stood in guilty disbelief at the horrific death of his older brother, Pahana. Their father, the Chief, crouched over his lifeless corpse and wept in painful grief.

"It was me, Father! I brought the girl, not Pahana!" Ahote broke down and fell to his knees. Between his tears and mournful groans he repeated, "It was me. I killed him because I was weak. It was me."

The attacking tribe had retreated back to their campground and was unaware that they had sought vengeance on the wrong brother.

When Ahote looked up, he observed his father placing Pahana's body on his horse. The Chief turned to his youngest son and commanded, "Quickly, gather mugwort, salep root and deer's tongue and meet me at the prayer circle."

He gazed through his wet and cloudy eyes in confusion at his father's request.

"Go! Hurry, Ahote!"

His guilt and anguish temporarily obscured his understanding of his father's intentions. He sprinted through the woods and toward his home. Focused on his task, he ignored every sharp rock and prickly thorn that stung his feet as he ran.

He reached the camp and headed for his father's dwelling. The eyes of his fellow tribesman and women guiltily darted away from him as he rushed passed them.

Inside his father's home, he easily identified the ritualistic ingredients. Always eager to learn as a young boy, he would ask endless questions of his father before falling asleep. Even as an infant, he would not easily take to slumber. The boy was aptly named, as Ahote means "restless one".

A powerful Shaman, the Chief indulged the young boy's curiosity and educated him on the magic of Earth's natural offerings. Ahote could name every herb, root and flower in the surrounding woods as well as their inherent, healing properties.

No one noticed as he darted back into the woods and to the prayer circle located next to the stream.

Out of breath, he arrived to the sacred spot with the ritualistic ingredients. He became increasingly uneasy as a growing and frightened understanding of his father's intentions surfaced.

Pahana's limp and bloody body was sprawled across the ground and enclosed by a circle of small stones. Four small fires sat outside of the rocky ring as representation of the four directions.

"Quickly, Ahote! Bring them to me!"

Ahote walked the items over to his father and placed them next to him. The Chief smeared lines of the blood of his dead son across his cheeks and forehead to begin the ritual.

"Stand aside, young one." He commanded Ahote.

The Chief smeared the mugwort on the chest, directly above the heart, of the shirtless Pahana. Next, he wrapped two pieces of the salep root on each of his limp wrists, leaving a foot of length on each. Finally, the deer's tongue was placed inside Pahana's mouth until only the tip was still visible.

With his hands reaching to the sky and a hauntingly desperate tone in his plea, the Chief chanted for the return of Pahana's soul from the spirit world.

Ahote watched in anticipation as his father begged the spirits to bring his dead son back to him. Several minutes passed and despite his father's request, Pahana remained void of life.

The Chief's grief over the death of his oldest became intense rage and an old injustice surfaced to fuel his anger.

He had accepted the loss of his son's mother and his loving wife when her life was taken by the intruding, pale-faced army. From that day, he had prayed for protection over his sons and his loyal tribe.

Today, he could not accept the loss at his feet and moreover, the enemy within. The people he tirelessly fought for had turned on his family and killed his son; his successor and their future Chief.

"Enough!" The Chief removed a bright, white, crystal stone that had been hanging around his neck and concealed by his colorful, tasseled leather coverings.

He tied the two ends of the salep root to the crystal and placed it on top of Pahana's heart, where it rested in the smeared mugwort.

Resuming his stance with his hands, once again, reaching high to the skies, he called upon the very essence of the Earth to restore life into his son.

Ahote incredulously watched his father's abandonment of their ingrained belief and respect of the natural order of life. He cringed as he considered the repercussions of his desperate father's actions.

His fears would prove to be well-founded.

The skies darkened and lightning flashed in between the eruptions of deafening thunder. Torrential rain poured down and formed sheets of water that robbed them of sight beyond a few feet in front of them.

Ahote blindly extended his arms to feel his way to his father. He could still hear the desperate, commanding chants despite the angry storm that suddenly appeared. Following his father's voice, he reached the edge of the prayer circle and he grabbed his father's arm.

Ahote embraced his father as they simultaneously watched the formation of a massive funnel. Wind and rain whipped around them in a fury and they, for the moment, remained safe inside the eye of the rapid whirlwind.

The Chief fell silent of his chanting and watched in amazement at the spectacular display of nature.

Ahote looked down and saw the crystal on Pahana's chest glowing and for reasons not consciously known, he was clear as to his next course of action.

He reached down and grabbed the brilliant, bright stone. Easily breaking it free from the sepal roots, he threw the stone through the wall of water and wind and into the raging waters of the usually calm stream.

The wind and rain instantly dissipated and the circling water fell to the ground. Thundering skies fell silent as dark thunder clouds were replaced with cotton-like, white sky-smoke. A calm, steady movement once again commanded the clear waters of the stream that provided drinking water to the nearby animal and human life.

Wet and bewildered, the Chief looked at Ahote in stunned appreciation of his actions.

Selene's motioned arm froze the final scene and she looked to Greer with continued patience.

Greer anticipated her usual question and addressed it before she could ask.

"Continuity, right? Well, the crystals are definitely a theme." After further consideration, he offered, "And, they appear to have considerable power… destructive power."

Selene's face displayed a proud, approving smile.

Reflection V

"So, how do destructive crystals help you save the world?" Sean asked as he opened a bottle of water that he had recently retrieved from the small cooler behind his seat.

Greer explained, "It doesn't and that's kind of the point."

Sean sighed. "I'm guessing there's no way to skip to the end of this book?"

Greer smiled and held back his laugh. "No, but there are only a few chapters left."

Sean was a lot more interested than he would ever admit, if not impatient, with regard to the nature of "the mission." He downed half of the bottled water and surrendered to the ongoing tale. "Well, don't let me stop you."

Selene continued to guide her student toward a spiritual awareness of the karmic thread woven throughout his lifetimes. She, again, raised her arm and the mirror reflected several fuzzy, rotating images. As they slowed, Greer's eyes observed another former self, not-so-coincidentally, in Chicago.

"Tomorrow we'll take a bike ride downtown; it's supposed to be warm." Charles stated.

"Sounds good, C. Love you." Julia smiled as she left the apartment for her night shift at her grandmother's bar.

For a moment, Charles stood deep in thought and staring at the closed door before eventually whispering, *I love you too*.

Charles went to his closet and pulled out the shoebox that contained the items he had secretly been collecting over the last few weeks. He placed it on the floor and took a deep breath.

Julia's grey tabby, Ruby, made her presence known as she stepped across the top of the box. Charles gently lifted her away and expressed only a slightly annoyance at the cat's characteristic determination to do, pretty much, what she wanted.

One by one, he pulled out the contents which included a small, oval mirror, a foot of copper wire and a large white crystal that he would later know to be selenite.

Julia had excitedly described her dreams of a monk who demonstrated the use of crystals to obtain personal desire. She was, however, unaware that Charles had his own dreams of the same "wish-making device".

Charles recalled his mysterious, recurring dream in which he watched his hands connect the objects. All the while, a large pyramid loomed in the distance; its limestone covered apex blindingly bright under the ancient, Egyptian sun.

First, he wrapped the wire around the shiny, selenite crystal. Then, he connected the wire to the mirror. He grabbed a piece of notebook paper and a pencil and wrote down the words, *I wish for money*.

Charles lit a candle and then placed the small piece of paper on top of the mirror.

He spoke aloud, "I wish for money."

Charles closed his eyes and repeated the scribed words a total of seven times. Opening his eyes, he felt silly and dismissed the exercise as a futile attempt at magic.

Charles walked away from the display in frustration and headed to the kitchen to get a beer.

Ruby returned to the bedroom from which she had recently been ejected. Her feline curiosity peaked at the sight of the shiny crystal and she moved closer to investigate.

Upon hearing that Julia had adopted a kitten, her grandmother had purchased an adjustable, pink collar for the feline companion.

Drawing on her deep-rooted metaphysical studies, she fashioned the collar with ornate stones and crystals. Julia understood that each provided health, balance and power for the physical, emotional and spiritual well-being of the kitten.

To the rest of the world, the shiny objects created an aesthetically pleasing and unique, cat collar.

Ruby stepped inside the magical arrangement of copper wire linked to a mirror and a shimmering crystal. The stones on her collar glowed brightly and created a beautiful, circular aura around her.

Charles returned with his beer and failed to notice the cat's soft aura or illuminated crystals on Ruby's collar. He, once again, removed the cat from the bedroom where her collar's crystals immediately lost their brilliance. Without detaching the wires from the crystal and the mirror, he dropped them back into the shoebox.

Once back in the kitchen, he took a swig of his beer and simultaneously dropped the box and its contents into the garbage can. He dismissed the entire concept and would not give the endeavor any further thought.

Following her long shift at the bar, Charles allowed Julia to sleep late into the next morning. They ate an early lunch and by mid-afternoon, Julia's arms were wrapped around Charles' wide torso as they were rode under a warm, May afternoon sun.

Greer interrupted Selene's presentation by holding up his hands and making an implied request. "Please, I know what happens from here."

She inferred and then granted his request to discontinue the image; confident that he was aware of the significant particulars of his incarnation in Chicago.

Sean waited for Greer to continue but he remained quiet. "Did you press pause?"

Greer laughed. "Yeah, man. I'm getting tired. Do you mind driving for a few hours?"

"No problem, G." replied his buddy.

Greer exited the truck at the next rest stop so everyone could get another bathroom break before the final leg of the trip.

Sean climbed in through the driver's side while Greer occupied the passenger seat.

With his buddy at the wheel, Greer managed a solid four hours of sleep until he was woken by the promised call from Ashley.

"Hey, Ash." His tired voice was deep with an overcompensating slow and deliberate delivery.

"Hi, Greer. I know that voice. Did I wake you?"

"Yeah. But it's alright. How was dinner?"

"It was nice." She paused. "Sorry to call so late but we talked for hours after dinner. I miss you!"

Greer smiled through his fatigue. "I miss you, too, Ash. We're only another..." He looked at Sean who then answered, "Five hours." Greer continued. "...five hours away."

Ashley laughed. "Yeah, I heard him. Hi, Sean. Are you driving for the big man tonight?"

"He needs his beauty sleep for the wedding." Sean joked.

Greer rolled his eyes. "Whatever."

Ashley suddenly remembered, "Oh, my dad wants you to call him when you get to the house. He gets up early so he'll let you in."

"Will do, Ash."

"Get some rest, Greer. I love you!" exclaimed his fiancé.

"I love you, too, Ash."

Ashley added, "Drive safely, Sean."

"I will. See you soon. Bye, Ashley."

"Bye, Guys"

With the call over, Sean told his buddy to go back to sleep and that he was good to drive a little longer.

Sean's selfless intention was to allow his friend to get the rest he needed for his big weekend.

His goal was realized when he later woke Greer at the same moment the truck passed the Chicago city limit sign. They had arrived at an early, or to Sean, late five o'clock a.m.

Best friend ever. Greer would later say to, pretty much, everyone.

Ashley's parents lived on the north side of the city so they had another forty miles to go. Thirty minutes later, the road trip trio arrived at Greer's future in-law's house where her dad met them at the door.

Sean introduced himself to Ashley's father to which he received the response, "Nice to meet you, Sean. I'm John, but please, call me Johnny."

Johnny stood six feet and four inches tall. A man in his early sixties, he had retained the majority of his thin, blond hair and appeared to be in very good, physical shape. His athletic build was the result of a retirement filled with tennis, golf and more water than beer.

Sobek lifted his leg on a rose bush.

Johnny laughed. "Who's this big fella?"

Sobek's tail whipped the air and he walked over to Ashley's father. Johnny bent down and received several, wet, Lab licks. He laughed as he scratched Sobek's neck which only seemed to increase the frequency of the canine kisses.

"That's Sobek and I'm sorry." Greer offered.

Johnny dismissed the apology. "No need to be. These guys are full of love. I had two Labs growing up. They were the best dogs I ever had."

I like this guy already.

"Let me show you to the guest room, Sean." He put his arm around Sean's back and looked over at Greer. "Then, you and I can chat."

Sean shot his buddy a look that clearly said, "Good luck."

Greer and his future father-in-law spent the next three and a half hours getting to know each other over several cups of coffee.

Ashley's dad had served four years in the navy. Once discharged, he found work loading mail into trucks for the U.S. Post Office. His strong work ethic eventually afforded him the role of a Plant Manager, from which he retired at the age of fifty-five.

Johnny and his wife, Karen, had raised four children and Ashley was their only daughter. They, understandably, worried about her, especially after she had moved to Florida.

Greer described his life growing up in Tampa. He had played soccer for seven years until his knees could no longer endure the constant, damaging impact of running.

He explained that his significant time at the gym not only provided a boost to his ego, but an opportunity to release the day's stress and was therefore, therapeutic as well.

"Plus, I look awesome and healthy." He only half-joked to Ashley's father.

Johnny stared at Greer as if expecting a follow-up comment. When he received none, he said, "As is your ego."

Hardly able to deny his assertion, Greer brushed off his comment and got serious.

"Johnny, I want you to know that I truly love Ashley."

"I know you do, Greer. In fact, I think you love her more than you love yourself." Johnny paused and then added, "And, from what I can see, well, damn boy, that's a lot!"

Once again unable to deny the brief personality assessment, Greer laughed and shrugged his shoulders.

Reflection VI

"Greer! Why didn't you wake me?" Ashley ran to the kitchen table to hug her soon-to-be husband.

"It's my fault, Ash. I've kept him here all morning, talking." Her father admitted.

Greer looked at Johnny and sincerely delivered, "I enjoyed it very much."

Johnny smiled. "Me too, Greer."

Ashley planted a long, wet kiss on her fiancé. The public display of affection taking place a short, three feet from her father made him a little more than uncomfortable.

Johnny observed his discomfort and excused himself. "I'll give you two some space." He kissed his daughter on the forehead and nodded to Greer. "Have a great day together."

"Thank you, Daddy. See you at the rehearsal." She turned back to Greer as her father left the kitchen. "I got up early so we could get our errands done and have lunch together."

Greer held back his laugh as the owl clock hanging on her mom's kitchen wall displayed the time of ten-fifteen in the morning.

To Ashley, that's an early start. He later told Sean.

Greer drove while Ashley called and confirmed the wedding photographer's time of arrival and the early morning appointment with her hairdresser, Liann.

Their first stop was to Macy's department store where Ashley picked up the bridesmaid's gifts.

I thought we were the ones who received gifts. Greer mused.

Next, they dropped off payment checks to the vendors that were supplying the bar and the band.

"Open bar, yes?" Greer asked

"Yes, Sweetie. And, you're on Sean-duty". Ashley informed him.

He was going to ask what she meant by that, but it was clear what she meant by that.

They stopped at an authentic Mexican restaurant for lunch. Greer deemed the salsa "sent from God" and also enjoyed three soft, chicken tacos.

Ashley put away a beef burrito that rivaled any regulation size football. Her dress would fit perfectly on the day of the wedding and confirm to an envious Greer that Ashley had an unnatural, yet extremely efficient metabolism.

After lunch they found a small park across from the restaurant and sat, embraced, on one of the wooden benches. In enjoyment of the warm, mid-May day that boasted high, blue skies, the park was filled with activity.

To their right, two middle age men threw a Frisbee back and forth. Their skill set included a behind-the-back catch and an under-the-leg throw. While their theatrics were limited, they kept the disc in the air in a competent, if not redundant exchange.

To their left, several families had converged on the lone covered wooden pavilion for a joint celebration of three, young girl's birthdays.

They watched as one dad manned the grill and nodded in pride at the random, "Smells good, Rick." and "Grill-Master Rick!" comments.

Two of the moms coached a volleyball game and separated the teams into boys versus girls.

Greer felt that the strategy was a clever attempt at gender segregation to delay their inevitable dating.

Ashley felt that he could find subterfuge in a rainbow.

In the center of the open field ran several small dogs. Their pet parents watched them chase each other while they exchanged "my dog has it better than me" examples.

My dog actually does have it better than me. Greer once said.

When Greer was done captioning the events in the park, Ashley asked him a question.

"So, are you ready to marry me?"

Greer pulled Ashley closer to him and the sweet fragrance of strawberry from her hair immediately put a wide smile on his face. "With all of my heart."

Greer leaned in and delivered a long, passionate kiss to Ashley.

The couple sat and chatted for another hour or so, wrapped in each other's embrace.

Greer circled back on a previously unanswered question and asked, "Are you going to tell me where we're going for our honeymoon?"

Ashley shook her head, "Nope. I told you that it's a surprise."

She caught sight of the time displayed on Greer's watch. "It's after three, Sweetie. We have to go."

Greer looked confused. "The rehearsal is at four. We have plenty of time."

"Father Gregory asked if we could get there a little early. He wants to meet you." Ashley explained.

The couple walked back to the truck and drove to the church that Ashley had attended as a child and would seat their family and friends on their special day.

At Father Gregory's request, they arrived fifteen minutes prior to the rehearsal. The priest was anxious to meet the man that Ashley had talked so excitedly about, in person.

The priest stood right at six feet tall with short, light brown hair. His childhood was spent in Ireland but as an adult, he had lived in Chicago. As a result, his voice had just the slightest remembrance of a once, strong Irish brogue.

For the most part, their short conversation went well. Things got a little tense when the subject of Sobek's presence at the wedding was addressed.

"We've never had a dog attend a ceremony before." Father Gregory explained.

Greer was direct. "Then, Sobek will be the first."

Ashley's family arrived at a punctual four o'clock along with the bridesmaids and Sean.

Since it wasn't a dress rehearsal, everyone wore casual clothing. Greer was about to chastise Sean for his sleeveless shirt until Ashley's younger brother, Kenny, walked over.

Greer did a double take.

Kenny wore a backwards, red ball-cap and a sleeveless t-shirt that displayed his defined arms. He stood next to Sean; a little shorter and a little smaller, but otherwise, eerily similar.

Kenny's like, Sean-Lite. Greer determined.

God help us, there's two of them. Ashley thought to herself.

The rehearsal took just under two hours and ended without incident. Everyone was clear on their placement and tasks both at the wedding ceremony in the church and the following celebration in the adjoining reception hall.

The group of family and close friends returned to Ashley's parent's house where her mom served a previously prepared meal of lasagna and homemade bread.

Greer's face displayed a familiar dietary concern at the meal.

"Sweetie, I love you but, if I hear the words carb-coma come out of your mouth, the wedding is off." Ashley delivered through a clenched smile.

"It smells wonderful. I can't wait to try it." Greer announced to anyone in ear shot.

Ashley's father had overheard their exchange and squeezed Greer's shoulder. "You're learning."

The evening was filled with joyous fun and laughter.

Ashley told the story of how they had worked together for a short time before they began dating.

Greer expressed his admiration for Ashley's philanthropic endeavors. He shared stories of her contribution of time and assistance at homeless shelters as well as her animal welfare efforts.

Ashley turned red in slight embarrassment as Greer bragged. He leaned in and kissed her. Immediately, a collective "aww" emanated from the crowd.

It was almost midnight when the festivities came to a close. Ashley was the first to call the day by citing her very early hair appointment.

After everyone had departed for their homes and Ashley's mother and brothers had gone to bed, Johnny opened his liquor cabinet and removed a twelve year old bottle of Royal Lochnager Scotch.

He handed Greer a thick, crystal glass and motioned to Sean. "Come on, best man."

Sean smiled and joined them. The guys stood in a circle and held their glasses out in a toast as Johnny spoke from his heart.

"I haven't known you long, Greer. But, I like you and more importantly, I trust you."

Greer beamed with delight at his soon-to-be father-in-law's words.

Their glasses still raised, Johnny toasted his future son-in-law. "To Greer and Ashley."

"To Greer and Ashley." Sean repeated.

Johnny closed his eyes. His appreciative palate enjoyed the smooth, aged Scotch's classic cereal barley and coffee malt taste as it slid down his throat.

Greer and Sean simultaneously choked on their first sip and, as much as they tried, could not contain their coughs and blatant inexperience with fine whiskey.

Johnny smiled and put down his empty glass. "There's more to life than Miller Lite, boys."

Pretending that their throats were not on fire, the guys laughed. Johnny retired to bed which left Greer, Sean and an already slumbering Sobek on the floor by the couch.

"Another beer, G?" Sean asked.

"Please!"

The guys cracked open their bottles and assumed seats opposite one another in the living room.

"Are you nervous, G?"

Greer was honest in his response. "No, I'm excited. But, not nervous." He paused and took a swig of his beer. "Mostly, I'm curious where Ash chose to go for our honeymoon."

Sean laughed. "She still hasn't told you?"

Greer shook his head. "No. I took two weeks of vacation and packed everything I own so I guess I'm ready for wherever we end up."

Sean had slept most of the morning and early afternoon after driving all night and was not yet ready to retire.

Trying to hide his curiosity, he stated, "So, I bet you're dying to tell me what happened next."

Greer's face displayed confusion.

"With Selene." Sean clarified.

Greer smiled at his buddy's poor attempt to hide his interest. "Yeah, man."

Greer was falling into despair at the repetitive occurrence of death amidst crystals and, from his narrow perspective, poor decisions.

Selene remained steadfast in her determination to help Greer identity the continuity in his previous lifetimes.

"Look at them individually, Greer."

He inhaled a deep breath and shook off most of the heavy frustration. With his head raised high, he worked to maintain an objective perspective as he recalled the significance of his previous incarnations.

"Let's break them down into very specific bullet points."

Selene smiled at his newfound commitment.

"In Maya, Tepeu blamed himself for the death of Itzel. Since he had taken a vow of celibacy, they weren't physical with each other. As a result, she remained a virgin and was taken for a sacrifice to the Gods, or rather, aliens."

His hand scratched the back of his neck and his head tilted slightly as he continued.

"He ended up killing her but not because of the sacrifice. When he pulled out that crystal skull, everyone was pulled into the ground."

Selene offered, "Indeed, into the Earth."

Greer raised his left eyebrow. *That's what I said.*

"Next, Miguel was killed inside a giant whirlpool."

Greer paused and made a connection. "He had crystals in his boat and was pulled down into the ocean." He looked at Selene and repeated her words. "Indeed, into the Earth."

She smiled, but not out of amusement.

Growing excited at the obvious pattern, his voice displayed excitement and confidence as he spoke. "The witches in Salem got their revenge using the crystals they wore. And, everyone was pulled underground…again."

Greer paused in silent reflection and his face displayed disgust in his actions of that lifetime.

"What is it, Greer?"

"Magistrate Wilcott was a dick."

Selene smiled patiently. "Indeed. Please continue with your previous train of thought."

Greer resumed his focus. "Ahote watched as the Chief used a crystal to try and bring life back to Pahana. It looked like they were headed toward the same fate but Ahote grabbed the crystal and threw it into the stream. How did he or, rather I, know to do that?"

Selene suddenly appeared serious and replied, "That is important, Greer."

He filed her comment away for future reference and continued with his past-life review.

"Charles didn't realize that Ruby's collar had charged the device. The result wasn't them being swallowed by the ground but they did endure a horrific accident."

A quick glance to Selene to verify that he was still on the correct path to understanding was met with, "Please continue, Greer."

He raised his eyebrows and initially drew a blank. "That was it. I mean, the only other lifetime where we used a crystal was in…"

Greer paused and looked at Selene while very sad memories flooded into his heart and head. He concluded. "…Egypt."

His guide watched as Greer struggled to connect the specifics of his Egyptian incarnation to those he had recently reviewed.

"They used crystals and had the same devastation but, Merkharu wasn't involved." Greer looked up. "Was he?"

Selene had already motioned her arm in response to his question. Blurry images became clear events on the oval mirror behind her.

Greer hung his head. It was obvious that she was about to reveal his participation in the catastrophe.

His overwhelming frustration returned.

What did I do now?

The magicians assembled in a desperate attempt to save their grey, deformed siblings. Holding hands, they stood in the center of the island and called upon the very essence of life within the planet.

A huge piece of selenite glowed in the center of their ritualistic circle while copper connected each priest to the charging crystal. As the gem pulled energy from the Earth, immense power moved through the priests. The energy intensified and grew stronger with each syllable of their chant.

Nookhotep monitored the increasingly dangerous surges of power and was prepared to break the circle when he received a telepathic message from the priestess that asked him to continue the ritual.

We're almost there. We just need to stabilize the...

Just then, the crystal imploded and created a fold in space that pulled five of the priests into a black hole of nothingness.

Nookhotep mentally told the priestess to move their ailing, alien siblings to safety. She ran, desperate to save them and implored them, telepathically, to join her, immediately, at the smallest pyramid.

The ground around Nookhotep disappeared to reveal an abyss of empty space. Luckily, he stood close enough to the edge of the massive hole to grab a hold of an exposed, thick root as he fell.

Desperate to complete the mission, he sent a telepathic message to Merkharu and informed him of their catastrophic blunder. Unselfishly, he asked for the Pharaoh's assistance in saving, not himself, but the priestess and the small, grey beings.

The priestess arrived to the pyramid and boarded the small disc-shaped craft. She helped as many of her brothers and sisters inside as she could until the ground beneath them began to crack. Feeling the very foundation weakening, she programmed the ship to ascend to the sky. Sadly, she only had time to send about half of the population to safety.

Merkharu arrived as the craft propelled itself into the sky. He stared, still mentally connected to Nookhotep, who was being pulled downward and hanging by a weakening root on the side of the newly formed crater.

The dirt and debris cleared to reveal the priestess. Merkharu took one step forward but she vanished as the ground collapsed beneath her.

The Pharaoh fell to his knees, unconcerned with the continued danger around him, and wept.

Nookhotep cried out, "No!" as he witnessed the death of the priestess through the eyes of his king.

Fate delivered its final blow when the remaining ground around the root to which he had so desperately clung, finally gave out and cast Nookhotep deep down, inside the Earth.

Crouched on the ground, Merkharu wept for the loss of his magicians. Finally, he picked himself up and walked directly to the magician's quarters. He retrieved the needed objects for the same failed ritual that claimed the life of his seven half-breed brothers and sister. Merkharu would attempt to bring them back, one by one, with one added element; his ankh.

The Pharaoh aligned himself due north and just on the edge of the deep crater that claimed the priestess.

This time, a large chunk of quartz claimed the center of the ritual. Connected to the crystal with copper wire and attached to his gold staff, Merkharu chanted for the return of his love.

The ground vibrated. Immense heat escaped between newly formed cracks. For hours, he chanted and his ankh glowed atop the staff with immense light.

Exhausted, he opened his eyes to see the pyramid with which he had aligned himself. He recalled his previous lonely climb down its spiral stairs and expectancy of his perished, grey siblings.

A smile ran across his weary face at the recall of their clever escape via an underground tunnel. They had enabled him to assist them with a second chance at life.

The bright limestone apex atop the pyramid shone blindingly at him under the hot, Egyptian sun and his eyes were forced shut as he collapsed in fatigue.

The distraught king returned for six more days and performed the same ritual a total of seven times. Each time, the ground shook and burning heat emanated from deep inside the Earth.

Finally accepting defeat, he returned to his chambers to live the remainder of his life in misery and solitude.

Greer almost yelled as he made the connection. "I figured it out!"

Selene motioned for the images to vanish and held her arms together at her waist in silent expectation of his explanation.

He began. "You said that in the future, the world is destroyed by natural disasters caused by an overheating of the planet's core."

Greer paused to give his guide an opportunity to correct his trajectory. Her silence was his approval to continue with the same thought process.

"The ground collapsed and killed Tepeu, Magistrate Wilcott and of course, the priests in Egypt." He paused and then added. "Miguel was on a boat but was still dragged down."

Another momentary glance at Selene yielded her trademark silence and patient smile so he moved forward with his determination.

"Merkharu did the ritual repeatedly and intense heat came up from the ground. He caused the core to overheat and the others made it increasingly worse over time!"

Selene's smile widened but she kept quiet.

"Well, am I right?" Greer held his breath in anticipation of her answer.

She stepped forward until she was an arm's length away from him and replied, "Indeed."

He exhaled and felt a rush of joy overcome him. His proud smile waned slightly as Selene maintained an ocular lock on him.

"What? I figured it out. All good, yeah?"

She replied, "Yes, you uncovered your actions that caused the end of the world."

Selene found herself conversing with "Oblivious-Greer" when he asked, "I'm missing something, aren't I?"

Her answer was direct. "How are you going to stop it from happening?"

"Oblivious-Greer" fell very, very quiet.

Reflection VII

"Holy crap, man!" Sean was more than intrigued by the story and abandoned all pretenses of disinterest. "You can't stop now, G!"

Greer laughed and then downed the last of his beer. He raised his empty bottle and asked his best man, "One more, buddy?"

"Sounds good, G."

Sean returned from the kitchen with two cold beers. He handed one to his buddy and sat back down in the brown recliner, directly across from him.

Impatient, Sean urged, "Come on, G. Tell me the end of story." He quickly excused his excitement with, "Who knows when I'll get to hear any more about your crazy adventures?"

Greer nodded in agreement and concluded a long story about the past, the present and the future.

"Oblivious-Greer" had been replaced with "Stressed-Greer" and was pacing as he muttered to himself.

The future hasn't happened yet but the past did so how can I change what happened from the present?

Selene patiently watched as he tried to sort through the confusing temporal elements of the problem. When she heard the appropriate keyword, she offered an assist.

How do I change the past?

"Indeed. How does one change the past?"

Greer looked around. "I don't know."

Selene chose a different angle. "What needs to occur for the past to change?"

Greer's eyes looked up as he considered the question. "Well, if Merkharu hadn't performed that ritual so many times he wouldn't have increased the core's heat."

Selene led him further into the thought. "And, what of the others?"

"What do you mean?" Greer asked.

"What is to stop them from causing damage and increasing the planet's internal heat?"

Greer suddenly had a moment of spiritual clarity that surprised even him. "They wouldn't have the idea in their head."

Selene waited for further explanation.

"The wheels were set in motion in Egypt. Merkharu, Nookhotep and the priestess, Sekhmet, continued to reincarnate together. Their need to balance the karma from the Egyptian lifetime surfaced as memories, dreams and subconscious instinct. They found each other in each new life and were drawn to magic and crystals. The cycle repeated until they, or more specifically, I destroyed the world."

Selene asked the question again. "What needs to occur for the past to change?"

Greer became exasperated. "I told you! Merkharu needs to know what kind of damage he causes by doing the ritual seven times."

His mind expanded just enough for a new consideration. "The stairs!"

Selene smiled. "Indeed."

His forehead wrinkled at his next thought. "But, the stairs took me to the future. I need to go to the past. Is there a staircase that goes backward in time?"

His spirit guide's face lit up. "Indeed."

Greer felt a rush of forced momentum and heard the sound of whirling wind in his ears. In an instant, he found himself standing inside a now long unused pyramid.

To his left, he recognized the stone, spiral staircase that Merkharu had descended down after imprisoning his deformed, grey siblings and found that his guilt was slightly assuaged when he discovered their escape via a recently dug tunnel.

He chuckled as comprehension tickled his mind. "Let me guess...the seventh step?"

"Indeed. The seventh step will take you back to a time of your choosing. Envision a specific event in your incarnation as Merkharu and concentrate on that image."

Greer began climbing up the stairs. With every step he envisioned Merkharu and other Pharaoh's as they descended down the stairs over the years. Their elite presence was a result of their knowledge and entry through the secret door located high up on the outside of the pyramid.

He reached the seventh step but before he could focus, Selene asked an important question.

"Greer, what exactly are you going to do?"

Not wanting to appear unconfident, his response was intentionally vague.

"I'm going to stop Merkharu from doing the ritual."

Selene offered one last bit of guidance. "Indeed. Greer, remember that your souls are one."

Now who's being vague?

She was unable to provide any further assistance with regard to his mission. Selene had faith in his abilities and while she could not intervene, she would monitor his progress from an elevated perspective.

Greer recalled the moment when Merkharu fell to his knees in despair at the death of his beloved priestess; just before he began the devastating ritual.

A white mist surrounded him and he felt the step beneath him vanish. Slight vertigo accompanied a sensation of rapid movement which forced his eyelids shut.

When he opened them, his eyes beheld a stunning structure known as a pyramid. Covered in limestone, it reflected the light of the sun; most assuredly a beacon for those descending from the sky. It stood in brilliant form; certainly a vast contrast to the pollution-blackened remains in the twenty-first century.

Greer observed ancient Egypt as a vibrant civilization full of color and life. Palpable electricity charged the air. Greer thought that it originated from the pyramids but he couldn't be sure.

Desert winds carried fine sand from miles away that challenged the people's vision and lightly coat any stationary structure.

The aroma of fresh bread that early Egyptians baked outside wafted through the air; an unfortunate stationary object forced to integrate sand as an unwanted ingredient that, over time, wore down their teeth.

Greer's attention was stolen by a loud rumbling just a few hundred yards away. He turned to investigate but already knew the reason for the calamity.

He mentally recalled and held the devastating image in his mind until he was instantly moved to the area of destruction. Greer stood adjacent to the weeping king and incredulously, his former self.

Greer could feel Merkharu's heavy sorrow as if it were his own. In many ways, it was. He was sadly reminded of Charles' similar despair after Julia's death caused by a horrific, motorcycle accident.

Additionally, the image of Ahote weeping over the loss of his older brother, Pahana, just after the death of the young girl he had tried to save, entered his mind.

Drifting off into a classic pensive state, Greer caught himself and forced his attention back to Merkharu.

The mission.

Greer spoke. "Merkharu, I need you to listen to me."

The king continued to sob, unable to hear Greer's voice.

Reaching out his hand, Greer tried to squeeze his shoulder. His hand moved through Merkharu's body as if it wasn't there.

Astral body. I keep forgetting.

Merkharu lifted his head and revealed his pained, tear laden face. As his anger fueled his desire to recover the loss of his beloved priestess, he stood up and began his march to the magician's chambers.

Greer recalled that Merkharu would retrieve the crystal and other objects needed to perform the ritual and return to the site of the accident.

Selene's words rang through his head and felt more like a forced insertion than a recalled memory.

Greer, remember that your souls are one.

Greer began to panic as Merkharu continued toward the chamber. His right hand rubbed the back of his neck as he repeated Selene's words in an attempt to discern their meaning.

Our souls are one. Our souls are one. So, that means we have the same soul? If we have the same soul then they are connected somehow? I know what he knows because he's in the past. How do I tell him what I know from the future?

Selene's voice sounded in his mind once again. "Greer, remember that your souls are one."

He yelled in frustration. "I heard you!"

Merkharu had gathered the necessary items and was walking out of the chamber when Greer turned to see him.

Unable to see, feel or hear Greer, Merkharu's arm went through Greer's as he moved past him. He would have been stopped by the contact had Greer been corporeal. Completely unaware of the occurrence, he continued out of the chamber.

Greer's body tingled with an intense vibration as a result of their contact. For a moment, he saw through Merkharu's eyes. Moreover, he heard his thoughts and felt his deep emotions. It was as if their minds had temporarily, been one.

Resonating with comprehension and running out of time, Greer moved himself back to the site of the implosion. He found the king chanting and beginning the ritual.

Hurry, Greer. Selene's voice urged.

So much for your noninterference clause. Greer later quipped.

He stood directly in front of the Pharaoh. His body vibrated and a buzzing filled his ears. Merkharu felt a slight tingling but dismissed it as a result of his focused chanting.

Their souls were slowly connecting and Greer felt his pulling him toward Merkharu.

As Merkharu chanted, his ankh glowed atop its gold staff and the ground underneath them began to tremble.

Suddenly, in a profound moment of understanding, the final act of Greer's mission was clear.

No longer confused by the vibrations that consumed his soul, he welcomed them with implicit trust. As a result, they intensified until he felt he could no longer remain whole.

Greer moved close to Merkharu and their energies began to merge. Merkharu was jarred out of his focused chanting by the intense vibration that surged through him.

In a bold and deliberate act, Greer stepped inside Merkharu's body.

Merkharu immediately froze as Greer mentally, emotionally and spiritually shared knowledge of his past which, of course, Merkharu interpreted as his future.

In his mind's eye, the king watched as he performed the ritual seven times and intensified the heat of the planet's core.

He observed the many subsequent lifetimes driven by personal gain and the use of crystals that often resulted in death and destruction.

Finally, he viewed the ending of the world, in 2026. Natural disasters destroyed the planet as a result of his actions at this very moment.

Greer was abruptly ripped from Merkharu's body. In the next instant, he stood disoriented and dizzy, on the seventh step of the stone, spiral staircase inside the pyramid.

Still light-headed and unsettled, he felt a rapid force of movement that was accompanied by a whirling sound in his ears. A second later he was, once again, standing in front of the oval mirror and a very proud, guardian angel.

Greer's senses quickly sharpened as the disorientation dissipated and his mind regained a clear focus.

Hopeful of his success, he looked to Selene. "Did it work?"

Rather than speak, she raised her arm one final time.

The oval mirror displayed swirling, hazy images that quickly took clear shape. The resulting display reflected a view of the Earth, as seen from space, in the year, 2026.

Greer smiled.

The continents had retained their land mass which meant the oceans had not risen to flood them amidst glacial melting.

The mirror zoomed in on the neighborhood street in which Greer had visited on multiple occasions and in multiple timelines.

Children played happily outdoors while adults conversed and prepared food for their afternoon meal.

The skies above them were blue and full of avian life while the ground boasted running dogs that chased, not people, but tennis balls and Frisbees.

The images inside the mirror faded. Greer held his hands out and exclaimed. "Mission accomplished!"

Selene smiled and her high cheekbones were red with pride. "Indeed."

Greer lowered his eyebrows. "There are a couple of things that I'm not clear on, though."

Selene tilted her head and awaited his questions.

"I understand that Tepeu's, Charles' and Miguel's desire to use crystals stemmed their early lifetime as Merkharu and each subsequent incarnation passed them down, so to speak. But, Ahote didn't use them. In fact, his understanding of their power and danger, for that matter, saved his father."

Selene adopted her patient smile and removed her student's confusion with her explanation.

"With the exception of Ahote, your previous selves used the crystals for personal gain. To obtain wealth, prosperity or the return a deceased loved one to the living. Ahote had studied the teachings of his tribe. He understood the sacred adherence to the natural order of life. During extreme grief and sorrow, his father momentarily discarded those beliefs. Luckily, Ahote was there to remind him."

"Sometimes intention is more powerful than action." Greer deduced.

"Indeed."

Greer was scratching his head and struggling to find the correct sequence of words for his other question. The result of his efforts was, "So, did I change everything? Did the things that I saw happen in all of my lifetimes…not happen?

Luckily, an ascended light being was the recipient of his query and understood what he meant.

"The insight in which you imparted to Merkharu helped him to determine his future choices. Keep in mind, that he, as well as your other personalities in other incarnations, retains free will."

Greer understood her words but was finding the potential changes hard to reconcile.

"Did I change the lives of Tepeu and Charles with the information I gave to Merkharu?"

"Indeed. But your involvement changed one, specific timeline."

Greer tried to wrap his mind around the temporal mechanics of altering the past and immediately felt a headache coming on. "Ya know, let's leave it as I saved the world and call it a day."

Selene, again, beamed with pride and smiled one last time. "Indeed."

With wide eyes and raised eyebrows, Sean leaned forward in his chair and stared at his buddy.

Greer looked to his left and then to his right in concerned expectation of his friend's next words.

Sean broke his silence and in a moment of honest and insightful feedback, he told his best friend, "I'm proud of you, G. You were able to see the actions of your past and makes changes so that you could have a better future."

Greer was speechless. He silently wondered if his buddy was speaking literally of the astral, time travelling events he described. Or, was he was referencing the mirrored particulars of his current lifetime?

It didn't matter. He determined and accepted his best man's blessing.

"Get some rest. I'll see you in the morning, G." Sean retired to the guest room and left Greer to his thoughts.

While Johnny hadn't specifically said it, Greer assumed he would prefer that he and Ashley not sleep together until after the wedding. Regardless of Greer's personal views and modern perspectives, he crashed on the couch, out of respect to Ashley's father.

Greer awoke to a soft kiss on his forehead from his future wife. Adhering to the traditional superstitions associated with a wedding day, she told him, "I'm going to the hairdresser and I don't want to see you until the wedding."

Greer laughed. "I'll be a ghost."

Ashley smiled. "I love you, Greer."

"I love you too, Ashley."

One by one, the members of the house filled the kitchen and chatted over coffee and bagels. Greer joined them at the same kitchen table where he and Johnny had talked for hours. As he sipped his morning java, the owl clock displayed the time of nine o'clock.

In four hours, I'm getting married.

The happy thought immediately brought a smile to his face and even slightly, watery eyes.

With not a lot to do besides put on his tux and repeat some mostly memorized vows, Greer easily convinced Sean and Johnny to nine holes of golf.

They played the round, hit the showers and arrived to the church just before noon. By twelve-fifteen they were dressed and patiently waiting for their cue.

The majority of Ashley's morning was spent in Liann's Beauty Studio and Spa.

Liann was a young, gorgeous, Korean woman boasting long, full, black hair with subtle, light brown streaks. She pretended that her stunning beauty took extreme effort but her soft, natural features begged to differ.

Ashley had chosen a "braided up-do" that presented a beautiful braid of Ashley's blond hair ceremoniously wrapped on top of her head. Her remaining hair would be pinned up and expose her delicate neck.

Liann worked feverishly on Ashley's hair and spoke mostly in witty, hairdresser quips.

"You have such beautiful hair, Liann. Is it hard to maintain?"

"It takes an hour every morning, Ashley. I'm so over my hair that I'm ready to chop it all off. And, by chop it all off, I mean trim it half an inch."

Ashley laughed. "An hour every morning? That must get old."

Liann explained, "I do hair morning, noon and night. On my days off, I limit my hair looks to three choices: shampooed, hat or homeless."

Ashley continued to laugh and asked, "What if someone comes over to visit or you have to leave the house?"

Liann smiled out of the corner of her mouth as she replied, "The solution to a bad hair day is to wear a low cut blouse."

As Ashley laughed, Liann swung her chair around to provide her a direct view of her finished hair-styling.

Ashley brought her hands to her face and began to cry.

Confident and experienced, Liann smiled in recognition of happy tears and handed Ashley a tissue.

"You look beautiful, Ashley."

"You made my day even more special, Liann. Thank you."

Greer was now pacing the dressing room. His cavalier attitude had completely vanished and he could feel the sweat underneath his tux.

Sean provided his familiar, supportive squeeze on his best friend's shoulder and nodded with an encouraging smile.

"It's go time." The wedding organizer, aka The Checklist Nazi, announced as she entered the guy's dressing room without knocking.

She herded Sean and Greer into the church and moved Johnny to the hallway where he waited to walk his beautiful daughter down the aisle.

Father Gregory nodded as Greer assumed his spot on the elevated floor. Sean and Ashley's brothers lined themselves on the right while the bridesmaids balanced the left side.

Greer's anxious, pounding heart almost stopped when the organ player began the march. Almost in perfect unison, the gathered friends and family turned their heads to see Johnny escorting a vibrant, glowing Ashley down the aisle.

Greer stared in awe of her stunning beauty.

Ashley's dress was a sheath, figure hugging design that reached down to her calves. Her well defined waistline showcased a modern woman's dress of confidence, strength and beauty. She had opted for a traditional, ivory white dress with soft, lace sleeves that matched the flowing gown behind. Warm and loving blue eyes sat beneath her tiara of braided, blond hair; the combination induced gasps from the guests.

She's a goddess. Greer thought to himself.

As she made her slow approach, Greer beamed with joy and wore the biggest smile she had ever seen.

Her eyes moved to Sean who nodded in reverence of their special day. She looked down to see Sobek, sitting in front of Sean and wearing a black bowtie around his thick neck.

She held back a giggle remembering the "extra" bowtie that she now understood had not been delivered in error.

Johnny presented his daughter to Greer and the guys exchanged respectful nods.

Greer and Ashley gazed lovingly into each other's eyes as the preacher explained the history and meaning of marriage.

When it came time to exchange vows, Ashley went first.

"I've never met anyone like you, Greer. And, that's what I love most about you. You're crazy, but confidently crazy."

A soft laughter emanated from the guests. She continued.

"You're strong, and it's a protective strength. You're true to your convictions, and I love that integrity. Our future together isn't written yet. But, it's a future together…always. That, I vow."

As Ashley finished speaking a tear fell from her eye. Greer softly wiped it from her cheek as the preacher nodded for him to begin his vows.

Abandoning his previously practiced words, Greer spoke from his heart.

"Ashley, I couldn't love you any more than I do, right now. I've spent a lot of time worrying about the future. And, I've spent even more time dissecting the past. It took a while, but I finally realized that what really matters is the present; our present."

Greer recalled Julia's wise perspective on destiny as she read Charles' palm. He then repeated the message, but in his own words.

"Destiny is only an indication of future possibilities. Above everything, we create our reality and nothing is set in stone or unchangeable. It's in the present that we'll find our happiest moments. And, in this present, I'm the happiest that I have ever been."

Ashley began to cry as Greer's eyes filled with water.

"I vow to love you in the present of each moment of our lives."

Nearly half of the guests were wiping tears from their faces in an emotional reaction to Greer's vows. The other half were hoping for a diagram to explain his liberal use of the word *present*.

An impressed priest smiled at Greer's words. He had, admittedly, not expected as much from the guy who brought a dog to his wedding.

He turned to the bride and asked, "Ashley, do you take Greer to be your husband for as long as you both shall live?"

She couldn't smile any wider as she replied, "I do."

"Greer, do you take Ashley to be your wife for as long as you both shall live?"

The big guy beamed with joy as he gazed into his goddess' eyes and delivered, "I do."

Father Gregory smiled at the childhood girl whom he had watched grow into a confident, young woman and pronounced the couple, "Man and wife."

Greer was already kissing Ashley when the priest turned to deliver his final line.

Immediately following the nuptials, the couple celebrated their union in the adjoining reception hall with their family and friends.

The next four hours consisted of photographs, dances, food and cake. The open cash bar was a useful tool for the skilled Sean in elevating his perceived charm to the tipsy bridesmaids.

"You can't tell me that you didn't see that part of the story coming." He said to Ashley when she displayed annoyance at Sean's behavior.

The event ended, the couple said goodbye to their guests and climbed into the long, black limousine that had been waiting for them outside of the church.

They toasted one another with the champagne provided by the elaborate compartment in the door. The driver raised the divider to give the newlyweds some privacy as he drove them to their resort.

Ashley snuggled up next her husband. "I love you, Greer."

Greer took her soft hand and placed it between his hands. "I love you, too Ash. So, are you going to tell me where we are going for our honeymoon?"

Ashley playfully paused as if deciding whether or not to tell him.

"Oh, come on, Ash!" Greer begged.

She laughed. "Alright. We're going to spend seven days in Ireland!"

Greer was thrilled. "Sweet! That's awesome, Ash!"

She explained her reasons for her choice. "The scenery is beautiful and I thought you would love seeing the castles."

Greer smirked. "I am definitely into seeing the castles."

Greer pulled his wife close and held her as he watched the passing scenery along Michigan Avenue.

The art deco seahorses that adorned the stunning Buckingham Fountain would have, at one time, filled his mind with the gory images of Julia and Charles' horrific accident.

Those memories now belonged to the past and had no place in Greer's present.

The End

The 7 Novellas Series is based on actual supernatural events that have occurred in my life. I describe those events in my book, The Dead: A True Paranormal Story.

Made in the USA
Charleston, SC
02 October 2016